Teaching Second Language Learners with Learning Disabilities

Strategies for Effective Practice

J. Dixon Hearne, Ph.D.

**Academic
Communication
Associates**

P.O. Box 4279
Oceanside, CA 92052-4279

Academic Communication Associates, Inc.

P.O. Box 4279
Oceanside, California 92052-4279

Printed in the United States of America
International Standard Book Number: 1-57503-057-8

Preface

This book is the culmination of years of teaching, learning, and searching. As I began my teaching career in a small preschool, I was ecstatic about the prospect of setting young minds on the road to knowledge and truth. With confidence that I that I would encounter the same eager minds at the secondary level, I left the preschool classroom to pursue loftier ambitions as an English teacher. With missionary zeal, I accepted a position at an inner city junior-senior high school, where I would push the limits of learning to new heights of understanding and appreciation for all the great books, all the great authors, and every writing convention. I had no idea how much learning still lay ahead for me.

Not long into my first year, I became painfully aware that there is really no common path for all students. There are many different roads through the K-12 public school system – some smooth, predictable, and rewarding, others mysterious, callous, and dead-end. Through the years – from preschool through college – I have attempted to shepherd students along these paths, consciously gathering knowledge and skill and forging them into an improved teaching repertoire. Nowhere have I gained greater knowledge and insight than from my many years in classrooms for students with learning disabilities and in settings where I worked with second language learners. Drawing upon these experiences in general and special education, I set about to develop the present resource book, an attempt to assist regular and special education teachers in blending theory and practice.

As the title suggests, the book addresses a topic of growing concern among educators, parents, and students. This book is aimed at a wide audience of readers in the fields of special education, speech-language pathology, bilingual-ESL education, and general education. It should serve as a practical resource for elementary school teachers, learning disabilities teachers and other special educators, bilingual teachers and coordinators, and elementary school administrators seeking to provide instructional leadership in these areas.

Each chapter in this book is written with the practitioner in mind, and careful attention is given to explanation, examples, and applications. The book includes a brief history of the field of learning disabilities (LD), a discussion of parallels between the LD field and bilingual education, and an examination of emerging theories on second language acquisition. Additionally, it offers extensive information about teaching and learning models and a host of promising practices for students with language and learning challenges (LLC) who have been labeled "learning disabled."

One particularly important feature of the book is the Adaptive Instructional Model (AIM). The approach lends itself to modifications and adaptations in each of the five components: Discussion, Instruction, Development, Performance, and Evaluation. I developed the plan as a means of reaching those students whose language and learning *differences* made them appear inadequate or deficient in the schools. It is actually an accountability model, which requires the teacher to consciously plan for students of varying ability levels and backgrounds. Units and lessons are enhanced by the development of Multiple Intelligences Matrices, application of skills from Bloom's Taxonomy, and the generous use of graphic organizers (webs, story maps, diagrams, etc.). It is my hope that the materials in this book will be valuable to you in helping second language learners to reach their full potential.

Dedication

To my parents –
Henry Drew and Wilda Elise Hearne

and

to the memory of
Duston Heath Allbritton

Acknowledgments

In various ways many persons have contributed to my work as an educator – former teachers, colleagues, and friends. It has been a circuitous route, but they made all the difference. I would like to acknowledge some of them here:

- Mrs. L. Bates, Dr. Nancy Fortney-Robinson, Dr. Virginia Bernhard – all teachers of the first order
- Dr. Alfred Louch, Dr. Mary Poplin, Dr. Linda LeBlanc – mentors and colleagues
- Rob Durham, John Schaub, and Carol Cover – sharp-minded friends
- Reviewers – Dr. Larry Mattes, Dr. Judy Montgomery, and Paul Locsch – whose encouragement made this book seem worthwhile
- Vern Cowles – technician-philosopher and friend extraordinaire

About the Author

Dr. J. Dixon Hearne has written extensively on topics in both general education and special education. He received his B.A. degree from the University of St. Thomas in Houston, Texas, M. A. Degree from Pepperdine University in Los Angeles, and Ph.D. from Claremont Graduate University in Claremont, California. Dr. Hearne has received numerous awards and honors – including *Teacher of the Year* and *Mentor Teacher* – and is listed in *Who's Who in California*. His current research interests include learning disabilities, the psychology of learning, literacy, and issues relating to the education of bilingual children with special learning needs. Dr. Hearne is currently on the faculty in the Education Department at Chapman University in Orange, California.

Table of Contents

Part 1
Background and
Perspectives

Chapter 1
Overview of the Problem

The first object of any act of learning, over and beyond the pleasure it may give, is that it should serve us in the future. Learning should not only take us somewhere; it should allow us later to go further more easily.

Jerome Bruner

The field of learning disabilities (LD) emerged as a separate field of study less than 40 years ago. During its relatively brief history, it has faced continual change and challenge. Nowhere has the challenge been more evident than in the areas of identification and service provision for students whose primary language is other than English. Bilingual education has endured an equally frustrating history in American public education. The fields parallel each other in several ways, most notably in their common struggles through legal challenges and legislative mandates such as the following:

Learning Disabilities
Public Law 94-142 (1975)
Public Law 99-457 (1986)
Public Law 101-476 (1990)
Americans with Disabilities Act (1990)
Individuals with Disabilities Education
Act (IDEA) (1990, 1997)

Bilingual Education
Bilingual Education Act (1968)
Lau vs. Nichols (1974)
Castaneda vs. Pickard (1981)
Keyes vs. School District #1 (1983)

Not until the passage of the Education for All Handicapped Children Act of 1975 (Public Law 94-142) were programs for students with specific learning disabilities mandated. Up to that point, students with LD typically struggled through the regular classroom curriculum and/or received special instruction along with other "slow learners" in remedial programs. Similarly, until the 1970's, students for whom English was a second language were generally placed in the regular classroom where they were expected to "sink or swim" in an all English learning environment. Several rationales have been offered for this "submersion" approach, but the most prevalent seem to be related to time-and-cost efficiency and the need for quick assimilation into mainstream American culture.

The submersion model failed the schools in several fundamental ways. Perhaps the most immediate and enduring effect has been the over-referral of non/limited-English speaking students to "special education" programs because of their language "deficits." During the 1970's, the number of referrals nationally – and particularly in the southwest – rose dramatically, creating in its wake a new tide of concerns and problems for the nation's special education programs.

Recent statistics (1995-1996) from the Office of Education show that students with learning disabilities represent approximately 47% of the total special education population in America's public schools. While the exact percentage of this population that speaks English as a second language is not known, it is suspected to be increasing rapidly. Hodgkinson (1993) estimated that 30% of the nation's school-age population are from linguistically and culturally diverse backgrounds, and that percentage is projected to be 36% by the year 2000.

The percentage of individuals from minority backgrounds has increased dramatically in recent years. During the 1980's, for example, there was a population increase of 53% for Hispanics, 108% for Pacific Islanders, 38% for American Indians, 13% for African Americans, and only 6% for whites.

Data reported by the California Department of Education (1996) and the California Teacher's Association (1996) revealed the following:

- More than 50% of all Limited English Proficient (LEP) children in the United States reside in California.
- English language learners (ELL) represent 24% of the total student enrollment in K-12.
- Approximately 78% of all identified English language learners speak Spanish as their primary language.
- The ethnic composition of students in California from Asian and Hispanic backgrounds is considerably higher than the national average:

U.S. Average		California	
African-American	16.5%	African-American	8.6%
Hispanic	12.3%	Hispanic	36.1%
Asian	3.5%	Asian	11.0%
White	66.7%	White	43.4%

- The top eight language groups of English language learners after Spanish were reported to be the following:

Vietnamese	49,778	Filipino	21,362
Hmong	28,494	Korean	16,366

| Cantonese | 23,728 | Armenian | 15,459 |
| Cambodian | 21,467 | Lao | 11,392 |

One final, alarming statistic warrants mention here. According to the U.S. Bureau of Census (1992), the dropout rate for Latino students in the United States was found to be 53 percent.

As recently as 1986, most states had not developed programs to serve the needs of this fast-growing population. Salend and Fradd (1986) sent a survey to all 50 states requesting information about availability of services for "bilingual special education students." From the survey responses, they reported the following findings:

- Five states had no definition of bilingual special education.
- Only two states had funding designated specifically for bilingual special education.
- Only four states had compiled a battery of "Recommended Assessment Instruments."
- No state had developed a curriculum for bilingual special education students.
- Only one state offered certification in bilingual special education.

While the overlap of these two burgeoning fields – bilingual and special education – brings together enormous and diverse databases, arguably the most valuable result has been the exchange of promising, field-tested teaching practices. Baca and Cervantes (1989) defined the aims of this joint mission as follows:

> Bilingual Special Education may be defined as the use of the home language and the home culture along with English in an individually designed program of special instruction for the student. Bilingual Special Education considers the child's language and culture as foundations upon which an appropriate education may be built. The primary purpose of a Bilingual Special Education program is to help each individual student achieve a maximum potential for learning. Above all, the program is concerned with the child's cognitive and affective development. It would be misleading to assume such a program is primarily concerned with teaching or maintaining a second language or culture. Here, language and culture are used as appropriate means rather than as ends in themselves. (p. 18)

Since the 1960's, research interests relating specifically to issues in bilingual and special education have increased dramatically. In 1970, the President's Committee on Mental Retardation (PCMR) published an alarming report, "The Six Hour Retarded Child," which brought to light how cultural differences were causing students to be mislabeled as "mentally retarded" (MR). Since that time, many students who might have been misdiagnosed as MR have been reassigned to learning disabilities programs. Although the label may have changed, misperceptions and misunderstandings are evident to this day. Discrimination in testing, for example, has been a topic of perpetual debate in education. What are the effects of cultural and language differences on I.Q. testing? On academic testing? How can we distinguish a learning disability from problems that can be attributed to limited proficiency in English?

According to Ortiz (1997), schools are faced with major problems resulting from a general lack of *knowledge* about culturally and linguistically diverse (CLD) learners. Until quite recently, minority populations – Hispanic and African American in particular

–were over-represented in learning disabilities programs (Harry, 1992). There have also been shifts in the labels assigned to bilingual children who are placed in special education programs. Rather than assigning the label "mentally retarded" when CLD students are placed in special education programs, labels such as "language- or learning disabled" are becoming more common (Beaumont & Langdon, 1992; Ortiz & Yates, 1987). Because of recent legislation, educators have become extremely cautious when placing culturally and linguistically diverse students in special education programs. There is now reason to suspect an under-representation of these students in many programs.

It is often difficult to determine whether the learning problems exhibited by limited English speaking students result from a true disability. A student should not be considered "disabled" if limited exposure to English is the cause of the learning problem (Mattes, & Omark, 1991; Roseberry-McKibbin, 1995). When tested using a standardized language assessment measure, a bilingual student may give the false impression that he or she has a language disorder (Mattes & Omark, 1991).

The limited availability of appropriate assessment instruments and bilingual assessment personnel make it difficult to identify second language learners who are truly in need of special education services (Campbell, 1999; Ortiz, 1997). Professionals in school settings, however, are expected to identify all students in need of special education programs. The nondiscriminatory clause of the Individuals with Disabilities Education Act (IDEA) (1990) mandates that every state develop procedures

> to assure that testing and evaluation materials and procedures utilized for the purpose of evaluation and placement of handicapped children will be selected and administered so as not to be racially or culturally discriminatory. Such materials or procedures shall be provided and administered in the child's native language or mode of communication, unless it is clearly not feasible to do so, and no single procedure shall be the sole criterion for determining an appropriate educational program for a child. (20 U.S.C. section 1412 (5) (C)).

Nonetheless, many children are erroneously labeled as "at risk" simply because they are second-language learners and/or from lower socioeconomic backgrounds (Cummins, 1989; Flores, Cousin & Diaz, 1991;). Flores et al. (1991) described the problem succinctly:

> For years our school system has identified students who differ from the mainstream with certain labels. As the decades change, so do the labels. But the same kinds of children are identified as slow learners, learning disabled, culturally deprived, semi-lingual, limited-English speaking, or the label of the late 1980's and early 1990's "at risk." (pg. 369)

Such perceptions have perpetuated myths that bilingualism and cultural differences have a negative effect on cognitive functioning. It is clear that the general public needs multicultural education programs to better understand the needs of the growing population of second language learners in our schools. Sleeter and Grant (1994) described the major approaches to multicultural education that have been implemented in the United States:

- *Teaching the Culturally Different* – This approach focuses on acculturation and transition into American culture.
- *Human Relations Approach* – This approach is aimed at sharing cultural differences, sensitivity and awareness of differences, and contributions of other cultures.
- *Single Group Studies Approach* – This approach targets single cultural/ethnic groups for deep study and uses that culture like a prism through which to examine its many facets. The approach is aimed at promoting social consciousness and activism.
- *Multicultural Education Approach* – This approach is designed to promote cultural pluralism and social equality.
- *Multicultural and Social Reconstructionist Approach* – This approach focuses on the same goals as the Multicultural Education Approach.

Qualitative Research and Placement Issues

From a longitudinal research project, Ruiz, Rueda, Figueroa, and Boothroyd (1996) identified three "profile types" of Latinos in bilingual special education: "(a) those with disabilities in the moderate to severe range; (b) those with mild disabilities or normal ability in conjunction with certain socioeducational factors, and finally, (c) those with normal ability" (p. 193). Their project, known as "Optimal Learning Environments" (OLE), is aimed at creating "effective learning contexts for bilingual children in pull-out special education programs" (p. 170). Information accumulated by OLE researchers supported earlier findings by Mercer (1973) that children from culturally and linguistically diverse backgrounds had been "overidentified" as needing special education services.

After reviewing 11 qualitative studies, Ruiz et al. (1996) reported strong evidence to indicate that both "ability" and "disability" are *socially* constructed. In addition, the studies revealed that holistic and learner-centered approaches showed more promise for diverse learners than did skills-based approaches. In one study, Goldman and Rueda (1988), found that two *self-directed* writing contexts – interactive journals and narrative writing with computers – were especially promising for bilingual special education students. Students selected the topics and successfully took control of their own writing, concentrating on *meaning* rather than form. In related research, Echevarria and McDonough (1993), described encouraging results using a reading approach guided by "instructional conversations." The aim was to create a *conversational* tone within the classroom so that students would feel free to discuss, question, and even *direct* exchanges of information. Over time, researchers noted an increase in student-initiated conversations and more time spent in conversational interactions. Students were able to participate in these interactions once they felt comfortable in the classroom environment.

When students enter our schools, their customs, values, and previous learning experiences have a profound impact on how they respond to the instruction that is made available to them. It is important for educators to be sensitive to cultural and linguistic differences when conducting assessment and developing instructional programs. Without this sensitivity, second language learners can easily be misdiagnosed and placed in programs that are inappropriate for their specific learning needs.

Implications for Students with Language and Learning Challenges (LLC)

- The fields of bilingual education and learning disabilities continue to face similar challenges and obstacles both inside and outside the schools.
- Schools must provide a continuum of approaches to language development and learning.
- Second language learners with learning disabilities, as well as their teachers, must create within themselves an attitude of openness and tolerance. Community-building begins at the individual level.
- Second language learners with learning disabilities seem to engage well in classrooms where language-rich activities, hands-on experiences, and personal choice are present.

Chapter 2
Learning Disabilities and Cultural Diversity

If there is one immutable feature in the landscape of learning disabilities, it is change.

Mary S. Poplin

Learning disabilities are often suspected by classroom teachers when students experience difficulties responding appropriately to instruction. When these students are referred for testing, a variety of measures may be administered to identify problems in perception, memory, and other areas that are believed to have an impact on learning in the classroom. Children who perform poorly on these tests often receive instruction designed specifically to remediate the identified "disabilities." Whether the deficits identified by many of these measures have much to do with classroom performance, however, must be questioned. Many of the norm-referenced tests commonly used in the identification of auditory and visual perception problems, for example, yield scores that are poor predictors of academic success (Hammill & Larson, 1974; Larson & Hammill, 1975). If the norm-referenced tests commonly in use are of questionable value in identifying why *English-speaking students* are not learning, professionals are presented with much greater challenges when students are referred who speak a language other than English.

The identification of learning disabilities is extremely difficult if a student comes from a background where a language other than English is used. To understand the dilemma faced by special education professionals in their efforts to identify second language learners with learning disabilities, it is important to understand the construct of learning disabilities and how it has evolved over the years.

The Field of Learning Disabilities

Following the emergence of the field of learning disabilities in the early 1960's, organizations such as the Learning Disabilities Association of America (LDA), National Joint Committee on Learning Disabilities (NJCLD), Division for Learning Disabilities (DLD), and Council for Learning Disabilities (CLD) have been established to address the needs and concerns of this newly formed field. It has been a rocky road to say the least, a journey marked by heated debate and political division. As Hammill (1993) stated, "The NJCLD was organized in 1975 to establish greater *cooperation* among organizations primarily concerned with individuals with learning disabilities" (p 297). The committee is comprised of representatives from the International Dyslexia Association, Learning Disabilities Association of America, American Speech-Language-Hearing Association, International Reading Association, and other organizations.

In recent years, various theoretical models have been used to "explain" learning disabilities. The models most often described are the (1) Medical Model, (2) Psychological Processing Model, (3) Behavioral Model, and the (4) Cognitive Strategies Model. The emergence of each has, in turn, contributed to division within the field. The schools (students, teachers, and administrators) have experienced this division in the form of windfalls of eclectic strategies, materials, and practices. Donald Hammill (1993) described the problem as follows:

> The sudden appearance and rapid growth of the field of learning disabilities presented serious problems for the American educational system because many administrators had little knowledge about learning disabilities, few teachers had been trained to handle students in this new category, and college programs for preparing teachers and other personnel to work with students with learning disabilities were almost nonexistent. (p. 299)

Issues in Defining Learning Disabilities

A major concern in the field of special education is that there is no clear definition of "learning disability." According to Gerald Coles (1987), the term itself emerged as a result of a national search by middle-class parents and professionals for an alternative to terms such as "mentally retarded" or "emotionally disturbed." These terms, along with, "culturally deprived," "seemed more appropriate for children from minority and poor communities, not children from the middle class" (p. xiii). The first usage of the combination of the terms *learning* and *disabilities*, however, is attributed to Samuel Kirk (1963), who described these disabilities as follows:

> . . . disorders in development in skills needed for social interaction. In this group I do not include children who have sensory handicaps such as blindness, or deafness, because we have methods of managing and training the deaf and the blind. I also exclude from this group children who have generalized mental retardation. (p. 3)

The characteristics commonly observed among children with learning disabilities are summarized in Table 2-1.

In a review of the literature, Cartwright, Cartwright, and Ward (1989) found at least 38 different definitions of learning disabilities. Nonetheless, two widely accepted definitions have emerged from research and debate. The 1977 Federal Register definition, which guided funding and subsequent legislation, is as follows:

> ## Table 2-1
> ## Primary Characteristics of Children
> ## with Learning Disabilities (LD)

General characteristics of learning disabilities include the following:

- By definition, the student with learning disabilities has average or above average intelligence and potential.

- The student does not achieve commensurate with age/grade level expectancy, when provided with appropriate learning experiences.

- An uneven pattern of development exists in intellectual, academic and/or social skills.

- A pattern of behavior problems is often evident.

- Attention problems are common during learning tasks.

The student may have difficulties in one or more of the following areas:

- *Listening Skills* - receptive problems, inability to comprehend what is heard

- *Oral Expression* - inability to express thoughts and feelings in an appropriate manner

- *Reading* - limited decoding skills and poor comprehension of what is read

- *Written Language* - difficulties with spelling, grammar rules, mechanics, and usage

- *Mathematics* - difficulties with calculation and basic operations (addition, subtraction, multiplication, division), reasoning, and problem-solving

Learning Disabilities are not likely to be the cause of learning problems under the following conditions:

- The student has had poor school attendance.

- The type of instruction being provided is inappropriate or inadequate.

- Instruction is not adapted for students with cultural and linguistic differences.

Learning disabilities do not exist if the student's problems can be attributed entirely to any of the following:

- Emotional disturbance

- Hearing loss

- Vision problems

- Motor problems

- Mental disability

"Specific learning disability" means a disorder in one or more of the basic psychological processes involved in understanding or in using language, spoken or written, which may manifest itself in an imperfect ability to listen, think, speak, read, write, spell or do mathematical calculations. The term includes such conditions as perceptual handicaps, brain injury, minimal brain dysfunction, dyslexia and developmental aphasia. The term does not include children who have learning problems which are primarily the result of visual, hearing or motor handicaps of mental retardation, or emotional disturbance, or of environmental, cultural or economic disadvantage. (U. S. Office of Education, 1977, p. 65083)

Many have challenged the Federal Register definition on the grounds that it is both inadequate and inaccurate. Smith (1991), for example, stated concern that the definition has not addressed non-academic manifestations of learning disabilities (e.g., abstract reasoning and social skills). Others have argued that all persons with LD have the same characteristics and causes and need the same treatment. Moreover, those holding this viewpoint maintain that the problem is intrinsic to the individual.

Whereas the federal definition is rooted in medical explanations and descriptions of learning disabilities, the definition put forth by the National Joint Committee on Learning Disabilities presumes the problem to be a "central nervous system dysfunction." The National Joint Committee on Learning Disabilities described "learning disabilities" as follows:

Learning disabilities is a generic term that refers to a heterogeneous group of disorders manifested by significant difficulties in the acquisition and use of listening, speaking, reading, writing, reasoning or mathematical abilities. These disorders are intrinsic to the individual, presumed to be due to central nervous system dysfunction, and may occur across the life span. Problems in self-regulatory behaviors, social perception, and social interaction may exist with learning disabilities but do not by themselves constitute a learning disability. Although learning disabilities may occur concomitantly with other handicapping conditions (for example, sensory impairment, mental retardation, serious emotional disturbance) or with extrinsic influences (such as cultural differences or insufficient or inappropriate instruction), they are not the result of those conditions or influences. (National Joint Committee on Learning Disabilities, 1988, p. 1).

Yet another important definition is offered by the Interagency Committee on Learning Disabilities (ICLD, 1987). Appointed by the United States Congress, the committee was comprised of members from 12 agencies of the Department of Health and Human Services and the Department of Education (Lerner, 1997). The committee was asked to review current legislation, research, and professional literature and to develop a clear definition of learning disabilities. In its final draft, the ICLD proposed that deficits in social skills be included in its set of characteristics that define learning disabilities.

Despite some distinctions along the finer lines, operational definitions reflect several common elements, among them:

Common Elements in Definitions

- **The exclusion of other conditions and/or causes.** For example, a student who is partially sighted might exhibit underachievement patterns similar to those of another student with a specific learning disability. However, the cause of the difficulty for the student who is partially sighted is clearly a medical condition.

- **Inconsistent patterns in performance and growth.** A student's pattern of performance is uneven and/or marked by inconsistencies. For example, a student who struggles in language arts might excel at math and computer-related tasks. Likewise, a student with LD might demonstrate what appears to be mastery of a given task on one occasion, only to fail at the same task when asked to repeat it later in the same day or the next.

- **Disorders and/or dysfunctions generally presumed to be neurological in nature.** In the study of learning disabilities, there has been a pervasive view that the cause lies within the person with LD. The brain and central nervous system have long been suspected as the area of dysfunction causing individuals with LD to think and perform as they do.

- **Discrepancies between perceived potential and actual achievement.** Frequently, teachers of students with LD report that they see these children excelling in areas such as art, music, athletics, use of computers, etc. In other areas of the curriculum, frequently language arts and/or math, these same students experience failure. While the causes for such underachievement cannot always be determined, the task for educators, parents, and specialists becomes the identification of discrepancies in one or more of seven areas (see federal definition above).

- **Problems with learning – academic and/or social.** The definitions point to several potential areas in which learning disabilities might be detected (e.g., listening, speaking, reading, writing, calculating). Because these activities are at the center of academic learning, any difficulties usually surface within the first few years of formal schooling. Closely linked to perception and thought, social behaviors might also provide some indicators of learning disabilities.

- **Heterogeneity.** Implicit at least in all operational definitions is the acknowledgment that learning disabilities is an "equal opportunity" condition. While males outnumber females in LD programs in the United States, learning disabilities manifest themselves similarly, if not identically, in both groups. Likewise, both definition and general characteristics are presumed to remain constant across races and cultures.

By definition, individuals with learning disabilities are of average or above average intelligence, as measured by standardized IQ tests. Most states have developed discrepancy formulas to aid in the identification and placement of students with learning disabilities. Typically, a discrepancy is derived by comparing an individual's IQ scores to academic performance on reading, written language, and/or math measures. This data, along with other relevant information, aids a multidisciplinary (I.E.P.) team in determining placement and deciding appropriate goals and objectives. However, the intelligence tests most commonly used to classify students yield little or no information about *how* the individual learns. (Cowles, 1991; Mercer, 1987; Poplin and Cousin, 1996). Additionally, Lerner (1997) raised three important issues: (1) the usefulness of IQ scores in determining a child's potential; (2) the fact that discrepancy formulas differ from state to state; and (3) discrepancy formulas are not generally useful in identifying learning disabilities in young children. It should also be noted that in today's multilingual schools, language barriers may prevent IQ testing. Moreover, norm-referenced IQ tests are not available in most of the languages spoken by second language learners in our schools.

In summary, there is no single definition of "learning disabilities." Without a universally accepted definition, how do professionals determine whether a child has a true disability? If the child is bilingual, how does one distinguish a disability from a "problem" that can be attributed to limited knowledge of English?

Challenges to Learning Disabilities

Several researchers (Coles, 1987; Poplin, 1988; Sleeter, 1986) have challenged learning disabilities as a verifiable phenomenon. In *The Learning Mystique: A Critical Look at Learning Disabilities* (1987), Gerald Coles suggested that "learning disabilities became prominent in the 1960's as a biological explanation of academic inequalities within the middle class. This explanation led to the establishment of methods and programs for ameliorating 'the problem' without demanding any structural changes in society – while at the same time suggesting that these children were bound to attain less." (p. xvi). Mary Poplin (1984) argued that, "Our entire field [learning disabilities] is deficit-driven; we spend millions of dollars and hours looking for deficits, defining them, perseverating on them, imagining that we are exorcising them, and sometimes even inventing them to rationalize our activities" (p. 290). These statements echoed the opinions of a growing number of educators and parents.

The label "learning disabled" may lead to the perception that a student is incapable of functioning normally when, in fact, many of these students function quite well in most situations. Teachers are likely to have lower expectations for children who have been labeled "disabled" than for other students. It might be more appropriate to describe these children as individuals with a "special need" rather than as "disabled individuals" (see Table 2-2). Armstrong (1994) stressed the need for educators to shift from a paradigm of "deficits" view to a paradigm of "growth" view of learners.

In the 1980's the Regular Education Initiative (REI) was one strong indication of a growing disbelief in the direction the field was headed. Spearheaded by Madeline Will (1986) and colleagues (Reynolds, Wang, & Walberg, 1997), as well as the Office of Special Education and Rehabilitation Services, there was a push to return all students with learning and behavior problems to the charge of the classroom teacher. Proponents argued that special education programs unnecessarily segregated school children and stigmatized students with learning disabilities. REI evolved into the present *inclusion model*, the goal of which "is to place and instruct all children – regardless of the type of disability or level of severity– in their neighborhood school, in the general education class" (Lerner, 1997, p. 154). The ultimate aim of full inclusion is the complete elimination of special education and the use of labels.

After decades of special education services in our schools, naturally there is disagreement about the viability of full inclusion. Certainly some parents and teachers are concerned that the general classroom is not the least restrictive environment for some students with learning disabilities. After all, the general classroom is typically where the child with learning disabilities was first identified. As Lerner (1997) put it: "One size does not fit all, and lumping students with learning disabilities into the general classroom ignores the notion of individual planning" (p. 155).

Table 2-2
Deficit Paradigm Versus Growth
Paradigm in Special Education

Deficit Paradigm	Growth Paradigm
Labels the individual in terms of specific impairment(s), e.g., ED, LD, EMR, BD	Avoids labels; views the learner as an intact person who has a special need
Diagnoses the specific impairment(s) using a battery of standardized tests; focuses on errors, low scores, and weaknesses in general	Assesses the needs of an individual using authentic assessment approaches within a naturalistic context; focuses on strengths
Remediates the impairment(s) using a number of specialized treatment strategies often removed from a real-life context	Assists the person in learning and growing through a rich and varied set of interactions with real-life activities and events
Separates the individual from the mainstream for specialized treatment in a segregated class, group, or program	Maintains the individual's connections with peers in pursuing as normal a life as possible
Uses an esoteric collection of terms, tests, programs, kits, materials, and workbooks that are different from those used in special education	Uses materials, strategies, and activities that are good for *all* students
Segments the individual's life into specific behavioral/educational objectives that are regularly monitored, measured, and modified	Maintains the individual's integrity as a whole human being when assessing progress toward goals
Creates special education programs that may not bring specialists and regular classroom teachers together as often as desirable	Establishes models that enable specialists and regular classroom teachers to work collaboratively toward goals

Source: Armstrong, T. (1994). *Multiple Intelligences in the Classroom*. Alexandria, VA: Association for Supervision and Curriculum Development. Alexandria, VA. Adapted from p. 135 with permission.

Shifting Models and Trends

Wiederholt (1974) and Hammill (1993) identified three distinct phases in the evolution of the field of learning disabilities: (1) Foundations, (2) Transition, and (3) Integrative. The Foundations phase (1800-1940) was guided primarily by a Medical model in research and development, i.e., guided by assumptions that learning problems have a medical (physiological and/or neurological) explanation and cure. When a child begins to experience failure in school, the process of referral for special services typically begins with a review of the child's medical history – and then an examination of other possible factors. Having contributed the earliest and traditionally most respected research, the medical field has maintained an authoritative and influential voice in dialogues on learning problems. Most of this early research, however, centered around the study of adults with specific physiological problems or acquired brain damage. Veterans with combat injuries and victims of accidents and strokes often participated in this research. Weiderholt traced the earliest formal attempts to study the phenomenon of learning disabilities to Franz Joseph Gall's research with language disorders (circa 1802). The Foundations phase resulted in erroneous assumptions about children's learning because the theoretical framework was based on information acquired by studying the behavior of *adults* rather than school-age children. Hence, questionable assumptions were made about how *children* learn.

By the turn of the century, systematic efforts were being made to quantify learning and intelligence in the newly created field of psychology. Alfred Binet's development of an "intelligence" test not only initiated a lasting fascination with mental measures, but also stimulated the developmental models and skills taxonomies which today underlie most educational curricula (e.g., Bloom's taxonomy).

With the failure of the Medical Model to provide an adequate explanation and "cure" for learning disabilities, psychological research during the ensuing Transition phase (1940-1963) focused primarily on children and the remediation of specific problems in spoken and written language, perceptual motor processes, and behavior. The Transition phase ushered in the age of "specialists," and, by the early 1960's, had also introduced a Psychological Processing Model in the study of learning disabilities. This model represented a shift from a medication approach to one characterized by concern with prerequisite skills for learning, e.g. sensory (auditory, visual, perceptual-motor) and memory training. Developed more fully during the subsequent Integrative phase (1963-1970), the Psychological Processing Model also failed to provide either a full explanation of the phenomenon of learning disabilities or practical methods and materials for educators who had to deal with the problem on a daily basis.

Medical and psychological research, however, had created in their wake a surge of public consciousness about the plight of exceptional populations. A grass roots movement among concerned parents and professionals, marked by the creation of the Association for Children with Learning Disabilities (1963), led to public demand and the eventual passage of Public Law 94-142 in 1975. This legislation assured equity in educational opportunity for all handicapped citizens. It also coincided with an educational movement toward a "behavioral model" of teaching and learning.

Because the Behavioral Model provided the first clearly defined and systematic plan for educating exceptional children, it was widely viewed as a panacea. As Poplin (1988) noted, "the behavioral model was so popular and pervasive by 1975 that Public Law 94-142 and subsequent regulations reflected the behavioral model, witness the 'least restrictive environment', 'short term instructional objectives', and 'significant discrepancy' criteria that still govern the identification and education of the handicapped" (p. 263).

By the late 1970's, however, skeptics had begun to argue that the Behavioral Model confined itself exclusively and erroneously to concerns for *what* one learns rather than *how* one learns. Behavioral approaches (behavior modification/behavior management) had become the overseers of public instruction that seemed to favor teaching (method) over learning. These approaches to learning transformed teachers into managers and created curricula based on questionable assumptions. Critics argued against assumptions (1) that segmenting and reducing information and skills leads to mastery, (2) that modifying behavior changes the child, and (3) that school goals can pre-empt personal goals. (Hearne, 1989).

Partly in response to a perceived need to humanize and dignify both the process of learning *and* the learner, the field of learning disabilities adopted a fourth model by the late 1970's – the Cognitive Strategies Model (CSM). Retaining some vestiges of behaviorism and psychological processing, the Cognitive Strategies Model may be characterized perhaps best by its focus on promoting self-knowledge and developing individual skills (learning how to learn). The intent was clearly to restore a sense of *ability* to the learner, rather than perseverating on *disabilities* with highly regimented instructional tasks. This new view of the student as *learning* rather than as *learning disabled* has contributed greatly to the wide popularity of the Cognitive Strategies Model. Despite some division in thought – between strict concern with learning strategies versus concern with cognitive and learning styles – proponents of the CSM point to both its success in helping students meet academic goals and its broad applicability in their personal lives.

Mary Poplin (1988) challenged the four models described above based on several shared and fallacious assumptions about the nature of learning: (1) Each model presumes that learning disabilities exist as a verifiable phenomenon; (2) Each model views the cause as being resident within the learner; (3) Each model attempts to reduce and segment learning to bits of information and skills; (4) Each typically places the learner in a passive role; and (5) Each purports to offer the best or "right" approach.

Drawing upon ideas from the fields of psychology, linguistics, anthropology, and physics, Poplin advocated a revised view of learning as a *holistic/constructivist* phenomenon. *Constructivism* is a term familiar to most educators. It refers to the process of constructing knowledge (learning) about constituent *parts* through study of the *whole*. Juliana Yanushefski (1988) offered a clear example in her discussion of the advantages of a constructivist approach in language arts, when she stated that the "mastery of subskills is a by-product of the overall involvement in the reading and writing process" (p. 280). *Holism* has been used by various fields to describe both philosophic and methodological perspectives. As it relates to general and special education, holism also encompasses emerging feminist theories and critical pedagogy. The latter has guided thinking and learning in some Latin countries and has begun to influence educators in America.

In recent years, extensive research in the fields of learning disabilities and bilingual education – particularly in the growing connection between the two – has resulted in shifts in views by *both* fields. These changing perspectives are described in great detail in a recent book, *Alternative Views of Learning Disabilities: Issues for the 21st Century* (Poplin & Cousin, 1996). In this book, it was suggested that general and special educators occupy themselves far too narrowly with content, pedagogy, and the ideology of schooling while substantially ignoring or discounting sociocultural factors. Curriculum and instruction that seemed to "fit" our needs 30 years ago fall short in today's multicultural schools and classrooms.

Because the schools are deficit-driven, English language ability has continued to over-influence placement decisions. Mehan, Hertweck, and Meihls (1986) proposed that schools label children based on availability of funding, program openings, school expectations, and finding the right test, rather than planning instruction around who the learners are and what they can do. The problem was described by Poplin (1996):

> The instruments we use carry with them enormous cultural 'baggage' (as does the education system itself), which makes it more likely that some people's children will be *disabled* [emphasis added]... We place children and adolescents in instructional settings more on the basis of current vogue, most recent law, or latest method than on the basis of individual needs. In our field, in this house called school, there should be many mansions, many possibilities. (p. 2)

The push toward "non-categorical services," spurred on by the Regular Education Initiative, has created a lasting impression on LD placement practices. Assistant Secretary for the Office of Special Education and Rehabilitation, Madeline Will (1986) expressed her support for the view that students who had been identified as learning disabled should receive services in the regular classroom, alongside their peers. Will argued that students would be better served by preventive measures than by remedial programs that labeled and stigmatized them within the schools. Along with Wang and Reynolds (1986), Will further argued that pull out programs perpetuated images of students with LD as failures and inadequate. She proposed that better teaching and awareness of student needs in the regular classroom would greatly reduce the number of students being identified as "learning disabled."

Predictably, Will and colleagues met with opposition from a large segment of the special education community – both peers and advocacy groups. The tenor of these discussions was captured in the following statement by Shepard (1987): "Brave talk about teachers learning to adapt to a wider range of differences is unrealistic when the sanctions for failing to teach or failing to learn are serious." (p. 329).

Smith (1991) stated that learning disabilities programs are "overused" by both small districts that bend criteria to place students and by large districts that look for placements when cutbacks occur in bilingual and remedial programs. Such placements are surely not in the best interest of students.

Referral, Assessment, and Placement: Process and Issues

When second language learners fail to experience success in the regular classroom, it is often difficult to determine the cause. Does the child have the language skills necessary to perform classroom language activities? Are the activities presented in the classroom culturally and linguistically appropriate? Is there a disability that affects learning in the classroom? Factors affecting the referral and placement of ESL Students in LD programs are listed in Table 2-3.

Children who have been identified as having learning disabilities often have problems processing and using language in both oral and written communication. A second language learner with limited proficiency in English may give the impression that he or she has a disability if unable to perform classroom language tasks.

If a disability is suspected, a team of professionals needs to conduct assessments to determine if placement in a special education program is appropriate. However, it needs to be made clear that placement in a special education program is appropriate only for students who have been identified as having disabilities. Issues that need to be considered prior to and during the assessment are summarized in Table 2-4.

The process for referring a student suspected of having a learning disability to a team of professionals is quite similar from state to state. The team that is assembled to consider

---

Table 2-3
Issues to Consider in Referral and Assessment

Pre-referral Variables and Concerns

- causes/basis for referral
- language ability - both primary language and English
- length of time in school and quality of instruction
- attendance record

Referral Variables and Concerns

- potential bias – by teacher or other party making the referral
- reliability/validity of instruments used to determine the need for referral (if any)
- qualifications of person making the referral

Assessment Variables and Concerns

- qualifications of person conducting assessment
- validity and reliability of tests and instruments used in the assessment
- timeline for testing and evaluation
- testing conditions – location, time, testing format
- student's language ability – both L1 and L2
- student's general intelligence
- student's academic skills and abilities
- student's motivation and general attitude toward school and learning
- parents' attitudes toward testing and assessment

Post-Assessment Variables and Concerns

- program placement options and availability – L1 and L2
- time frame and follow-up
- program transition

**Table 2-4
Factors Affecting Referral of ESL Students
and Placement in Learning Disabilities Programs**

- Proficiency in the primary language (spoken and written)

- Proficiency in the English language (spoken and written)

- Age and grade placement

- Prior school experience and placements (e.g. preschool, Head Start, special programs)

- Levels of academic achievement

- Native intelligence (IQ) as determined from standard measures

- Alternate forms of assessment

- Type and severity of disability

- School attendance patterns

- Progress reports and/or anecdotal records of success and/or failure

- Health and physical/mental condition – medical records

- Presence of disabilities or handicapping conditions occurring concomitantly

- General level adaptive ability

- Social behavior

- Classroom behavior (e.g., attentive, disruptive, passive, apathetic, positive)

- Multidisciplinary team decisions

- Parent/Guardian decisions

- Availability of space and/or appropriate programs

a referral is known as the Student Study Team (SST) in many school settings, but names such as Child Study Team, Multidisciplinary Team, and School Assessment Team are also common. The intent of a multidisciplinary team is to bring differing perspectives, knowledge, and expertise to the discussion, in a word, *objectivity*. For purposes of discussion here we will use the term, Student Study Team (SST).

Typically, a child is referred to the SST when he or she is experiencing difficulty or failure in the regular classroom. The function of the Student Study Team is primarily (1) to review each child's case individually, (2) to develop a plan for intervention, and (3) to assure safeguards against misplacement in the school system. For this reason, both federal and state governments have developed guidelines and imperatives, among them, that the SST be a multidisiciplinary team. The guiding principle in determining placement of any student is least restrictive environment (LRE). One common misunderstanding about the role of the SST has been that it is convened only for the purpose of discussing children with learning problems or disabilities. It should be noted that the functions of a Student Study Team extend beyond the mere exploration of students' deficits.

The Student Study Team is a regular education function – not a special education function. The over-arching purpose of the SST is to build partnership with the parents/guardians and to share decision-making. Parents and guardians are often intimidated by the process and the persons involved. The more tactful and caring the team appears, the more likely they are to establish trust and partnership.

When a child who has limited English proficiency is demonstrating problems learning in the classroom, the SST should include individuals who understand issues relating to bilingualism and cultural diversity. Professionals in special education and bilingual education need to combine their efforts to plan assessments and to develop culturally and linguistically appropriate programs of instruction.

In the wake of the "inclusive schooling" movement, there has been a greater trend toward *collaborative* and *consultation* models of service delivery. Many schools and districts across the nation have seen a redefining of the roles of Learning Disabilities Specialists/Resource Specialists (RS), Categorical Program Specialists (CPS), and other support personnel. In brief, the consultation approach typically brings together the teacher and consultant (e.g., Resource Specialist) to explore strategies and interventions and to develop a plan of action. The consultant may monitor the child's progress under the action plan, and, along with the teacher, assess student progress and make adjustments based on student needs.

Whereas the specialist is viewed as the expert in the consultation model and the primary voice in developing an action plan, the *peer collaboration* model promotes partnership. The referring teacher, along with peers, parents, and specialists work together to hammer out plans of action, including ways of assessing program effectiveness.

Assessment

Assessment represents perhaps the most controversial facet of special education. In addition to controversy over the value of IQ testing, as discussed above, there is equal disagreement over which achievement tools and measures to use. Selecting appropriate tests is extremely important, especially if they will be used in placement decisions. There are virtually hundreds of achievement and aptitude measures available, many of which are seriously lacking in two critical areas – **validity** and **reliability**. In her *Guide to 100 Tests for Special Education*, Carolyn Comption (1995) reviewed the strengths and limitations of widely used tests and measures and the implications of their use by special educators. The following is a listing of primary weaknesses that were identified.

- Insufficient information on standardization procedures and populations
- Insufficient standardization samples (by race/culture, age, gender, geographic region, etc.)
- Insufficient data on reliability studies
- Insufficient data on validity studies
- Misleading and/or inaccurate statements
- Vague, inadequate, and/or misleading directions
- Technical inaccuracies and inconsistencies

Such caveats are certainly important to school psychologists, resource specialists, speech-language pathologists, and other persons engaged in special education assessment. Inadequate and/or inappropriate instruments have long been the culprit of wrongful placement of second language learners in special education programs.

Least Restrictive Environment

The guiding principle in all educational placements is *least restrictive environment* (LRE). Generally speaking, the general classroom is viewed as the least restrictive environment for all learners. Under the Individuals with Disabilities Education Act (IDEA, 1990) and its reauthorization (1996), all students, regardless of the severity of their disabilities are to be included as fully as possible in general classrooms at their neighborhood schools. This legislation, along with Public Law 94-142 and Section 504 of the Rehabilitation Act, guide schools and other education agencies in placement decisions. Parents and guardians play a prominent role in the decision-making process.

Certain procedural and legal safeguards for individuals with disabilities and their families are provided by IDEA, among them:

- the rights of both student and parent/guardian to review all data accumulated during the referral process and placement decisions
- the right of the student to testing and assessment in the primary language
- the right to be assessed with instruments that are racially/culturally bias-free
- the requirement of written consent by parents/guardians before assessment can proceed
- the right of parents/guardians to assessment information in their primary language
- assurance of confidentiality of records and information accumulated in the referral-placement process

Cultural and Linguistic Considerations

Some children who are labeled "learning disabled" have problems processing and using the spoken language. If the student comes from a home where a language other than English is used, the deficiencies observed in comprehending and using the spoken language can have an effect on learning.

Asian speakers learning English, for example, produce a variety of "errors" similar to those commonly observed among children with language disorders. Examples from a list reported by Roseberry-McKibbin (1995) are presented below:

Language Characteristic	**Sample English Utterances**
Omission of plurals	Here are 2 piece of toast.
Omission of copula	He going home now. They eating.

Misordering of interrogatives	You are going now?
Omission of articles	I see little cat.
Misuse off pronouns	She husband is coming.

Although language differences such as those listed above can have an effect on learning, the observed "problems" reflect limited experience with the English language and should not be viewed as evidence of a "disability" (Mattes & Omark, 1991; Roseberry-McKibbin, 1995).

Cultural differences also can affect how behaviors are interpreted by assessment personnel and may lead to erroneous conclusions about children and how they learn. Recent immigrants from Asian countries, for example, may be unaccustomed to participating in groups of mixed gender. They may not "take initiative" or ask questions in the classroom. In some Asian countries, it is considered rude to ask questions during class. Students are expected to sit quietly and not to question the teacher. (Cheng, 1991; Roseberry-McKibbin, 1995). In American schools, however, such behavior might be viewed as evidence of passivity, poor attention skills, or lack of interest.

When interviewing Asian parents, the response "yes" may mean "I hear you" rather than "I agree" (Cheng, 1991). When American teachers ask parents to take a specific course of action, a "yes" response indicates that the request was heard. This response, however, does not necessarily mean that the parent will follow through with the requested action. Therefore, American teachers need to learn how to ask questions and how to present information to individuals who may perceive the "problem" quite differently from themselves.

Parents who came to the United States from another country may be offended if a teacher suggests that there is something wrong with their child. How can there be a disability if that child looks normal and doesn't show any evidence of something being "wrong" in the home environment? If the child shows no obvious evidence of being "different" at home, the parents may wonder why the school is concerned.

Although it is important to consider cultural differences, it is also important to avoid stereotyping students based on where they come from. Religious differences, living environment, social status, and a variety of other factors influence one's values and behavior. By learning about different cultural groups, professionals become aware of behavioral *tendencies* that may have an effect on performance in school. It is harmful to assume that all students from a particular country share the same values and behave in the same way. By studying cultural tendencies, professionals can reduce the likelihood of confusing *differences* with *disorders*. This information is also critical in developing culturally and linguistically appropriate instructional programs for individual students (See Table 2-5).

Implications for Students with Language and Learning Challenges

As indicated in the above discussion, the field of learning disabilities emerged in the early 1960's as a result of pressure from parents from the middle class for an alternative to labels such as "mentally retarded." To this day, however, many of the tests used in the identification of learning disabilities are of questionable validity, and the construct "learning disabilities" means different things to different people.

Since the emergence of the field of learning disabilities, educators have become increasingly more aware of the effect of culture, language background, and environment

---

Table 2-5
Cultural and Linguistic Considerations Related to IEP Development

Selection of IEP Goals and Objectives

Considerations for IEP Development	*Classroom Implications*
IEP goals and objectives accommodate student's current level of performance.	- At the student's instructional level - Instructional level based on student's cognitive level, not the language proficiency level - Focus on development of higher level cognitive skills as well as basic skills
Goals and objectives are responsive to cultural and linguistic variables.	- Accommodates goal and expectations of the family - Is sensitive to culturally-based response to the disability - Includes a language use plan - Addresses language development and ESL needs

Selection of Instructional Strategies

Considerations for IEP Development	*Classroom Implications*
Interventions provide adequate exposure to curriculum.	- Instruction in student's dominant language - Responsiveness to learning and communication styles - Sufficient practice to achieve mastery
IEP provides for curricular/instructional accommodation of learning styles and locus of control.	- Accommodates perceptual style differences (e.g., visual vs. auditory) - Accommodates cognitive style differences (e.g. inductive vs. deductive) - Accommodates preferred style of participation (e.g. teacher- vs. student-directed small vs. large group) - Reduces feelings of learned helplessness
Selected strategies are likely to be effective for language minority students.	- Native language and ESL instruction - Teacher as facilitator of learning (vs. transmission) - Genuine dialogue with students - Contextualized instruction - Collaborative learning - Self-regulated learning - Learning-to-learn strategies
English-as-a-second language (ESL) strategies are used.	- Modifications to address the student's disability - Use of current ESL approaches - Focus on meaningful communication
Strategies for literacy are included.	- Holistic approaches to literacy development - Language teaching that is integrated across curriculum - Thematic literature units - Language experience approach and - Journals

---

Source: Garcia, S.B. & Malkin, D.H. (1993). Toward Defining Programs and Services for Culturally and Linguistically Diverse Learners in Special Education. *Teaching Exceptional Children, 26 (1),* pg. 115. Reprinted with permission from the Council for Exceptional Children.

on learning. What appears to be a learning disability can often be explained by differences in a child's experience background. Children who are referred to special education often come from backgrounds that are different from that of most of their classmates. Drug use in the home, child abuse, poor nutrition, and a variety of other factors will influence learning in the classroom. If a child has difficulty understanding the language or the cultural norms of the classroom, learning difficulties may also be experienced.

When faced with the complex task of determining whether or not a second language learner has a learning disability, it is important to keep the following factors in mind:

- Cultural bias is inherent in many of the instruments used in assessment. How can the schools provide bias-free testing and assessment for students from so many language and cultural backgrounds? The response, at least for now, is that we *cannot.*
- The construct "learning disabilities" has become a controversial topic. Performance on many of the norm-referenced tests used in the identification of "disabilities" may have little or no relationship to the "problems" that are affecting learning in the classroom. If the procedures used to identify native English speakers with learning disabilities have questionable validity, how can educators be expected to identify second language learners who have disabilities that require special education intervention?
- Most of the research and development in the field of learning disabilities has been conducted among English-speaking populations. Hence, there is a lack of valid and reliable assessment instruments (e.g., achievement, aptitude, and IQ tests) in languages other than standard English.
- Second-language learners often receive less comprehensible instruction than their English proficient peers, and therefore perform more poorly in the classroom. Poor performance frequently leads to referral and placement in special education programs.

A comparison of referral and instructional practices used with ESL students and students with Learning Disabilities is presented in Table 2-6.

General Suggestions for Assessment and Instructional Programming

While there is no single "best" method for promoting learning and language acquisition, Table 2-7 includes some "pointers" on assessment, motivation, instruction, and evaluation. An effective program includes an assessment of student strengths and interests – as well as needs and motivation. Professionals must become familiar with a student's background and experiences in order to provide culturally and linguistically appropriate programs of instruction. Information that needs to be obtained includes the following:

- Level of proficiency in the primary language
- Level of proficiency in English
- Instructional needs in academic areas
- Social needs and/or problems
- Personal motivations that influence classroom behavior and academic functioning

Table 2-6
Comparison of Referral and Instructional Practices for ESL Students and Students with Learning Disabilities

	ESL	LD
Identification	referral based on language deficits (speaking/reading/writing)	referral typically based on language deficits (reading/writing skills)
Assessment	diagnostic: oral and/or written tests	diagnostic: oral and written tests
Service Model	pull-out program/ ability grouping	pull-out program/ ability grouping
Instruction	deficit/product-driven, remediation, drill and practice, Direct Instruction	remediation, drill and practice, Direct Instruction
Evaluation	verbal and written tests	verbal and written tests

(For related information, see Drecktrah, M. E. & Chiang, B. (1997). Instructional strategies used by general educators and teachers of students with learning disabilities. *Journal of Learning Disabilities, 18 (3)*, pp. 174-181).

Other Commonalities

- Drop-out rates for both groups are well-above the national norm.
- Both groups are stigmatized by their labels and school placements.
- Both groups are often ridiculed and ostracized by peers.
- Expectations of academic success are frequently low.

Table 2-7
Promoting Learning and Language Acquisition

Assessment – The Starting Point
- Identify students' individual levels of language ability and stage of development.
- Identify students' individual strengths, learning styles, and multiple intelligences (MI).
- Determine students' needs – academic, socio-emotional, and physical.

Motivation
- Create a language-rich learning environment, complete with L1 and L2 literature.
- Create reasons for students to listen, speak, read, and write – authentic purposes.
- Provide comprehensible input as a bridge to new learning and language development.
- Encourage parents/family members to visit your classroom.

Instruction
- Create opportunities for all students to experience academic success.
- Simplify input as needed for students with LLC – content is secondary to communication.
- Provide both verbal and non-verbal input and instruction, e.g. gestures, realia, visuals.
- Engage students in meaningful activities; capitalize upon their interests.
- Provide high context and low context instruction – monitor and adjust to student needs.
- Model language in its many forms – read texts, magazines, drama, poetry, lyrics, etc.

Evaluation
- Accept progress – even small gains – as evidence of learning and personal growth.
- Use broad assessment/evaluation tools, e.g. portfolios, performances, rubric scoring, etc.
- Allow adequate time and assure proper conditions for test-taking.
- Provide encouragement; reassure students of the progress they have already made.
- Utilize assessment/evaluation data in planning future instruction.

Remember

- Do not expect failure from students with LLC in your classroom or program.
- Do not perseverate on students' language and/or learning deficits.
- Do not correct every error – it is often counterproductive.
- Do not forbid use of the primary language – it serves as another cueing system.

Teachers should begin instructional planning by capitalizing the strengths and areas of interest that were identified during the assessment. Students are much more likely to engage in classroom activities that incorporate their interests. Frequently, students from diverse cultural backgrounds share common interests, and this provides wonderful opportunities for class projects and cooperative grouping. Shared interests help to create *authentic purposes* for students with LLC to speak, read, and write (in either or both languages). Classrooms should abound with books and literature in the languages of the students. However, reading and instruction, if they are to be effective, must be comprehensible to the learners. Table 2-8 provides additional suggestions for teachers of students with language and learning challenges in the general classroom.

Two additional elements critical to school success are acceptance and empowerment. The lived experience of each child is reflected in his or her school performance— good or bad. It is impossible for students with LLC to dissociate thoughts from feelings in academic situations that pit them against peers in the regular classroom. Language is power and a lack of power can easily lead to frustration and failure. Table 2-9 offers some ways to empower language-minority students in our schools.

Table 2-8
Students with LLC in the Regular Classroom
General Suggestions for Teachers

Sample Modifications/Adaptations:

Classroom Environment - *It Begins Here*
Create a classroom atmosphere that values differences – where all students are welcome.
- Plan welcoming activities that encourage student interaction.
- Accommodate students' learning styles by varying physical arrangements (i.e., some students work best in groups, others independently).

Socio-Emotional Considerations - *Nurturing the Heart*
- Conference with students individually, to assure them of their value and to encourage their trust and commitment.
- Meet with parents of every student to gain insight into the child's background, interests, ideas, and feelings – as well as insight into the child's home life.

Assessment - *Gaining Access to the Child's World*
A broad assessment might include the following:
- Interest Inventories
- Language Dominance Tests (e.g., IPT)
- Language Proficiency Tests (e.g., SOLOM)
- Multiple Intelligences (MI) Assessment
- Learning Styles Profile
- Academic Assessment, (e.g., criterion-referenced measures)
- Modality Preference (visual, auditory, kinesthetic, tactile)

Instruction and Interventions - *Nurturing the Mind and Body*
The Preview-Review method is a powerful tool for use across all disciplines. The student may need modifications and/or alternate assignments in some of the following activities:

Activity/Skill	Intervention/Strategy
Listening	- repetition, recorded lessons (primary language), interpreter
Speaking	- microphone, peer interpreter, reduced assignments
Reading	- reduced assignments, alternate/abridged stories and/or books
Written Language	- word processors, dictated in primary language
Math	- calculators, bilingual math partners, cooperative groups
Science	- bilingual science partner, simplified hands-on tasks
Social Studies	- reduced/simplified assignments, cooperative groups
Art	- alternate art activities/medium
Music	- peer interpreter, music in primary language
P.E.	- adapted/alternate activities as needed

Table 2-9
Ways to Empower Language Minority Students

- Help language minority students develop lessons to teach the class about their culture.

- Encourage language minority students to teach children's songs in the primary language (L1) to the class.

- Organize and/or participate in a school-wide cultural fair.

- Encourage multiple intelligences (MI) throughout the school year.

- Have students explore their interests/talents and possible career options.

- Create a multicultural environment in the classroom.

- Create opportunities to praise the student for development in both languages.

- Maintain a class library rich with books in all the languages of your students.

- Provide opportunities for students to use the second language in other school settings.

- Help the student locate appropriate reading and learning materials for use in the home by family members.

- Teach the child ways of teaching other family members.

- Take the students on walking field trips to visit neighborhood businesses.

- Encourage students to write letters, cards, and notes to relatives and friends in L1.

- Provide instruction at the child's language developmental level in the primary language (L1) and English (L2).

- Infuse the curriculum with the students' real world experiences.

- Use students as cross-age tutors for younger minority language students in the school.

- Have minority language students make audio tapes of stories read for other students.

- Have minority language students make cards and gifts representative of their culture.

Chapter 3
Models and Options for Language Learning

The cat chased the mouse into its hole and waited beside the hole. Then it barked like a dog. The mouse, thinking the cat had gone away, came out of its hole and was pounced on. Then the cat said archly, You see, 'it pays to be bilingual.'
George A. Miller

Diversity is a fact of American culture. Nowhere is this more apparent than in the nation's schools, where more than 100 languages are spoken in some sectors. The responses of schools to the growing demands for quality education, according to some, have been inadequate and slow, although not without reason. Over the years, researchers have offered a virtual continuum of linguistic theories and models, along with impressive data to support them. However, like the field of learning disabilities in its earlier days, few researchers have translated their theories into usable or practical models for teachers. The mere variety of theories has brought some confusion to the task of developing second-language programs in the schools. When programs and models are reviewed by educational agencies, the following factors need to be considered:

- theoretical soundness of the program or model
- the viability of implementing the program
- the applicability of a plan or model for general/specific populations
- adequacy of available personnel to effectively implement the plan
- availability of appropriate materials to enhance the chances of success
- adequacy of funding to assure long-range planning

- procedures for monitoring and adjusting to learner needs as they arise
- procedures for formative and summative evaluations of the program itself

Paul Loesch (1998), a former "Principal of the Year" in a predominantly Hispanic elementary school, expressed the following concerns about bilingual and second-language program assessment:

> It may be useful to note that most [second language] approaches are not matched to adequate assessment plans. Thus, there are no real examples of proven approaches to second language instruction. Almost all approaches seem to work on faith – 'This ought to work.' District programs are handicapped by three things: (1) *very* limited resources; (2) teachers ill-trained to meet the need and overwhelmed by the scale of that need; and (3) an uncertain foundation based upon questionable assessments.

Efforts to develop bilingual programs have been further complicated by uneven population growth *and* uneven school planning. For example, immigrant and bilingual populations are not spread evenly across most school districts. Redrawing school attendance boundaries has undoubtedly helped, but natural borders created by ethnicity and/or language define many neighborhoods and communities and the schools that serve them.

While educational planning for second-language learners continues to be a formidable task, assessment of *individual* achievement presents even greater problems. Assessment practices vary from state to state, district to district, and sometimes from school to school. Second-language learners create a dilemma for schools and districts with state-imposed standardized testing. Basically, the tests are designed to assess verbal and logical-mathematical abilities. Students in schools driven by whole language instruction, project/inquiry-based instruction, or a multiple intelligences model may be unfairly challenged and ill-prepared to demonstrate the breadth of their knowledge and skills in a paper-and-pencil test. For second-language learners, the task can be even more frustrating – perhaps even meaningless. The mismatch between classroom instruction and standardized testing is often a concern.

Should state education agencies and school districts provide alternate forms of assessment for second-language learners? Assessment issues seem to confound educational planning for this population of students.

Trends in Second-Language Instruction

• *ELD (English Language Development)*
In California, the state with the largest concentration of second-language learners, the term English-as-a-second-language (ESL), has begun to be replaced by the terms *English language development* (ELD) and *Specially Designed Academic Instruction in English* (SDAIE). In ELD classrooms, emphasis is given to vocabulary development and the teaching of language through content (Freeman & Freeman, 1994). Through the use of visuals, realia, and picture dictionaries, students begin to build bridges to English. At the Pre-production stage, for example, teachers attempt to communicate with students through Total Physical Response (TPR), by using gestures, voice tones, and body language to communicate ideas, information, and commands. Simple commands might include "Open your book," "Come to the board," or "Write your name." Over time, students

are typically able to move from simple to complex tasks and responses. The use of other visuals helps students to progress from simple to advanced levels of language ability. Providing comprehensible input is paramount to students' oral and written language development. It is therefore imperative that the difficulty level of the language used in instruction approximate the language level of the students. Freeman and Freeman (1994) identified several characteristics of teachers who were effective in meeting the learning needs of second-language learners:

- Effective teachers celebrate both the learner and the act of learning.
- Effective teachers value cultural and linguistic differences.
- Effective teachers are guided by constructivist principles in which holism is emphasized.
- Effective teachers encourage multiple ways of constructing meaning.

• *Sheltered English (K-3)*

The term "Sheltered English" refers to controlled language instruction in meaningful contexts. ESL (English-as-a-second-language) and sheltered English are often used synonymously, although ESL was intended as an intervention for students at the beginning stages of second-language development (Freeman & Freeman, 1994). Instruction in this approach is "content-based." Thus, content area subject matter is used to teach English. Selection of appropriate literature is a critical factor in planning instruction. Au (1993) urged teachers to select not only developmentally appropriate literature but also stories and books from many cultures.

• *Specially Designed Academic Instruction in English (SDAIE)*

This approach is widely used with second-language learners in grades 4 through 12. Generally speaking, candidates for SDAIE should be at least at the intermediate stage of fluency. The approach is content-driven and typically follows the core curriculum of the district and/or state frameworks. Information and skills are not watered down and stretched out. Nor are they "dumbed down" by a presumption that second-language learners are inherently less capable, intellectually or otherwise. However, careful effort is given to "contextualizing" lessons so as to make them comprehensible and relevant. Lessons should be designed so that they help students activate their prior knowledge and experiences as a bridge to new learning. It is therefore imperative that teachers get to know their students and what they are capable of doing with language. An integral part of a successful SDAIE program is attention to study and learning skills. Devices used in learning disabilities classrooms – mnemonics, chunking, acronyms, and other cognitive strategies – are equally valuable to second-language learners who are struggling with cognitively demanding instruction. Likewise, modified or alternative instruction and/or assignments may become important options for teachers. Regardless of their subject areas, it is imperative for SDAIE teachers to have a broad knowledge of English and how to teach it to second-language learners.

• *Biliteracy Approach*

Thinking of biliteracy as as instructional objective is difficult for many educators because "schools appear to face an increasingly uphill battle in their efforts to develop literacy in just one language" (Cummins, 1993, p. 9). The general decline in national test scores over the past 20 years, findings from the Carnegie Report and other alarming research "findings" in the 1980s have all contributed to a growing skepticism about the effectiveness and efficiency of bilingual education. Cummins (1993), however, presented a strong argument to show that biliteracy is a feasible educational outcome. The theory underlying biliteracy is that both cultural and critical literacies are not only relevant but also necessary to the achievement of national educational goals. In other words, learners should retain rights to their individual identity formation and their cultural perspective on the world. Language is thought and vice versa. Thinking in two languages allows us to operate in our own world and connect with those of others. Other arguments that might be made for biliteracy include the following:

- Literacy in two languages increases a child's future career potential in American and international markets.
- Literacy in more than one language allows the individual to construct broader meanings. Literal translations are not possible for many of the expressions used within a particular language. A thought that can be expressed in a few words in one language may require several sentences when translated.
- Literacy in more than one language allows a person to utilize and enjoy good literature in its original text.
- Literacy in two languages enables an individual to help others learn English.

Painstaking as it may seem, educating second-language learners solely in English – a language of exceptions – is a reality in many schools and districts. Consider the following riddle.

Hints On Pronunciation For Foreigners

I take it you already know
Of tough and bough and cough and dough?
Others may stumble but not you
On hiccough, though, laugh, and through.
Well done! And now you wish, perhaps,
To learn of less familiar traps?

Beware of heard, a dreadful word
That looks like beard and sounds like bird,
And dead: It's said like bed, not bead
For goodness' sake don't call it deed.
Watch out for meat and great and threat
(they rhyme with suite and straight and debt.)

A moth is not a moth in mother
Nor both in bother, broth in brother,
And here is not a match for there
Nor dear and fear for bear and pear
And then there's dose and rose and lose
Just look them up and goose and choose,

And cork and work and card and ward,
And font and front and word and sword,
And do and go and thwart and cart,
Come, come, I've hardly made a start!
A dreadful language? Man alive!
I'd mastered it when I was five.

-Anonymous

Methodologies for Teaching Language Skills

The ESL methods described below have provided a framework for various programs of instruction used in our schools:

- *Direct Method*

   In this approach, also known as an immersion method, the guiding principle is that language learning takes place through the association of words with objects. For this reason, instruction relies heavily upon the use of "realia," that is, pictures and objects from everyday life. Translation is *not* allowed. The expectation is that, through constant usage, learners will eventually acquire both the **vocabulary** and **form** of the language.

   Implications for Students with LLC - Students who have difficulty with memory and recall tasks will probably struggle if this method is used. Moreover, based on what is currently known about the process of acquiring a second language, this approach has serious limitations. Children learn language most efficiently when it serves a useful function. Direct approaches often focus on teaching various language structures in isolation. Therefore, students often experience difficulty generalizing what is learned in the classroom to natural communication contexts.

- *Audio-Lingual Method*

   In this approach, imitation and practice are emphasized as various language skills are modeled for students. The belief is that second language acquisition occurs through hearing, repeating, and reinforcement.

   Implications for Students with LLC - Students who have been diagnosed as having auditory memory problems will probably have difficulty recalling the messages and dialogues to be imitated.

- *Grammar Translational*

   This model may be thought of as a *form* before *function* approach. The learner is encouraged to learn the rules of the language (grammar, mechanics, and usage) by rote and by written translation. The emphasis, therefore, is placed on language structures rather than functional language use.

   Implications for Students with LLC - Complex written language is commonly a difficult task for students with LD. Likewise, rules of grammar may remain meaningless for some time to the child who is still struggling with concrete, functional language.

- *Pragmatic (Notional/Functional)*

   The guiding principle in this model is to teach students to use language for specific purposes that have relevance to their daily life experiences. An emphasis is placed on the pragmatic aspects of communication. From that base, the child can build vocabulary and meanings from both languages. Rather than teaching students various language "structures," children are provided with feedback to help them use language to express needs, request information, etc.

   Implications for Students with LLC - Children learn language because it helps them to satisfy needs and achieve goals in their interactions with others. This model makes use of what the child knows about language to expand his/her linguistic capabilities. An effort in made to relate new learning to the child's previously acquired knowledge.

• *Natural Approach*

The Natural Approach has become an exemplary model for second-language programs. Terrell (1977; 1981) documented predictable patterns and identified a hierarchy of language skills. Language acquisition in both the first and second language begins with *listening* and advances naturally through the remaining stages of *speaking, reading,* and *writing.*

Implications for Students with LLC - This approach provides teachers of students with LLC with a developmental model for selecting content, language and learning experiences, and age/stage-appropriate materials. The approach also provides a basis for assessment and evaluation.

Structure vs. Function

Prior to the 1970s, most language acquisition models focused only on the structural aspects of language. Language was often viewed as a series of structures that were mastered one at a time. Researchers now recognize the important role that the social context has in the learning of language. Language learning requires much more than the learning of words and grammatical structures. From the very early stages of language acquisition, children use language for specific purposes. They learn what they need to know to achieve specific goals.

The process of learning a second language is very similar to that of learning a first language. Second language learners who speak their first language fluently, however, already know quite a bit about language and how it works. This knowledge and experience background facilitates learning to speak a second language. Moreover, if the child is able to read in the native language, this knowledge of the reading process can be used to facilitate learning to read in English.

Dimensions of Language Proficiency

Cummins (1981;1991) proposed a theory of language acquisition based upon five principles that relate to both innate and environmental influences.

1. *Common Underlying Proficiency* - Success in acquiring oral and written communication skills in a second language is influenced by the knowledge and experiences that the individual has had in learning the first language. In other words, there are underlying factors and conditions common to language acquisition in any language.

2. *Linguistic Threshold* - There is a point at which the student's cognitive and linguistic ability merge. When the student is proficient in the primary language (L1), he or she has already developed the strategies necessary to understand and use language, and this knowledge facilitates second language learning. Nonetheless, inadequate and/or ineffective learning experiences may adversely affect the acquisition of high levels of proficiency in either or both languages.

3. *Two Dimensions of Language Proficiency* - Cummins used the image of an iceberg to illustrate the principle involved here. As most people are aware, the visible portion of the iceberg is but a small part of the whole. As applied to language acquisition, daily conversational language is the mere tip of the language requirements for success with a demanding and complex curriculum. Although *basic interpersonal communication skills* (BICS), are often mastered in two or three years, the cognitively demanding language skills necessary to complete classroom assignments take much more time to learn. Based on a review of research, Cummins reported that it takes five to seven years for students to acquire

cognitive-academic language proficiency (CALP). Unfortunately, teachers often assume that students are ready for academic instruction in English only when these students have mastered the basic skills necessary to respond appropriately during informal conversations. Students who can carry on a simple conversation in English, however, may experience difficulty manipulating language and performing the cognitively demanding language tasks necessary to complete worksheets, take tests, and complete various other classroom activities.

4. ***Second Language Acquisition*** - Acquisition of both the first and second language, according to Cummins, is dependent upon comprehensible information and a positive environment in which to experiment with language. Skills mastered in the first language facilitate learning in the second language. A student who reads well in Spanish, for example, has learned the processes necessary to construct meaning from print. This student can apply this knowledge when learning to read in English.

5. ***Student Status*** - The final principle relates to matters of self-image, self-esteem, feelings, and emotions. The status of the student within the school and/or community may well be the strongest predictor of attitudes toward learning. If learning is prevented by feelings of inferiority or defeat, the value of the instruction that is being provided might seem questionable at best.

Cummins (1989) advocated an interactive approach that engages students in meaningful language, instruction, and experiences. In Cummins' interactive model of instruction, the importance of providing *meaningful* opportunities for learning is emphasized. The following points are especially important for elementary school teachers:

- Learning should be a guided experience, rather than a purely teacher or curriculum-centered pursuit.
- Classrooms should encourage student-student discussion for both social and academic purposes.
- All content areas should be infused with language use and development.
- The emphasis in the language curriculum should be meaningful dialogue rather than drill activities that focus only on language structure. Students must be provided with opportunities to learn language in situations where they are communicating for a purpose.

Stages in Language Learning

Krashen (1982) emphasized the importance of creating inviting and language-rich environments for second-language learners at all levels. He identified five important factors or hypotheses directly related to language acquisition:

1. ***Natural Order Hypothesis*** - According to this hypothesis, language development follows a natural and predictable order. From the field of physics, educators have long applied the principle that "form follows function" in academic learning. Nowhere is this principle more applicable than in language development. First and second-language learners acquire language through experimentation and language play. Language learning begins with listening and then proceeds developmentally toward speaking. After learning to speak, children acquire reading skills followed by skills in writing.

    Implications for Teachers of Students with LLC – Learning language takes time and, therefore, students may not begin speaking English immediately.

While listening to the language around them, students learn new concepts and acquire insights related to how language works. Attempting to "hurry" students to speak English often results in frustration for both student and teacher. Speech-language pathologists, special education teachers, and bilingual education specialists should work as a team to help classroom teachers develop an understanding of the processes involved in learning language.

2. *Input Plus One (+1) Hypothesis* - The best predictor of what will be learned, it is said, is what is already known. Krashen applied this principle to language acquisition by asserting that new learning must approximate the level of knowledge or the experience the child has had with the subject/concept. Learning, then, is a matter of stretching the learner by adding new information or experiences at a level just beyond that of the student.

   Implications for Teachers of Students with LLC - All too frequently, there is a mismatch between a student's present level of operation/experience and the new information or skill being introduced by the teacher. Instructional planning should begin at the student's level of language development.

3. *Acquisis Versus Grammar* - Like the hypothesis of natural order, there appears to be a natural acquisition process for language form. Form is acquired over time as the child learns the various grammatical distinctions that affect meaning. Children do not consciously think about "grammar" as they learn language. Language, according to this hypothesis, is holistic in nature, learned without conscious knowledge of individual language rules, and it is self-regulating.

   Implications for Teachers of Students with LLC - Attempting to impose form (grammar rules, mechanics, usage) too soon might be described as "teaching against the grain." By emphasizing *form* over *function,* the instruction provided may make little sense to the student. *Emphasize function, more than form.*

4. *Monitor Hypothesis* - According to Krashen, there is within each of us a self-regulating editor that monitors and decodes incoming messages and then attempts to formulate comprehensible responses. The more complex the information, the more processing time it takes to mentally interpret and apply language rules to one's response. For this reason, many second-language learners continue to be perceived as "slow."

   Implications for Teachers of Students with LLC - This problem, coupled with learning disabilities, can be a prescription for failure in English-only (EO) or "transition classrooms." Teachers of students with learning disabilities can mediate instruction by working closely with regular classroom teachers in adapting the curriculum and methods.

5. *Affective Filter Hypothesis* - Similar to the monitor hypothesis, Krashen described an internal process whereby the learner's performance is filtered through an affective screen of feelings, emotions, and attitudes. Such factors directly influence the student's level of anxiety and disposition toward schoolwork.

   Implications for Teachers of Students with LLC - ESL students with learning disabilities may have high levels of anxiety directly related to levels of confidence, school failure, and placements. Teachers should plan for success, no matter how small that success might be.

Language Differences and Language Disorders

When students learn a second language, they may exhibit "errors" resulting from the influence of the first language. In the Spanish language, for example, the only consonants that ever occur at the end of words are /d/, /l/, /n/, /r/, and /s/. In English, however, most consonants can occur in the initial, medial, or final position of a word. When learning English, Spanish speakers frequently omit final consonants. This difference is to be expected and should not be viewed as an abnormality (Mattes & Omark, 1991; Roseberry-McKibbin, 1995). Differences commonly observed among Spanish speakers when speaking English are listed in Table 3-1.

Although some grammatical errors produced by second language learners result from the influence of the first language, many reflect the student's progress in acquiring a new set of language rules. Thus, when learning English, sentences may be produced that are similar to those produced by first language learners in the early stages of language acquisition. Therefore, it is quite easy to confuse language differences with language disorders (Roseberry-McKibbin, 1995).

If a student has a language disorder, deficits will be evident in both the primary language and English (Langdon & Merino, 1992; Mattes & Omark, 1991). Children with limited proficiency in English need to be provided with opportunities to listen to the language and to practice using it in functional speaking situations. If there is no evidence of an abnormality, however, these students should *not* be placed in any type of special education program. Rather, programs should be provided within the regular education curriculum to meet the needs of these students.

Bilingual children who have limited opportunities for functional use of the primary language often experience a loss of proficiency in that language. If they have not yet mastered English, they may score low on tests administered in both the home language and English. These students may give the impression that they have communication disorders if their background experience is not considered in the assessment. Language loss is a normal phenomenon that occurs when opportunities for continued practice in the use of a language are reduced (See Langdon & Merino, 1991; Mattes & Omark, 1991).

Barriers to Language Learning

Thonis (1993) described the challenge facing monolingual teachers in schools with large populations of limited English proficient students. She emphasized that language is *content*, but it also carries content. If children in the classroom "do not understand the language of the teacher and if the teacher does not understand the language of children, both are at a very serious disadvantage in the teaching and learning efforts" (p. 148). She advocated beginning reading and writing instruction in the dominant home language of the student population. Johns and Espinoza (1992) proposed three major barriers to language acquisition in our schools:

1. *Reductionism* - The belief that the language can be broken down into discrete units that can be taught individually has resulted in programs that are often ineffective.
2. *Cultural barriers* - Linguistic and cultural differences are often misperceived and/or undervalued by educators.
3. *Inadequate communication* - There may be limited communication between the adults who interact with the child at home.

A primary reason for pushing the use of reductionist teaching methods, according to Johns and Espinoza, is that these methods "are seen as a way to help children do better

Table 3-1
Articulation Differences Commonly Observed Among Spanish Speakers

Articulation Characteristics	Sample English Patterns
1. /t, d, n/ may be dentalized (tip of tongue is placed against the back of the upper central incisors).	
2. Final consonants are often devoiced	dose/doze
3. b/v substitution	berry/very
4. Deaspirated stops (sounds like speaker is omitting the sound because it is said with little air release).	
5. ch/sh substitution	Chirley/Shirley
6. d/voiced th, or z/voiced th (voiced "th" does not exist in Spanish).	dis/this, zat/that
7. t/voiceless th (voiceless "th" does not exist in Spanish).	tink/think
8. Schwa sound inserted before word initial consonant clusters	kate/skate; espend/spend
9. Words can end in 10 different sounds: a,e,i,o,u,l,r,n,s,d	may omit sounds at ends of words
10. When words start with /h/, the /h/ is silent	'old/hold, 'it/hit
11. /r/ is tapped or trilled (tap /r/ might sound like the tap in the English word "butter.")	
12. There is no /j/ (e.g., judge) sound in Spanish; speakers may substitute "y"	Yulie/Julie yoke/joke
13. Frontal /s/ -Spanish /s/ is produced more frontally than English /s/.	Some speakers may sound like they have frontal lisps.
14. The ñ is pronounced like "y" (e.g., baño is pronounced "bahnyo.").	

Spanish has 5 vowels: a,e,i,o,u (ah, eh, ee, o, u) and few diphthongs.
Thus, Spanish speakers may produce the following vowel substitutions:

15. ee/I substitution	peeg/pig; leetle/little
16. E/ae, ah/ae substitutions	pet/pat; Stahn/Stan

Source: Roseberry-McKibbin, C. (1995). *Multicultural students with special language needs: Practical strategies for assessment and intervention.* Oceanside, CA: Academic Communication Associates. Reprinted by permission.

on standardized tests" (p. 11). Teachers have often allowed these assessment tools to influence how instruction is provided to students.

As to the second proposition, Cummins (1989a) suggested that students from other countries are driven, at least initially, by different values, perceptions, and experiences. In American schools, these students may be asked to perform tasks and assignments that are so foreign to their ways of thinking that they question or misperceive the purpose. Problem-solving in some cultures is a collaborative process. Students may have difficulty following classroom procedures when completing tasks that are done individually. We must sometimes ask ourselves what the real goal is: If we want our students to master subject matter, should they be allowed to learn it in their own way? Or, are we more concerned about their proficiency in completing worksheets independently?

To the third proposition, I would add, *inaccurate communication*. Language differences in themselves create ample opportunities for misunderstanding. While some of the problems facing parents and families of immigrants are self-imposed, others are clearly the result of years of oppression in their native lands. Thousands of students from other cultures enter our classrooms every year. Lack of effective communication has become the single biggest problem in some sectors.

Part 2
Paradigms and Promising Practices

Chapter 4
Views of the Learning Process

Abandon the notion of subject matter as something fixed and ready-made in itself, outside the child's experience; cease thinking of the child's experiences as something hard and fast; see it as something fluid, embryonic, vital; and we realize that the child and the curriculum are simply two limits which define a single process. Just as two points define a straight line, so the present standpoint of the child and the facts and truths of studies define instruction. It is continuous reconstruction, moving from the child's present experience out into that represented by the organized body of truth we call studies.

John Dewey (1964, p. 344)

In recent years, researchers and educators have gravitated toward one of two philosophical perspectives, namely *reductionism* or *constructivism* (See Figure 4-1). Each represents a unique paradigm of thought and practice – a way of viewing the world. Schools and classrooms reflect these sets of beliefs and views. This chapter includes information about the major principles of the two paradigms and their implications for educational planning, particularly as they relate to language and learning-challenged students.

At the classroom level, reductionist pedagogy is much more familiar to parents and teachers who have gone through America's public schools. It conjures images of traditional classrooms with desks all-in-a-row, lecture/expository teaching, note-taking, paper-and-pencil tests, and letter-grade report cards. It suggests a skills-based, product-driven curriculum in which information and instruction are reduced and segmented in the belief that learning is a **linear** phenomenon. Freire (1970) referred to this approach as a "banking system of education" and described it as follows:

Figure 4-1
Paradigms of Teaching and Learning

Reductionism	Constructivism
• Learning is a linear process.	Learning is a holistic process.
• Learning occurs part-to-whole.	Learning occurs whole-parts-whole.
• Information/skills are reduced and segmented into discrete parts.	Learners search for and construct new meanings.
• Teaching imposes form first, e.g., language rules, mechanics.	Form follows function.
• Product-oriented, e.g., test scores, immediate work samples.	Process is primary.
• Learning is primarily a passive process.	Learning is active, experiential.
• Curriculum is deficit-driven.	Curriculum is strength-driven.
• Teacher's role is to present material.	Capitalize on teachable moments.

Respective Models / Approaches

• Skills-based instruction	Integrated Thematic Instruction
• Phonics	Whole Language
• Programmed Instruction	Inquiry/Discovery
• Basal Reader	Literature-based Reading
• Direct Instruction	Project Approach
• Mastery Learning	Process Writing

. . . the teacher teaches and the students are taught; the teacher knows everything and students know nothing; the teacher disciplines and the students are disciplined; the teacher chooses and enforces his or her choice, and students comply; the teacher acts and the students have the illusion of acting through the action of the teacher; and the teacher chooses the program content and the students adapt to it.

Constructivists, on the other hand, are guided by the integration of multiple approaches to teaching and learning. Teachers and students work together to construct a classroom curriculum that helps students make meanings. Constructivist principles most closely match our present knowledge about how learners construct new meanings and acquire language. Linguist Roger Shuy (1984) emphasized that language development is a predominantly constructivist – not a reductionist – activity. Learners acquire functional language first – that which they need to communicate and make sense of their worlds. Language form (both spoken and written rules), follows function. Nonetheless, there is disagreement in some circles as to the viability of constructivism as a model for *all* populations, particularly students with learning disabilities.

In the past 15 years we have seen some evidence of transition from reductionist (skills-based) education to constructivist pedagogy in the forms of whole language instruction, process models in writing, hands-on mathematics, project approaches in science and social studies, integrated curriculum, and holistic/rubric assessment in most of the disciplines. The effects have been extremely promising (Poplin & Cousin, 1996). However, as we enter the new millennium, there is once again a concurrent movement back to basics.

When we speak of "back to basics," we are generally referring to an emphasis on skills-based approaches to teaching and learning. The term itself has become synonymous with reductionist philosophy. While constructivist teachers incorporate many reductionist practices (e.g., phonics, directed instruction) into their teaching, – reductionism does not allow for that which cannot be segmented, quantified, and measured. So long as this polarity exists, there is little or no chance that the pendulum will rest.

In the meantime, we are spending countless dollars and hours vacillating between two extreme points. As we cannot prove a single "best way" to teach all second language learners with learning disabilities, should we not be allowed to select methods and materials on an individual basis? Should the students themselves be allowed to participate in planning their own learning? What are the strengths and limitations of existing approaches and practices? Are there ways of bringing the two paradigms into concert? Perhaps the following sections of this book will provide some answers or, at least, responses to these questions.

Constructivism Paradigm

Constructivism is a "supply-side" perspective. It requires that we know what we have to work with in our classrooms, in our students, and in ourselves. This means getting to know the strengths and talents that permeate our schools and using them as organizing centers for curriculum and instruction. It means challenging traditions and culling from them their lessons and wisdom to be integrated into an ever-expanding spiral of knowledge. An abundant knowledge of deficits without a clear knowledge of potential is virtually useless. As stated by Catherine Twomey-Fosnot (1990), constructivism is a theory about knowledge and learning. It refers to what the learner knows and does – not what the teacher knows or does.

With respect to the principles of constructivism presented in the following pages, Mary Poplin (1986; 1988) has written extensively about their implications for the fields of learning disabilities and bilingual education. Other researchers in the field of special education have also begun to explore the implications of constructivism for our schools, from instructional considerations and approaches to assessment issues. In contemplating what constructivism has added to traditional educational assessments, Meltzer and Reid (1994) noted several new approaches in schools, including the observation that assessment is becoming more holistic, dynamic, and multidimensional. This stands in sharp contrast to the traditional psychometric testing approach in which structured measures are used to quantify specific behaviors related to achievement and intellectual ability.

The emergence of constructivism in education, according to Gredler (1997), can be linked to educators' "dissatisfaction with the cognitive perspective" (p. 57) and their concerns that teaching decontextualized skills and information were of lesser value to their students than experiential, hands on learning. It might be helpful here to peek inside a classroom driven by constructivist principles.

A Visit to Room 2-1

Even before the school day begins, Room 2-1 is abuzz with activity – sounds of a vacuum cleaner picking up elusive remains of the previous day's activities, the low hum of the air conditioner, the syncopated beat of a familiar sixties tune, and a soulful pantomime sure to please the Beatles themselves. Today is like any other day in Room 2-1. It is a rule – not an exception – to begin the day with music and self-amusement. The doors swing open at 8:15 sharp, although occasional intruders empty the room of its smaller occupants – rabbits, turtles, snakes (the friendly kind), and rats – hiding them beneath their shirts and jackets long before students are supposed to enter the classrooms. The room is alive with the minds and spirits of its human inhabitants, overflowing with artwork, writings, models, books, displays – the magnificent, if messy, triumphs of child over matter. On the board is written this message: "The best journeys begin within." I cannot think of a better metaphor to guide us.

Ms. Page is an educator in the truest sense. Her sacred trust seems to be the "drawing out" from within her students the uniqueness which they alone possess. This fourth grade classroom is filled with eager bilingual students in need of diverse and activity-rich experiences through which to hone their dual languages (English and Spanish). Within these walls can also be found students with learning disabilities whose needs are being met equally well. The curriculum is strength-driven, drawing on the gifts, talents, and multiple intelligences of its designers. It is evolutionary, neither contrived nor confined. It is guided by opportunity and the sensitive blending of needs and ideas, theory and practice. There is a pervasive air of hope and openness which invites learners into worlds beyond the books and material boundaries of the common classroom. They are encouraged to see themselves as they are and how they wish to be. They are stretched and challenged and occasionally hurt by their own limitations. And they learn that this, too, is growth.

At present, students are working on the production of a musical, *Hansel and Gretel*. What is unique about this project, as is true of most of their works, is that it is written, produced, and performed entirely by the students themselves – both in English and in Spanish. Daily, we hear the pounding out of the show's tunes on an old, slightly out-of-tune piano which is perched in a corner amid the clutter of several concurrent projects. Auditions are held by the parents, a classroom aide, and Ms. Page. Parts are assigned for both the English and Spanish productions. Students not auditioning are engaged in a variety of activities that contribute to the productions. Inside the classroom, they work on scenery, props, refining the script, and discussing their roles. Rehearsal for auditions takes place in the lunch area. Every student is involved and committed. Following auditions, all students return to the classroom to rehearse the songs they have written. They are especially excited about these performances because they are learning to produce the lyrics in sign language as they sing them.

This student project is both interdisciplinary and pedagogically sound. Learners are engaged in authentic work for authentic purposes. They are immersed in the exploration of languages, the arts and humanities, the study of mathematical principles and scientific inquiry. They must read, write, revise, edit, translate, calculate, predict, construct, and perform to degrees far more rigorous and superior to a textbook approach. They undertake the challenge and privilege of educating themselves, rich with many voices and many viewpoints. On any given day, one can find evidence of many modes of inquiry in the various subjects of study. To some persons on some days, it might appear to be an explosion of ideas, an uncontrollable tangle of activity, even chaos. To the constructivist educator, however, it is learning in a purer form. Writing in Ms. Page's classroom, for example, has as much to do with mold and mice and meteors as it does with semantics, syntax, and symbolism. Math lessons might well be played out through music – through meter and measure and mode. When asked what he liked about Ms. Page's class, one second language learner stated, "We get to learn things a lot of different ways."

Spiral of Learning Principle

At the heart of constructivism is the belief that learning and experiences are intertwined as a personal "spiral." The spiral model is used to describe Piaget's conception of learning as the constant *transformation* of individual knowing and how it becomes *personalized*. With each sensory impression, the child receives throughout the day, the child's thought and knowledge are changed forever. Billions of bits and pieces of information are constantly interacting within the mind (brain), and they constantly collide to form leaps of insight. These leaps are described by Piaget (1955) as "Aha experiences" – or *learning*. Hence, each learner brings different background experiences to the act of new learning. These experiences predict to some degree how new information will be perceived and integrated into the learner's spiral of knowledge. A student from Chinese culture, for example, would bring her own set of beliefs, values, and views to bear on daily classroom learning. Her interpretation of *The Good Earth* might differ dramatically from the meanings gleaned by her American peers. This model differs sharply from a reductionist view, which holds that learning is linear, occurring as bits and pieces of information that are assembled into "building blocks." Several principles of constructivism are outlined in the following section.

The Constructivist's View of Learning

Poplin (1986) described views of the learning process proposed by Constructivists. These views have been adapted in the list that follows for use in guiding program development for *students with LLC*:[1]

- **The whole is greater than the sum of its parts.** Teachers must be aware that studying isolated parts of a concept, skill, or language obscures from the

[1]Adapted from *The Quest for Meaning* by M. Poplin (1986). Used by permission from The Claremont Reading Conference, Claremont, CA.

learner the connections of the parts to the whole. Use of a whole-part-whole approach is recommended. We would not have students study or draw reams of pages depicting the feet in various positions as a reasonable approach to either teaching or learning a new dance.

- **The construction of new meanings transforms both the individual's spiral (whole) and the newly learned experience (part).** Language-rich experiences and environments aid learners in: (1) acquiring new knowledge, (2) transforming existing knowledge, and (3) constructing and applying new meanings to new situations.

- **Learners are always actively searching for and constructing meanings.** Teachers must recognize that learning is both an internal and eternal quest for meaning. Students are **always** engaged in learning. It may not be what teachers, peers, parents, or caregivers want or expect them to be learning, but when questioned about their interests, students can often dazzle us with skills and knowledge – evidence of learning. Students should be provided with opportunities to share their talents and interests.

- **The best predictor of what students will learn next is what they already know.** Teachers must determine students' strengths, talents, and interests, as well as present levels of language development, if they truly seek to maximize opportunities for school success. We all build upon our present knowledge and skills, and we grasp most easily new knowledge and skills that have familiar aspects or applications. It is important to start where the learner is. Students' interests can be broadened by addressing their present interests.

- **The development of form (structure) follows the emergence of function.** It cannot be emphasized too sharply that language development follows a predictable pattern in which function precedes form. In planning instruction for students with LLC, teachers must be aware of what their students know about language. Attempting to impose rules of grammar when students are struggling to acquire basic interpersonal communication skills (BICS) is often confusing because students have limited understanding of the purpose of the instruction. Instructional programs should present activities using language that is comprehensible to the students.

- **The learner's spiral of knowledge is self-regulating and self-preserving.** Teachers should be aware that learners are drawn most toward pursuits that interest them personally. The spiral of learning is "self-selecting." There must be sufficient reason, desire, or specific need for the new information before it will be constructed as new "learning." When a student with LLC is repeatedly confronted with academic failure, his or her spiral of knowledge acts to reject and devalue school learning. It acts to preserve individual dignity.

- **Errors are critical to learning.** Classrooms – indeed entire schools – should operate on the premise that failures and errors are evidence that learning is taking place. Jean Piaget's interest in the errors that children made was not without basis. They revealed much about the workings of the mind and its ability to conceptualize, organize, and apply new knowledge. Therefore, classrooms with "penalty-free" errors are to be encouraged.

- **The role of the teacher is to touch the students' "spirals" at just the right time and in just the right way.** Teachers must recognize the teachable moment when it arises and actively plan to create such moments. We must ask ourselves if we wish merely to be technicians who distribute, collect, score, record, and redistribute the same texts and materials to all students with LLC. Or, do we wish to select our own methods and materials, based on the individual needs of these learners. Students should be empowered to take part in planning the classroom curriculum.

Reductionism Paradigm

American public education has been guided primarily by a reductionist philosophy. Evidence is everywhere, from the way in which we carve up the typical school day into content areas and daily schedules, to our reduced and segmented skills continua. Such planning is no accident or natural occurrence. It derives from decades of research particularly from the fields of behavioral psychology and the physical sciences – which has been translated into implications for America's schools. Behavioral psychologists focused on what was happening in the classroom between the teacher and students–observable and measurable behaviors. Modeling, reinforcement, feedback, and successive approximation are key concepts in this approach (Joyce & Weil, 1986). By the early 1970s, behaviorism became the dominant and exclusive model of choice in special education. According to Reid (1998), behaviorists advocated direct instruction in the "three R's" because "they believed students were predominantly passive and reactive and, therefore, we could devise materials, often referred to as 'teacher-proof' (cf. DISTAR, by Englemann & Bruner, 1969), to elicit desired responses" (p. 397).

Jean Piaget's stage-developmental model, gave quick rise to skills and developmental taxonomies, such as Bloom's (1956) taxonomy of educational objectives (cognitive domain), Krathwohl and Bloom's (1964) taxonomy of educational objectives (affective domain), and Kohlberg's (1983) stage-developmental model of moral development. All of these have exerted impressive forces on educational planning in the United States.

As it relates to classroom learning, reductionism has been a boon to a host of related models and strategies, including mastery learning, task analysis, criterion-referenced testing, direct instruction, computer-assisted instruction, and even *accountability* procedures for schools and teachers. With the push to reduce, quantify, and measure learning, the nation's schools became a booming market place for publishers and developers of reductionist programs by the 1970s. One widely known program, DISTAR (Direct Instruction Systems for Teaching Arithmetic and Reading) emerged as an effort to help disadvantaged black children and those identified as "slow learning." (Gearheart & Gearheart, 1989). Joyce and Weil (1986) reported that early research (before 1986) suggested that direct instruction was "effective in promoting student learning in reading and math, especially for students from lower socioeconomic backgrounds" (p. 326).

About the same time, a similar and widely-used approach, Mastery Learning, was developed by Benjaman Bloom and John B. Carroll – applying systems analysis procedures to curriculum materials development. The result was a program in which subject area content and skills were reduced and segmented into *specific behavioral objectives*. The primary goals of Mastery Learning, according to its developers, were to: (1) allow learners to work at their own pace through sequences of "individually prescribed instruction" (content and objectives); (2) to encourage self-direction and motivation; and (3) to help learners achieve acceptable levels of mastery. (Joyce & Weil, 1986). Both DISTAR and Mastery Learning models bear marks of behaviorist theory, as do most subsequent reductionist programs and approaches. Even Madeline Hunter's (1984) seven-step lesson design reflects a behaviorist emphasis on *teaching* over *learning*. The notion that there is a correct way to teach presumes that there is a correct way to learn. For example, the Hunter model includes the following components as a condition for learning:

- *Anticipatory Set* – This is a focusing procedure in which it is presumed that learners must somehow be ready to learn. Since learning is a fluid, continual process – albeit not always what the teacher has in mind – one must question the value of this component.
- *Input* – This includes the lesson content or target skills to be taught.
- *Modeling* – The teacher demonstrates the behavior first, with the expectation that students will replicate the act.
- *Checking for Understanding* – The work completed by students is monitored.
- *Guided Practice* – Students are guided through activities relating to a skill until the teacher decides that the skill has been mastered.
- *Closure* – The teacher poses questions to determine if students will be able to transfer the skill to a new situation.
- *Independent Practice* – All students are expected to practice the skill independently.

Joyce and Weil (1986) reported that, while initial research supported direct instruction, subsequent studies and reviews of research did "point out that other teaching strategies may be more suitable for promoting such educational goals as *abstract thinking, creativity,* and *problem solving*" [emphasis added] (p. 326).

However, as mentioned earlier, the field of learning disabilities extended an equally warm welcome as behaviorism made its way into the schools. At last, special educators felt that they had a systematic way to approach daily instruction and behavior problems. Perhaps the prime exemplar of approaches used by behaviorists is behavior modification (BM). B. F. Skinner, most often credited with inspiring systematic approaches to behavior management has left an indelible mark on American education. From time to time we read or hear that BM had reached its zenith in the late 1970s, but one need not look far to find vestiges of BM in many areas of daily school life today. Behavior contracts, behavior charting, reward systems, time-out – they seem to have become a permanent feature in the landscape of public education.

Influence of Reductionism

Among the assumptions underlying reductionism, the notion that learning is fundamentally a linear process is perhaps the most contested. Reductionist philosophy asserts that learning is the acquisition of bits and pieces of information and skills. Reductionists predetermine the parts and instruct students in these parts (Poplin, 1988; Poplin & Stone, 1992). While many reductionists agree that the brain or *mind* is "pattern-seeking," the presumption is that it seeks *linearly* and therefore *logically*. For example, the reductionist wishing to teach the concept "bush" to a student with language and learning challenges would have the student examine the concept in terms of its constituent parts or attributes. The child is expected to study the parts and add them up to make the whole – *bush*. There is no overt attempt to identify and build upon the child's prior knowledge about similar or related concepts (e.g., tree, shrub, plant). Each concept remains static. Hence, learning is viewed as a linear phenomenon which can be matched to linear instructional models (e.g., programmed instruction, mastery learning, direct instruction, etc.).

Conversely, constructivism holds that the learner is constantly and actively engaged in a search for *meanings*. As new information is acquired, it interacts with all the information the child has already acquired. Jean Piaget used the metaphor of a "spiral of knowledge" to represent what he believed this phenomenon of learning to be. The spiral is dynamic and constantly transforming the learner's knowledge into new meanings. The two concepts – *tree* and *bush* – interact in a dynamic way to *transform one another*. That is, the learner actively participates in concept development by selecting what is needed to construct meanings. Since *tree* is already in the child's spiral of knowledge, the concept *bush* is more easily learned. Once the child integrates *bush* into his/her spiral, both concepts are transformed, giving the child greater knowledge of the two concepts than the mere sum of their constituent parts. The child not only knows what the bush is by its attributes, but he/she also now knows what a bush is not (a tree) – and vice versa.

Reductionist Principles and Instruction

Reductionism has had a profound influence on educational programs and how they are implemented.

- ### Expository Teaching as a Model

    Direct instruction and related expository approaches are offered as models of correct teaching. The premise is that what is important to know and be able to do have been identified, isolated, and arranged in logical and organized sequences of knowledge and skills. Hence, it is the job of the teacher to dispense, monitor, and evaluate. In many cases, if not most, procedures and answers have been carefully prepared and published in easy-to-use manuals. "Why reinvent the wheel?," pre-service and in-service teachers frequently ask. "I learned just fine this way when I was in school." The honest response is that many children do not. One expository approach, the Madeline Hunter model, offers a step-by-step approach to classroom instruction which presumes learning to be primarily a linear phenomenon. While entire schools and districts bought into the model since it was introduced to educators, the advent of renewed interest in experiential learning has replaced many such direct instruction approaches over the past 20 years.

- ### Skills-Based Continua

    A purely skills-based approach exposes students to a microscopic view of the curriculum. We would find students immersed in the acquisition of reduced and segmented pieces of information and the mastery of skills and subskills. Information and learning are carefully controlled by prescribed books, materials, and instruction. Skills acquisition is viewed as a developmental process, i. e., from simple to complex, concrete to abstract. By arranging tasks in such a linear fashion, it is believed that learners will more readily master them. Some further believe that this principle applies to all or most content areas.

- ### Product-Oriented Goals and Objectives

    From a reductionist's viewpoint, *products* are more primary than *process*. Products can be used to establish goals, objectives, and learning outcomes and evidence that learning has taken place. This notion is clearly evident in I.E.P.'s where learning is reduced, segmented, and quantified.

- **Quantifiable and Measurable Learning**

     Ultimately the schools must arrive at decisions about success, failure, learning needs, progress evaluation, and grade promotion. Parents and the general public want to see evidence that the schools are doing a good job. The traditional and most typical form of such evidence is test scores. We know that test scores drive most schools and districts. Even at the writing of this book, the state of California is in the midst of transition from one standardized measure to another. Challenged by a rapid growth of second-language learners in the public schools, some districts have begun to question the reliability and validity of standardized testing. Nonetheless, it has remained the most efficient means of sampling learning across large populations of school-age children. Standardized testing has also been used to measure teaching effectiveness across districts and within schools. At least some education agencies favor publishing such information in newspapers for reasons of public awareness.

Sample Reductionist Approaches

     Reductionist approaches might be fairly characterized as expository and linear in nature. The general aim is to reduce learning and knowledge into information and skills continua so that aspects of behavior can be quantified and measured. Despite this central and unifying philosophy, reductionism has taken many forms in the schools.

- *Direct Instruction* – In this approach to teaching, information and/or skills are broken down into component parts, arranged in sequential order, and presented to learners. In reading, for example, decoding and comprehension are broken down into subcomponents. Sound-symbol relationships and phonemic awareness might be isolated for drill-and-practice as prerequisite to *decoding*. In *comprehension*, targeted subcomponents singled out for drill might include context clues and vocabulary. This approach is clearly a part-to-whole process. The ultimate target is getting meaning from reading. Planning an entire reading or math unit would follow a similar approach, i.e., reducing the unit to lessons complete with specific objectives and further segmenting the lesson to address subskills and prerequisite knowledge.

- *Phonics* – Phonics is a word analysis skill and a term often used to describe a general approach to language development and teaching reading. Because the aim is to "analyze" the printed word for clues relating to pronunciation (graphophonic), it reduces language information to basic components, i.e., phonemes and morphemes. Teachers who swear by phonics as the best approach to teaching reading are probably stating as much about their own learning style and beliefs as the method they embrace. Belief in *any* method is the first step to success in using it. Whole language proponents too believe in the merits of phonics in teaching reading, but their approach is not limited to phonics only. Special educators and bilingual teachers also recognize the inherent value of phonics in building bridges to reading. Word families and language cognates are viewed by many learning disabilities teachers as logical starting points and as tools to further learning.

- *Computer-Assisted-Instruction (CAI)* – as it has been most widely implemented, CAI is patterned after a direct instruction approach. The most common criticism of CAI has been its overuse as a teacher and underuse as a creative medium. Publishers of school materials have long recognized that the groundwork for instructional software has been done for them by educators themselves (e.g., transferring learning from desktop to computer screen).

- *Programmed Instruction* – Often called "canned instruction" or "controlled learning," programmed instruction refers to any approach in which attempts are made to package and dispense learning in discrete parts. Programmed instruction is presented in small doses and steps with frequent feedback. The learner proceeds at his/her own pace. The approach may be helpful for organization, structure, and guidance purposes (Smith, 1991).

- *Mastery Learning* – This is a formal instructional program aimed at individual learners. The general goal of the approach is to allow students to proceed at their own rates and level of comfort until specific goals and objectives have been mastered. Naturally, content and skills have been controlled to accommodate a range of student entry levels and prerequisite knowledge and skills.

- *Task Analysis* – Perhaps the clearest example of reductionism, task analysis specifies behaviors required to complete a task. The teacher evaluates the student's level of development or performance and then identifies all the requisite behaviors or components that will lead to a targeted behavior or task. In essence the teacher is shaping behaviors along the way. In other words, the teacher determines exactly what he/she wants the student to do, then maps out all the intermediate behaviors required to reach the goal. This approach has been widely used in special education, particularly among populations with more severe and/or restrictive conditions.

- *Behaviorism* – Probably the best known exemplar of reductionist teaching, behaviorism refers to a systematic approach to changing behavior through rewards and punishment. The aim is to promote positive behaviors and reduce undesirable behaviors. In schools, BM has been played out in a variety of ways, ranging from elaborate behavior management programs aimed at entire school populations to simple "prizes" for correct responses (e.g., candy) at the individual and classroom levels. Drawing upon behaviorism, educators have experimented with virtually every principle, including approximation and shaping, positive and negative reinforcement, and extinction. Nowhere has this been more true than in special education classrooms where, unfortunately, many students with behavior problems have been assigned. Behavior contracts have been a common feature in Individualized Education Plans for many years.

Sample Tools and Materials

The tools most often used in reductionist approaches to teaching and learning have traditionally been:

- *Basals* – Basals are typically used in reading, math, social studies, and science. The basal approach has been widely used for several reasons. Perhaps the most obvious is efficiency – content has been pre-selected and organized into lessons, chapters, units, and tests. Basals have provided a means of standardizing curricula within states, districts, and/or schools to assure that all students are exposed to the same information over time. It is not unusual to see a textbook series span the entire K-12 curriculum. Textbooks in reading and literature, for example, have often divided the K-12 curriculum into attractive grade-level themes and titles. Another attractive feature to educators is that many textbooks have included vivid graphics and illustrations. Basals have also provided an accountability tool, whereby instructional planning could be monitored and measured.

- *Workbooks/worksheets* – Basal series often include supplemental materials – workbooks and/or worksheets – to enhance learning and to extend lessons beyond the text. Generally speaking, these materials have been used for drill and practice to help students acquire new skills and/or to reinforce previously learned knowledge and skills.

For some students, additional examples and practice are needed, and ready-made materials have allowed teachers to use their time more efficiently and wisely.

- **Computers and Word Processors** – As mentioned elsewhere in this book, computers have been disproportionately used to remediate and/or reinforce information and skills. The educational software market abounds with drill-and-practice programs and titles. Even word-processing has followed the reductionist tradition in many classrooms. It is not uncommon to find students drilling themselves by typing their spelling words 10 times each or copying rather than creating print. Some educators find such pursuits to be worthwhile.

Criticisms of Reductionism

Approaches used by behaviorists generally reflected a belief that there is a correct or best way to teach – which in turn presumes that there is a correct or best way to learn. If there has been anything made clear by researchers and practitioners in the fields of learning disabilities and bilingual education over the past 30 years, it is that there is no single best way to either teach or learn. The more cerebral and less dimensional our assessments, the more needy and less capable our students with LLC appear. At the school and classroom level, paper-and-pencil assessments may not produce a thorough picture of actual learning. How can we expect to capture every dimension and nuance of knowledge and knowing with a single instrument? In his discussion of reading instruction as a prime exemplar of reductionism, James Astman (1986) stated it this way:

> [a] reductionist framework has guided the development of virtually all skills-based reading programs. The appeal of these programs is not very difficult to understand. After all, the guesswork is taken out of teaching when there is a clear sequence of skills that can be identified, taught, and tested. This is the implicit promise evident in the program scope and sequence charts which preface one reading text after another. Skills are defined and plotted over the span of school-age years; they are coordinated with and subordinated to one another, being variously assessed, introduced, practiced, reviewed, and applied. Within those charts, general headings suggest a clear framework for the teaching and analysis of reading: visual discrimination, auditory discrimination, decoding, including phonics and structural analysis, vocabulary, and, at the end of the list, *comprehension* [emphasis added]. However appealing this kind of skills-based framework may be, it is a fallacious one. It proceeds from a set of assumptions that altogether ignore the nature of perception, of meaning, of awareness itself. It identifies comprehension as one achievement among many, and it takes as given the notion that the categories of linguistic analysis somehow parallel the stages of children's language development. Finally, the conventional skills-based framework is based on the view that reading skills are individually knowable and subject to the reader's control. (pp. 30-31)

Such perseveration on parts may obscure or delay understanding of the target goal itself – *reading*. Consider for a moment the second-language learner who is struggling to make sense of both the rudiments of language itself and the rules that govern both his/her primary and a second language. When language is segmented, the learner is not provided the advantage of all the cueing systems. For example, reading words in isolation is void of syntactic, semantic, and pragmatic cues. The student must rely solely on graphophonic cues. Therefore, learners who have difficulty with language are not only being robbed of opportunities to practice using the linguistic cues, but they are also being forced to rely on one cueing system – one that may not be well developed. (Keefe & Keefe, 1993). A reductionistic bits and pieces continuum may indeed prove helpful for some students – those learners whose primary language is intact – but for students who have difficulty understanding the whole of what is to be done, sometimes nothing except direct experiences in meaningful contexts will suffice.

Reyes (1992) suggests that because of the high regard and respect Hispanics generally hold for teachers, some students may feel more secure with *direct instruction* as a methodology. School success is not only contingent upon language and academic development, but also acceptance of learning differences and degrees of dependency. While direct instruction and other reductionist strategies might well provide the degree of structure and step-by-step support required by some students with LLC, they should be alternated with other, more learner-centered methods if we hope to build self-sufficiency and divergent thinking skills.

Chapter 5
Language, Literacy, and Learning

Reading does not consist merely of decoding the written word or language, rather, it is preceded by and intertwined with knowledge of the world.

Paulo Freire

Before we walked, we crawled and explored and experimented; no one stopped and corrected our learning. Before we spoke, we babbled and experimented with language; no one demanded that we first learn the alphabet. Before we wrote, we scribbled and scrawled our way across reams of paper, sidewalks, sand, and walls; no one criticized our neatness or form. Before we read, we stumbled through words, made up new sounds for words, read picture books; no one came along and told us we were wrong. In all these cases, we owned our experiences. They defined and guided our early paths toward literacy.

Literacy approaches must therefore reflect the lived experience of the learner. We must, as Freire (1970) contended, *infuse* the curriculum with lived experiences. Reading derives from these experiences – some of them richer and more varied; some less. These experiences form the *roots* of literacy and reflect to some degree the perspective of a culture towards literacy. In the schools, we can control for the amount of encouragement learners receive and the contexts in which language learning and reading take place.

Prior to formal reading instruction, learners must be prepared and receptive to the event. They must feel comfortable in the instructional setting and secure enough to experiment with the language. LeBlanc (1998) stressed that reading involves risk-taking by both learner and teacher. This is especially true for students for whom language is a formidable barrier.

Readers construct meaning as they read. To do this, they must use the print on the page (external text) to comprehend at the literal level. At a deeper level, they must also make inferences by filling the gaps left by the author (text-based inferential comprehension) and by using background knowledge and experiences (knowledge-based inferential comprehension). It is important to allow the reader the luxury of engaging in a trial-and-error process of 'making meaning.' Readers gradually form an idea, read more, alter their ideas, and so on. By using internal and external text, by inferring and guessing, readers constantly alter and refine their ideas as to what the text is about. (p. 1)

LeBlanc emphasized that readers utilize *all* clues, strategies, and cueing systems in deriving meaning from printed text. Readers experiment with sound-symbol relationships (graphophonic and phonemic awareness) and then move toward words and meanings. The process of learning to read is the same in both native and second language acquisition (Cummins, 1984; Krashen, 1982).

Learners acquire vocabulary words in many ways and through many contexts (conversation, instruction, incidental learning, etc.). According to Graves (1985), the ease or difficulty with which students acquire new words is linked to the *relationship* between the learner and the words. He describes four such relationships:

1. *Sight words.* These words are in the students' listening and speaking vocabularies, but they do not know how to read them.
2. *New words.* These are words that the learners know conceptually, but they are not in their vocabularies.
3. *New concepts.* These are words for which students do not have a concept. Neither are they in their vocabularies.
4. *New meanings.* These are words that already exist in the learners' vocabularies, but additional connotations of the words must be learned.

Although eventually the *printed* word becomes the primary cue for readers, listening remains central to reading and literacy development. Students acquire much of their learning through listening – both in and out of school. Tompkins and Hoskisson (1991) have identified three purposes for listening, all of which are relevant to both second language learners and students with LD. *Comprehensive listening*, the most common type of listening in school refers to the use of hearing to understand a message. Examples include listening for instructions, listening for content and main ideas, and listening for answers. Students with LLC typically spend a large portion of their school day immersed in comprehensive listening.

Critical listening engages the student in listening for critical pieces of information. It requires the learner to carefully, consider, analyze, synthesize, and evaluate. These skills are particularly important in situations involving propaganda and persuasion. Even small children are subjected to such devices when listening to the radio or watching television. Advertising permeates the *lived experiences* of virtually all children in America.

By contrast, *appreciative listening* is used in social contexts for enjoyment. Examples include conversation, listening to music, shared reading, and storytelling. It is this type of listening that learners know best and where they feel most comfortable. Generally speaking, it levels the playing field for many minority students and students with LLC. Second language learners, particularly those in the *silent stage*, may have great difficulty differentiating between important messages and casual comments in the context of classroom learning.

Reading and Literacy: What the Experts Say

Spanning a 10-year period, Rona Flippo's (1997) research focused on literacy and what we have learned about promising and unproductive practices in the schools. She reported the following insights from her studies:

- We know that neither phonics nor whole language is a method. Phonics is a word-analysis skill that involves the use of symbol/sound relationships; whole language is a philosophy that includes the belief that all language systems are interwoven.

- We know that phonics and other necessary skills can be taught by teachers who have whole-language philosophies.

- We know that many "whole language teachers" have been teaching phonics, as well as other skills of word recognition and analysis, as part of their reading programs. *However* – they teach these skills within the context of the students' reading materials, rather than by focusing on them in isolation.

- We know that teachers should not be required to teach by one approach alone.

Flippo asked each of 11 experts in the field of reading to develop lists of things they believed teachers should do and shouldn't do in their classrooms to promote reading development. Her findings revealed practices and contexts that the experts agreed would tend to make learning to read difficult for children; they also agreed on a variety of practices for facilitating the learning of reading. Practices that were believed to promote learning to read included (1) a whole language approach that integrates listening, speaking, reading, and writing, (2) literature based reading programs that emphasize the importance of real books – as opposed to abridged or leveled readers, and (3) modeling of reading for learners, and identifying authentic contexts and purposes for reading.

Conversely, the experts reported that many of the reading practices common in our schools tend to make learning to read difficult for students, including an over-emphasis on phonics; the use of decontextualized reading materials (e.g., basal reader selections) and instruction (e.g., drill-and-practice, worksheets); and a lack of *authentic* purposes for learning to read (see Flippo, 1997 for more information).

Written Language Development

In *Art, Mind, and Brain* (1982), Howard Gardner examined the evolution of children's literary imagination by tracing its development from imitative play in the second year of life to the creative imaginings of preadolescents. With young children, Gardner observed:

> A three-year-old can concatenate a couple of episodes, generally in the appropriate order. By the age of four most children have command over a sheaf of episodes; they can combine them into sets and order them in diverse ways to achieve contrasting effects . . . [and] by the age of five the child has acquired a 'first draft' knowledge of the literary realm. The child understands the centrality of problems in stories and generally solves at least simple problems by exploiting the resources of the story itself. (p. 176)

In related research, Catherine Twomey Fosnot (1989) described six stages of development in children's writing from preschool to adolescence. Her descriptive analyses of stages 1 through 4 parallel closely the findings of Gardner, especially as they reflect students' close adherence to conventions such as, "Once upon a time," or "One day...,", and "The End." Interestingly, she found that students who were engaged in a "process approach" came to "discover" for themselves the importance of each phase in the process – *prewriting, writing, and postwriting* – as they became more proficient with the act of composing itself. By allowing students to immerse themselves as "authors" first, their work was given purpose and drive. The need for improving their work came from within, not from coercive efforts by teachers.

Drecktrah and Chiang (1997) conducted a survey among 300 elementary school teachers, one-third of whom were teachers of students with learning disabilities. A 21-item questionnaire was developed by the researchers to explore what approaches these educators were using to teach reading and writing in their classrooms. Of the 183 usable surveys, results indicated that teachers – including LD teachers – employed *both* whole language and direct instruction methods in their teaching. A variety of reasons was offered, but responses indicated several important factors such as variations in teacher-training, varying degrees of understanding of whole language principles, and varying levels of personal commitment to either approach.

In her review of literacy research, Goldstein (1995) found evidence that effective methods in general and bilingual education were also effective for students with learning disabilities. The use of authentic tasks that were relevant to students' backgrounds and experiences worked well in both settings. Studies by Rueda (1989) and Ruiz (1989) indicated that whole language was an effective model for bilingual students and limited-English-proficient students with learning disabilities. Conditions that were found by Ruiz, Rueda, Figueroa, and Boothroyd (1995) to facilitate language and literacy learning are listed in Table 5-1.

Stahl and Miller (1989), on the other hand, concluded from their quantitative studies that there were no significant differences in reading improvement achieved by students receiving whole language instruction and those in basal reading programs. Although Stahl and Miller were subsequently criticized for excluding supportive studies on whole language (e.g., McGee & Lomax, 1990), their work signaled the need for an ongoing critique of instructional practices, as does that of Drektrah and Chiang.

Cultural differences can affect how a student will respond to a particular approach to instruction. In American schools, students are often encouraged to compete with one another, to ask questions, and to show what they know. In many Asian cultural groups, students are expected to be silent in the classroom and strive *not* to appear smarter or better than their peers. Many Hispanic and Asian parents view the child's role as the passive receptor of knowledge (Cheng, 1991; Roseberry-McKibbin, 1995). Hence children new to American schools frequently bring with them conceptions of schooling that are at variance with what they observe in the classroom.

Oral traditions are stronger and more respected in some cultures and therefore present special challenges to American educators – challenges that sometimes result in mislabeling and misplacement of minority students (Sleeter, 1986). According to Paulo Freire (1970), "Only dialogue, which requires critical thinking, is also capable of generating critical thinking" (p. 81). Hence engaging children in meaningful dialogue is at the heart of reading and literacy development.

Moreno (1993) advocated using the Creative Reading Method developed by Alma Flor Ada (1986) in working with limited-English-proficient students. The method includes four phases:

Table 5-1
Conditions for Optimal Language and Literacy Lessons:
An ESL Perspective

Student Choice	Students exercise choice in their learning, writing topics, book projects, thematic cycle.
Centered on Student	Lessons begin and revolve around students' personal experiences, background knowledge, and interests.
Wholeness (whole-part-whole)	Lessons begin with whole texts (e.g., books, poems) to maximize the (whole-part-whole)construction of understanding, then move to the analysis of small units of language (e.g., phonics, spelling, punctuation), returning to the text as a whole.
Active participation, Peer interaction	Students actively engage in lessons with frequent and long turns of talk.
Primacy of Meaning (then form)	Students' good ideas get communicated first, and then move to a focus on correct form or mechanics, such as spelling and grammar.
Authentic purpose	The end products of lessons have a real-life function.
Approximation	Students are encouraged to take risks and successively approximate language and literacy skills (following a developmental course).
Immersion in language and print	The classroom is saturated with different print forms and functions, as well as opportunities to hear and use language for a wide range of purposes.
Demonstration	Teachers demonstrate their own reading and writing and share their ongoing efforts with students.
Immediate response	Students receive a response to their oral and written literacy tasks; they are encouraged to give personal responses to others' efforts.
Community	Students, parents, and teachers form a community of readers, writers, and learners who explore a range of questions relevant to them.
Expectations	Teachers, parents, and the students themselves expect that students will become proficient and independent speakers, readers, and writers.

Source: Ruiz, N.T., Rueda, R. Figueroa, R. R., and Boothroyd, M. (1995). Bilingual special education teacher's shifting paradigms: Complex responses to educational reform. *Journal of Learning Disabilities, 28 (10)*, 622-635. Reprinted by permission.

1. *Descriptive Phase* - This phase centers on the *who, what, where, when,* and *why* aspects of a story.
2. *Personal Interpretive Phase* - In this phase, students are required to use their own backgrounds and experiences when interpreting the information in the story/text.
3. *Critical Phase* - In this phase, listeners and/or readers reflect and infer. The students establish a connection between what is read or discussed and what they have experienced.
4. *Creative Phase* - In this phase, students apply learned information to improve and empower themselves as they make decisions relating to their daily lives.

Maldonado-Colon (1993) emphasized that language acquisition and ultimately reading are not disconnected from culture. Rather, culture is the lens through which individuals view the world and draw meaning from it. These meanings emerge eventually through their writings and oral sharing. This information joined with that accumulated from literacy research provide a structure for long-range educational planning.

Implications for Students with LLC

- The research summarized in this chapter indicates a need for both broad and balanced approaches to instruction e.g., scaffolded instruction, Specially Designed Academic Instruction in English (SDAIE), and whole language.

- We know that no single approach should be used exclusively.

- We know that assessment should be formative (ongoing), broad-based, and conducted in the primary language as necessary.

- We know that English language learners should be integrated with native English speakers for much of their instruction.

- We know that the English language instruction is most effective if presented in meaningful wholes rather than segmented into structures that are taught one at a time.

- We know that teachers need to determine ways to make reading functional and purposeful so that students will be motivated to learn.

- We know that teachers must create inviting and safe risk-taking environments in order to reach all the students in their charge.

- We know that teachers must be prepared and willing to repeat, restructure, and/or abandon instruction as the need arises.

- We know that we do not need to measure every utterance, writing stroke, or reading attempt for grading purposes.

Models for Developing Literacy

Three popular models that have been used as the framework for literacy programs in our schools are described in this section.

Model I: Constructivist-Whole Language

> *Whole language is whole. It does not exclude some languages, some dialects, or some registers because their speakers lack status in a particular society. Every language form constitutes a precious linguistic resource for its users.*
>
> *Kenneth Goodman*

Rona Flippo (1997) reported startling headlines about the controversy surrounding reading instruction in the nation's schools – a controversy that pitted *phonics* against *whole language*. However, as Twomey-Fosnot (1997) asserted, neither phonics nor whole language is a "method" of instruction. Rather, phonics is a word-analysis skill that involves the use of symbol/sound relationships; whole language is a philosophy that includes the belief that all language systems are interwoven. Phonics is an integral and necessary part of a balanced curriculum – a whole language curriculum.

Those who have followed the development of the whole language movement know that leaders – such as Kenneth and Yetta Goodman, Jerome Harste, Donald Graves, and Lucy Calkins and their colleagues – all recognize that phonemic awareness and skill in phonics facilitate the acquisition of literacy skills. There can be little doubt that such knowledge and skills are likewise imperative when learning to read in a second language.

A phonics approach in any language, however, places the onus on teachers to assure an adequate and appropriate cueing system. For example:

- oral language modeling in L1 and/or L2 – proper pronunciation and inflection
- visual cues – print, pictures, graphics, realia
- learning devices – audio/video tapes and players, TV, computers

One excellent visual aid, popularized by Wagstaff (1994), is the creation of a classroom "Word Wall" for learners to use in their reading and writing. Students generate the wall list, which contains a variety of words from classroom reading and study. It serves as a ready reference – highly visible and uncluttered with irrelevant words and terms. The Word Wall is an excellent cue for second language learners and students with LD. It sharpens their skills in the following areas:

- studying patterns as clues to decoding other words
- determining correct spelling and pronunciation
- discovering correct usage

Whole language teachers create ways of utilizing such cueing systems naturally in the classroom. They recognize the importance of activating students' present linguistic knowledge, and they provide both informal and formal contexts for language skills development. They also acknowledge the need for interventions – for example, direct instruction in specific subject matters, additional practice on certain skills, and differentiated instruction for students with language and/or learning problems. Although certain approaches to teaching phonics are viewed as "questionable," whole language teachers *do* make use of strategies to enhance skills in phonics.

While negative comments about whole language have appeared frequently in the press, such comments reflect a "serious misunderstanding of what whole language is really about" (Newman & Church, 1991, p. 25). The notion that phonics is avoided in whole language instruction is simply not true. Other common myths about whole language include the following:

- There is no structure in whole language curriculum and teaching.
- Whole language teachers aren't concerned about spelling, grammar, mechanics, and usage.
- Tests aren't used in whole language and there is no objective proof of learning.
- The whole language curriculum revolves only around the interests of students.
- Whole language means that products aren't important – only the process is.
- Whole language teaching makes it necessary to eliminate the use of textbooks completely.
- Whole language teachers are born – not made!

The only item in this list which might be argued defensibly is perhaps the last one. We are all attracted to ideas and methods that match our own personal teaching style, but we must not allow personal comfort to limit us in any way. To presume that there is a *right way to teach* presumes that there is a *right way to learn*. Such a notion would seem absurd on the face of it. Hence, as teachers we must not allow a self-imposed blindness to obscure other views and other voices. Teachers must be open to the use of more than one approach in their instructional programs.

Imagine for a moment how American education might have evolved in the absence of persons such as Jean Piaget, B. F. Skinner, or Jerome Bruner. How would instructional programs be implemented without a developmental model to guide us in designing curricula, without behavioral models to guide us in planning classroom discipline, and without inquiry models to promote scientific method in our science and social studies classes? Had they not envisioned differing constructs of learning and motivation, American public education might have changed little over the past century. While change is not always *progress*, it does allow us to critique our past and to examine our present work through *new lenses*.

Keefe and Keefe (1993) identified the following marks of whole language classrooms. Each of these observations seems not only relevant to learning, but is also highly conducive to second-language development.

- Students perceive reading and writing as do-able and owner-able.
- Students are provided with models of good reading and writing.
- The classroom is structured with routines of reading aloud, reading predictable texts, independent reading, and reading and writing for a purpose.
- Repetition is ongoing.
- Skills and explicit information about reading and writing are shared through demonstrations of purposeful reading and writing.
- Students gain confidence in their reading and writing ability.
- Positive expectations are provided.
- Supportive and constructive responses from teachers match the learners' current level of performance.
- Opportunities for independent problem solving are provided.

- Individualized demonstrations occur.
- Mistakes are viewed as approximations that mark growth.
- Generalization occurs (pg. 177).

To this list of attributes, I would add the following:
- Whole language encourages self-monitoring – a valuable life-skill.
- Whole language facilitates the development of problem-solving and planning skills.
- Whole language encourages divergent thinking and develops higher order thinking skills.
- Whole language reduces dependency among students with LLC, a concern commonly expressed by teachers.

Language Experience Approach (LEA)

Sometimes used synonymously with whole language, the Language Experience Approach has been popular for many years in both regular and special education programs. In this approach, students use their own ideas, backgrounds, and experiences as content for writing and reading. Examples of topics used within the Language Experience Approach are listed in Table 5-2. The underlying theory is that students learn best and most quickly those things that approximate their own interests. Because students create their own stories for use as reading material, they become active participants in the learning process. Hence their stories and writings become a prominent part of the language arts program. Typically, LEA takes the learner through the processes of thinking, telling, listening, reading, and reinforcement, as follows:

1. The student thinks of an event or idea to write about.
2. The story is dictated to the teacher, aide, peer interpreter, or volunteer.
3. The story is recorded precisely the way it is dictated.
4. The story is then read back to the student.
5. The student then attempts to read the story – both silently and aloud.

The stories may be used in a variety of ways to engage cueing systems (i.e., syntactic, semantic, and graphophonic) as illustrated by the examples below:
1. *Syntactic* - Have the student focus on the word order of one or two sentences. Rearrange the word order, and ask the student to reread the sentences to see if they make sense. Seeing that they do not, the student is then asked to place the words into an order that does make sense.
2. *Semantic* - Have the student focus on two specific words that have been used in the sentences. Discuss other words that might be used to replace the targeted words. Then ask the student to reread the sentences to see if they make sense after the words have been replaced. Has the meaning of the sentence changed? If so, how has it changed?
3. *Graphophonic* - Ask the student to focus on the printed words themselves. Select words that share a common pattern, e.g., *pat, hat, sat*. Discuss the regularities in the sound patterns of these words.

The Language Experience Approach can be used to facilitate both the development of oral and written language skills. Speech-language pathologists, for example, can use students' stories to stimulate the development of vocabulary, sequencing skills, phonemic awareness, and other "skills" that are critical for effective communication. Special

---

Table 5-2 **Topics for Language Experience Approach**

Home

Foods

Cooking
Favorite foods
Family meals

Family

Autobiography
About My Family
Pets
Vacation and travel
Celebrations
Shopping
Dining out
Favorite movies, TV shows

School

Social Studies

Personal/family history
What it would be like to be a
    doctor, police officer, farmer, etc.
Cultures
Celebrations
Transportation
History of a country
Holidays

Science

Plants and gardening
Classroom experiments
Weather and climate
Rocks

Animals
Water (rain, snow, clouds)
Oceans, lakes, rivers
Walking field trip

Reading

Library books
Classroom literature
Shared reading
Personal journal
Comic books
Writing (letters, stories, etc.)
Storytelling and retelling
Reader Response Journals

Math/Computers

Games
Math Field Day
Math story books

Arts and Music

Favorite songs, singers
Favorite instrument(s)
Dances and music
Favorite actor/actress
Movies and television shows
Personal drawings, paintings
Class/school plays
Personal performances/demonstrations
Museum trips

Miscellaneous

Trips to a: doctor, veterinarian, farm,
beach, relative's home, zoo, ball game, etc.
When I grow up, I'd like to . . .
"How to" (make a sandwich, play a game
    etc.)
My favorite sport(s)
My favorite team(s)
The Best/Worst Day of My Life
Dreams

education teachers can use the stories to strengthen sight vocabulary, word decoding, use of contextual information, and various other skills. The Language Experience Approach provides opportunities for learning within contexts that are relevant to the experiences of the learner.

Literature-Based Reading

Literature-based reading, which presents literature in both primary and second languages for students with LLC, is generally associated with whole language. It contributes greatly to a comprehensive literacy program. As an approach, it introduces the learner to whole stories and books rather than small pieces of literature. Children of all ages cultivate a desire for reading by being exposed to good literature. Students with LLC should be encouraged to select books and stories that interest them. This practice motivates students to focus on content as they make decisions about which books to select.

Process Approach – Writing and Reading

Over the past 30 years, reading researchers and teachers have amassed enough data to question traditional skills-based approaches to reading and writing, and to support an alternative – a process approach. In essence, a process approach considers the acts of reading and writing as integrative and dynamic. The aim is to actively engage students through their own creative energies and interests. In writing, for example, students are typically encouraged to both create and respond to print. They might begin their writing by engaging in brainstorming, discussion, and sharing, followed by low-risk creations of first-draft samples. Along the way, students share, revise, and polish their work into its finished form. Frequently, these works are "published" in the classroom and shared with others. The belief is that, over time, learners will acquire improved writing skills and knowledge of conventions (grammar, mechanics, usage, spelling), as well as improved reading skills and creative talents. Hopefully, they will also come to recognize the value of the process itself and its applications across the curriculum.

Assessment in the Whole Language Approach

An important distinguishing feature of the whole language approach is the use of authentic assessment. Authentic assessment implies that learners will be assessed in ways that reflect both the breadth and depth of their knowledge and skills. It proceeds from the premise that the "learnings" to be assessed have some **authentic purpose** beyond the classroom. Likewise, authentic assessment takes into account the **audience** for whom the work (products/performances) is intended. One guiding belief in recent years has been that the more actively engaged learners are in all aspects of their learning, the more powerful and meaningful it becomes. Students preparing to perform before an audience of parents and peers are more likely to put forth greater effort than they would on paper-and-pencil tasks or rote assignments. Hence, the teacher capitalizes upon both the clearly identified purpose and the audience while engaging the learners to greater depths.

One widely useful assessment tool, **rubric scoring**, has made its way into many areas of education – from classrooms to teacher certification exams. If properly designed, it can be used to assess aspects of learning that elude traditional testing and measures. "A rubric is a scoring tool that lists the criteria for a piece of work, or 'what counts' (for example, purpose, organization, details, voice, and mechanics are often what count in a piece of writing); it also articulates gradations of quality for each criterion, from excellent to poor." (Goodrich, 1997). Rubrics may range from simple Likert scales to detailed written assessments. They may be used to assess achievement in almost all areas of the curriculum. For example, a rubric detailing the primary traits of a superior report in language arts class might require only minor "tweaking" to be equally useful in assessing students on science reports. Goodrich (1997) maintained that rubrics are useful for two key purposes: (1) to define quality, and (2) to encourage students to become more critical and reflective about their work.

Portfolios have become as common as report cards in many districts across the nation. They are used throughout the curriculum to assemble artifacts and benchmark samples of student work. However, they need not – indeed, should not – be used merely to document performance and accomplishments. Rather, they should be a reflection of the students themselves. When they become simply another assessment tool, they lose their powers to reveal hidden qualities and characteristics – individual tastes, interests, talents, self-perceptions, and pride. When students are allowed to self-select items for inclusion, they learn to discern the important from the trivial, the valuable from the inferior.

Benefits of the Whole Language Approach

In summary, whole language has been successful for many reasons and continues to hold special promises for second language learners and students with reading and writing disabilities. The emphasis on language-rich and print-rich school environments encourages the development of linguistic and academic skills. Providing a range of authentic learning experiences also enhances opportunities to connect prior knowledge to new learning. Using authentic assessment in making curricular decisions simply demonstrates good pedagogical sense. This is not to suggest, however, that whole language should mean the complete abandonment of basics and/or directed instruction. Embedded in whole language are rich opportunities to facilitate and direct learning. The key elements of a whole language classroom are summarized in Table 5-3.

Model II: Skills-Based - Expository - Product Model

> *The rule, or measuring rod, which the behaviorist puts in front of him always is: Can I describe this bit of behavior I see in terms of 'stimulus and response'?*
>
> *John B. Watson*

Dewey's (1964) discussion of traditionalist ideas also characterizes contemporary expository methods. The same principles that have guided regular education have driven special education practices. (Kugelmass, 1995). Skills-based instruction focuses specifically on the teaching of a predetermined set of skills. Teacher-centered, textbook-centered, and/or learning-centered approaches are generally based on this instructional model. Table 5-4 shows the critical differences between skills-based and whole language approaches to instruction.

Direct Instruction

Direct instruction (DI), sometimes called *directive teaching*, "involves students in teacher-directed interactive instructional groups, with emphasis on sequential skills" (Drektrah & Chiang, pg. 174). Features that distinguish it from constructivist approaches include the following:

- Instruction is generally product-oriented.
- Instruction in reading, writing, and math proceed from part-to-whole.

Table 5-3
Key Elements of a Whole Language Classroom
Meeting the Needs of Students with Language and Learning Challenges

---

Immersion

Immerse students in a rich language and literacy environment. In whole language classrooms, learners are surrounded by and interact with language in its many forms – books, stories, magazines, notes, letters, poetry, song lyrics, and so on. Nothing is "held back" under the presumption that some genres absolutely precede others. Second-language learners, like their English-speaking peers, have varied literary interests. The use of realia in the early stages of second-language development may be critical to a balanced literacy program.

Opportunities And Resources

Provide ample time, materials, and space for learners to be listeners, speakers, readers, and writers. Plan activities that invite as well as instruct. Opportunities should abound for students with LLC to demonstrate their understanding – in all its many forms – without penalty for failure.

Meaningful Communication

Focus on the whole. The mind is pattern-seeking and constructs meanings from experiences in listening, speaking, reading, and writing when these activities are communicated as *wholes*. Generally speaking, language development is need-driven. It begins "naturally" with a need for meaningful and interpersonal communication in the early stages and progresses toward "academic language proficiency" over time. Like most learning tasks, literacy development is strongly related to personally meaningful experiences.

Modeling

Act as a communication role model in listening, speaking, reading, and writing so that instruction and purpose are meaningful. Encourage all learners to become "models" themselves. Create opportunities to demonstrate effective communication and literacy practices in the classroom and in the school.

Acceptance

Accept students as readers and writers capable of whole – and thus meaningful – communication. Literacy and learning begin with the learner, not the teacher.

Expectancy

Create an atmosphere of expectancy, an affective, attitudinal climate that is encouraging and supportive, where children are expected to continue in their literacy development.

Table 5-4
Comparison of Skills-Based
and Whole Language Methods

Reading Method Used by the Teacher

Skills Based

Teaches segments from part to whole
in a hierarchical order
> Letters
> Sound symbols
> Words
> Phrases
> Sentences

Drills words
Uses controlled texts
Teaches skills in isolation

Whole Language

Models the reading process from
whole to part
Reads whole stories (literature,
dictated stories)
Invites child to get involved in the
reading process
Invites child to:
> reconstruct a whole story through
>> retelling or rereading
> discuss the meaning of the text
> predict events
> apply concepts in the story to
>> his/her own experiences
> read and reread familiar stories
> read independently

Learning Process Used by the Child

Skills Based

Learns letter names
Learns sound-symbol relationships
Learns isolated words
Reads controlled vocabulary in phrases
Reads controlled sentences
Reads stories with simplified text

Whole Language

Seeks to understand the whole text
Learns from whole to part
Reconstructs the whole story in a
> literature selection or dictated story
Understands the meaning of the text
> matches story to a specific page
Develops directionality and tracking
Uses picture clues
Identifies repeated sentences and
> phrases
Identifies familiar words
Develops phonemic awareness

Reading Material

Skills Based

Controlled vocabulary texts
    basals
    phonic booklets

Whole Language

Predictable texts
Literature, dictated stories,
    strips, pattern books, student
    published material
Trade books, novels, factual books

Evaluation

Skills Based
Phonetic knowledge

Word knowledge
Worksheets
Skills tests
Basal level
Standardized tests

Whole Language
Observation or language behavior
    as children are engaged in reading
    and writing

Reading
    use of meaning
    use of pictures
    use of patterns
    use of tracking (pointing)
    use of phonetics
    comprehension through class
        discussion
    reading behavior inventories

Writing Method Used by the Teacher

Skills Based
Emphasizes skills before composing
Teaches skills of spelling
Teaches grammar in isolation
Teaches punctuation and usage separately
Controls topics and genre
Controls format of writing
Expects transfer of learning to students'
    compositions

Whole Language
Promotes daily writing
Encourages experimentation (allows
    invented marks and spellings)
Encourages drafting and revising
Emphasizes composition development
Encourages growth of spelling, grammar,
    usage within process of writing
Links literature to writing
Encourages development of composition
    through conference interviews and
    drafting
Recognizes developmental stages

Learning Process by the Child

Skills Based

Learns spelling lists
Learns phonic rules
Learns punctuation
Learns grammar rules

Whole Language

Gets hooked on writing
Enjoys writing
Drafts and revises
Learns conventional spelling, grammar,
   usage within process of writing
Attends to grammar, spelling, revising,
   editing, and publishing processes

Writing Experiences

Skills Based

Teacher assigned
Skills-oriented exercises
Teacher-controlled topics
Teacher-controlled genre
Weekly writing opportunities

Whole Language

Daily writing opportunities
Student-selected topics
Student choice of genre
Revising encouraged
Draft writing encouraged
Publication of student efforts
   emphasized

Evaluation

Skills Based

Emphasizes knowledge of isolated skills
Spelling tests

Grammar tests
Usage tests
Compositions evaluation based on deficits
Grammar, usage

Whole Language

Emphasizes integrated growth of
   composition and conventions as
   students write
Observation of growth in:
   composition
   symbolic representation of spelling
   spelling
   conventions
   publishing, revising, editing
Writing behavior inventories of actual
   behavior of students in writing
   process

Source: Excerpt from Heald-Taylor, G. (1989). *The Administrator's Guide to Whole Language*, Katonah, New York: Richard C. Owen Publishers, pp. 13-15. Used with permission.

- Control over curriculum decisions generally resides with the program developer and/or teacher.
- Classroom "scripts" are used by teachers to direct, monitor, and control learning.

Direct instruction (DI) can be traced to the mid-1960s, with the development of the Direct Instruction System for Teaching Arithmetic and Reading (DISTAR) (American Teacher, 1997). This program was initially aimed at children who were suspected of being at risk for academic failure. The term "direct instruction" is now commonly used to describe highly structured programs in a variety of disciplines. In a recent review of research, DI was found to produce favorable results in both the elementary and secondary schools – as well as in special education classrooms. (American Teacher, 1997). One "testimonial," Mabel B. Wesley Elementary, in a lower socio-economic area of Houston, Texas has gained national attention for academic achievement using this approach over the past 20 years.

In subsequent studies, involving ninth-graders in comparable metropolitan areas, students receiving direct instruction maintained above average achievement in both reading and math until they were placed in traditional classrooms. Concurrent studies in Baltimore and Broward County, Florida have produced even stronger support for direct instruction. In Broward County, for example, schools reported a significant drop in the number of students reading below grade level. (American Educator, 1997). The coordinator of the Broward County program and the principal of Wesley Elementary both acknowledged the real key to success in their programs – faculty and community "buy-in." In the case of Wesley Elementary, the school principal reported that success was greatly dependent upon proper training for both teachers and paraprofessionals *and* availability of needed materials. Proponents were also quick to point out that the DI model is not a panacea.

Phonics

Phonics is a system for teaching students to associate sounds with letters. For example, when students confront the word *bed*, they decode by breaking down the word into three sounds. Phonemic awareness is critical for success in phonics instruction. While phonics instruction is helpful to many students, it can also be counterproductive and impede the development of other strategies that are critical for comprehension. Some students learn more effectively when whole word units are emphasized rather than isolated sounds. Instructional programs that focus on "phonics" can be problematic for many students with learning disabilities who have difficulties with sound discrimination, letter sequencing, and/or auditory memory. Some students, for example, have difficulty holding sounds in memory and may forget the beginning sounds within a word as they progress to the sounds that follow. Trying to decode words one sound at a time can be quite frustrating for these students.

Basals

Basals are texts that have been designed for use in teaching specific skills and presenting specific types of information. Lerner (1989) reported that for the past 40 years, the basal reader has been, "the predominant instrumental tool in reading in 90 to 95 percent of the classrooms across the country" (p. 102). Hence a large portion of instructional decision-making has been handed over to program developers and textbook publishers. Because districts often adopt textbooks and/or programs for a block of several years, and at great expense, there is generally a strong commitment to the adopted programs and texts. In many cases, this means reduced autonomy in decision-making for the classroom teachers who know their students far better than the publisher. An argument frequently used by educators and parents in large districts is that adopting basals for use across the district is inappropriate. This has been argued eloquently by teachers in the Los Angeles Unified School District, one of the largest and most culturally and linguistically diverse districts in the country. In reading, for example, what criteria does one use in selecting a basal reader series intended for use with all students in the district?

Some basal reading programs embrace grouping and follow strictly "lock-stepped" sequences that rarely consider the immediate needs of the child. If learners "don't get it," they may simply be referred to remedial or learning disability programs where the same information is taught in smaller steps.

Mastery Learning

Mastery learning focuses on the content to be learned. In reading, for example, the presumption is that by mastering *component skills* (phonological/phonemic awareness, structural analysis, etc.), the child will be able to read. In writing a friendly letter, the teacher must identify the skills and subskills associated with letter-writing, arrange them sequentially/hierarchically, and monitor student progress at each stage of development, as illustrated in Figure 5-1.

Once the student has attained the level of proficiency predetermined by the teacher or writing program, he/she is ready to move on to skills development in related areas. This approach presents a clear example of how step-developmental models of learning have been hammered into a workable format for daily instruction. This does not, however, reflect Piaget's conception of the *phenomenon* of learning – which he described as sudden leaps of insight, or the "aha" experiences discussed elsewhere in this book. Rather, it generalizes the stage-step aspect of Piaget's developmental model in linear skills hierarchies. With respect to such instruction among students with LLC, highly reduced and segmented instruction has not enjoyed wide success (Hearne & Stone, 1996; Poplin, 1988; Poplin & Cousin, 1996).

Task Analysis

Task analysis (TA), as applied to teaching and learning, is a highly reductionistic approach. The teacher may focus on the learner, the task, or both in TA. In the former, the teacher must analyze the strengths and abilities of the student in terms of what is needed to accomplish the identified task. For example, if the task is to write a summary of a short story, the teacher must first determine if the student has requisite reading, writing, and comprehension skills to accomplish the task. In the latter, the teacher must determine what steps are required to accomplish the targeted task. In other words, the teacher must identify the hierarchy of components for each task. The use of TA is not common in programs for students with LLC. These students typically are capable of learning without having the activities broken down into minute "pieces." Task analysis is typically reserved for cases where there is a truly justifiable need for a highly structured program of instruction.

Product Orientation

The primary difference between process-oriented approaches and product-orientations is that the former is viewed as a key product in itself – that is, an understanding of the process. In terms of goals and objectives for students with LLC, for example, it is important that they learn how to arrive at solutions, answers, relationships, and products – not merely the single right or best answer identified by the teacher or the text. Products,

Figure 5-1
Skills Hierarchy for Writing a Friendly Letter

Product Level

- correct letter formation, spacing, slant, and size
- correct grammar, mechanics, usage, and spelling
- correct format for letter writing
- correct addressing of envelope

Prerequisite Skills Level

- pen/pencil held in correct position
- paper oriented properly for ease of writing
- 100% correct spelling of words in the letter in 9 of 10 attempts
- correct letter format in 9 of 10 attempts
- 100% correct usage of comma and period in 10 of 10 tests
- correct addressing of envelope in 10 of 10 attempts

Subskills Level

- correct formation of individual cursive alphabet letters
- correct use of comma in simple sentences
- correct use of period in simple sentences
- correct use of question mark in written language
- correct position of fingers for cursive writing
- correct orientation of writing paper

as delineated in textbooks are generally aimed at the typical classroom learner, not the student with language and/or learning difficulties. Hence, it becomes incumbent upon the teacher to adapt the material or develop alternative materials to meet the needs of students with LLC.

While a product-orientation may satisfy school board and/or public concerns about tangible proof that students are achieving, there is perhaps a more persistent need to educate the public in the processes of learning. When a child reports home with products from the day's classwork, parents might probe with *how* and *why* questions, e.g., How did you make this? How is yours different from the ones created by other children? Why did you make this? Tell me about the lesson/subject you are studying. By probing and questioning, students are encouraged to engage in reflective thinking and analysis. Asking the child to compare his work to that of other students provides the parents with insight into the thinking processes used by the child. For limited or non-English speaking parents of a student with LLC, this activity may serve two additional purposes: (1) It may increase awareness of the child's abilities and needs, and (2) it presents opportunities for the parent(s) to acquire/improve English language skills.

Implications for Students with LLC

- Leveled texts and materials imply "standards," in many (if not most) cases, the very kind of standards that mismatch the levels and abilities of students with LLC.

- While skills continua are an integral part of all good planning, the exclusive use of a lock-step "drill until skilled approach" will often preclude success for some students with LLC in the classroom.

- Because DI presumes that thinking and learning are linear processes, the model itself is problematic for some learners whose thinking processes don't match those of the model and/or teacher.

- For students with LLC, language-rich activities (including instruction in phonemic awareness) should promote knowledge of linguistic rules and usage.

- *Process* is more primary than *product* for students with LLC who are struggling to grasp meanings in the general classroom. Some students with LLC may appear to be "slow learners" because of difficulties understanding task instructions. Students with limited proficiency in English will often require more time to figure out tasks than classmates who are native English speakers. Teachers need to "tune in" to what these students are understanding and how they approach tasks rather than evaluating performance based entirely on the accuracy of responses.

Model III: Project-Based Experiential Approach

> *It is in fact, nothing short of a miracle that the modern methods of instruction have not yet entirely strangled the holy curiosity of inquiry; for this delicate little plant, aside from stimulation, stands mostly in need of freedom; without this it goes to wreck and ruin without fail. It is a very grave mistake to think that the enjoyment of seeing and searching can be promoted by means of coercion and a sense of duty.*
>
> *Albert Einstein*

Integrated/Interdisciplinary Curriculum

The integrated curriculum approach, known alternately as *interdisciplinary curriculum, cross-curriculum,* or *multidisciplinary curriculum* weaves the disciplines in ways that enhance and enrich learning. Generally speaking, an integrated-curriculum approach creates wonderful opportunities to *actively* engage students in projects, inquiry, and meaningful learning. Students are encouraged to construct their own meanings from direct, first-hand experiences, rather than merely accept the meanings and understandings of others. For students with LLC who need to make use of more sources of information and cueing systems than those provided by direct instruction, experiential approaches may hold great promise. Ten Models for integrating the curriculum are presented in Table 5-5.

Known widely for her work in the area of interdisciplinary curriculum, Heidi Hayes Jacobs (cited in Brandt, 1991) made the following observation: "The biggest obstacle to interdisciplinary curriculum planning is that people try to do too much at once. What they need to look for are some, not all, natural overlaps between subjects" (p. 24). Selecting contexts for integrating curriculum is not an easy task for some teachers. For others, the approach itself may seem overwhelming and/or inappropriate for students struggling with English and/or students with learning problems. To these teachers, I would pose this question: Would literature be a sensible, even comfortable starting point for exploring connections among content areas? Literature is not only accessible to many learners but also rich with possibilities for such exploration. Lauritzen, Jaeger, and Davenport (1996) described the issue clearly:

> It is fairly common practice to plan a unit from a chosen concept or topic and then seek literature that is related in some way to the concept or topic. What we are urging is that the *story* [emphasis added] is the integrating force in the curriculum. It provides a multifaceted context for learning from which the areas of study will develop naturally due to the children's and teachers' interests and questions. (p. 405)

Alejandro (1994) suggested that the visual arts offer another avenue to curriculum integration. She emphasized that "when we read and write, we use the same critical thinking and decision-making brain power that we use when we paint or respond to paintings" (p. 13). Using quality art (pictures/paintings from magazines, calendars, etc.), Alejandro transformed her classroom into a mini museum and transformed her "at risk" third-graders into thinkers, critics, and creators. Students in her classroom were able to construct their own personal stories about the pictures they liked – original stories, with

**Table 5-5
Ten Models for Integrating the Curricula**

Model	Descriptions	Examples
Fragmented	This is the traditional model of separate and distinct disciplines, fragmented by subject area.	The daily schedule shows distinct time slots with topics from two areas that are only occasionally intentionally related.
Connected	The teacher deliberately relates ideas within each discipline, rather than assuming that students will understand the connections automatically.	The teacher relates the concepts of fractions to decimals, which in turn relates money, grades, and so on.
Nested	Within each subject area, the teacher targets multiple skills; a social skill, a thinking skill, and a content-specific skill.	The teacher designs a unit on photosynthesis to simultaneously target consensus seeking (social skills), sequencing (thinking skills), and plant life cycle (science content).
Sequenced	Topics or units of study are rearranged and sequenced to coincide with one another. Similar ideas are taught in concert while remaining separate subjects.	In language arts, students read a historical novel depicting a particular period, while the teacher covers that same period in social studies.
Shared	Shared planning and teaching takes place in two disciplines in which overlapping concepts or ideas emerge as organizing elements.	In science and math, a teacher uses data collection, charting, and graphing as shared concepts that can be team-taught.
Webbed	A fertile theme is webbed to curriculum contents and disciplines; subjects use the theme to sift out appropriate concepts, topics, and ideas.	A teacher presents a simple topical theme, such as the circus and webs it to the subject areas. A conceptual theme, such as conflict, can be webbed for more depth in the theme approach.
Threaded	This approach threads thinking skills, social skills, multiple intelligences theory, technology, and study skills through the various disciplines.	The teacher targets prediction in reading, math, and science experiments; and targets forecasting current events in social studies. Thus, she threads the skill of prediction across the disciplines.
Integrated	This cross-disciplinary approach blends the four major disciplines by finding the overlapping skills, concepts, and attitudes in all four. Matches are made among them as commonalities emerge.	According to whole language philosophy reading, writing, listening, and speaking skills spring from a holistic, literature-based program.
Immersed	The disciplines become part of the learner's lens of expertise; the learner filters all content through this lens and becomes immersed in his/her own experience.	A six-year old is consumed by an interest in insects. She writes, reads, and dreams about them. Like an artist or writer, this learner is constantly making connections to her subject.
Networked	The learner filters all learning through the expert's eye and makes internal connections that lead to external networks of experts in related fields.	A fifth grader interested in Native Americans meets an anthropologist and archeologist on a summer dig. The learner's networks begin to take shape.

Source: Fogerty, R. (1991) *The Mindful School: How to Integrate the Curriculum*. Arlington Heights, IL: Skylight Training and Publishing. Adapted from page xv with permission.

minimal discussion and prompting. The teacher let them discover their own genius and helped them to appreciate the varied and individual forms they took. As for advice to other professionals, Ms. Alejandro stated emphatically: "*Never* remediate. *Always* enrich. Treat students as if they were all gifted and talented, and they will show you in some way or in many ways that they are" (p. 20).

Winograd and Higgins (1995) also provided an unusual (and interesting) approach by engaging students as authors of math story problems. They described a whole language approach in which mathematics was linked to language arts. A math story-problem writing program was implemented in which students openly shared their story problems with peers, discussed these problems, and explained them. The authors concluded that, "When invited and trusted to do so, these students were willing to initiate and sustain their own mathematics problem writing, reading, and solving with enthusiasm and thoughtfulness" (p. 316).

Inquiry Approach

I chose to address *inquiry* apart from *integrated/interdisciplinary* curriculum, although inquiry frequently engages students in learning that stretches across the curriculum. Student research at the elementary level, however, has been confined primarily to "in class" and "at home projects" (e.g., Science Fair projects, History Day projects, etc.). Investigations and inquiry have been limited for a variety of reasons, including lack of time, lack of materials, and/or lack of teacher interest. It is probably safe to assume that such approaches have been used even less among language minority students and students in special education programs. As pointed out by Poplin and Stone (1992), the same kinds of misperceptions and misdiagnoses that have forced some learners into special education programs probably unfairly influence some educators' views of second-language learners as well. Traditionally, students in learning disabilities programs have spent a large portion of their time engaged in activities aimed at "remediating" their deficits (Poplin, 1988; Poplin & Cousin, 1996). While these learners may have difficulties with reading and writing, they may also have wonderful ideas to share in cooperative groups and inquiry projects. Likewise, simply because students are limited in their English proficiency does not imply that they cannot contribute admirably to group investigations and other activities.

One highly underestimated source of inquiry-rich ideas is literature. Reading and social studies programs, for example, share several common goals, including (1) a general shift from reducing and segmenting instruction, to one that considers the "whole" of what is to be learned, (2) a de-emphasis on decontextualized learning and materials, and (3) a general shift from product-driven instruction to one that emphasizes process. (Hearne & LeBlanc, 1991). Lauritzen, Jaeger, and Davenport (1996) stressed that "a good story captures the imagination of its audience and invites the audience to consider possibilities. It is from these possibilities that curriculum arises. "

Graham and Harris (1994) offered the following observation:

> Educators with a constructivist orientation contend that when learners construct their own knowledge, they understand it and can apply it. According to this perspective, constructing knowledge leads to ownership, which is accompanied by an understanding of how to use the created knowledge. Many constructivist educators further contend that discovery-oriented approaches to teaching should be used to promote such construction and understanding. This is, whenever possible, teachers should structure situ-

ations so that learners use what they already know to discover knowledge, strategic processes, and so forth (pg. 275).

Inquiry Within Reach

One of the primary purposes of inquiry and project approaches is to encourage development of higher order thinking skills among students. This can be accomplished at any grade level through thoughtful planning. The "Inquiry Within Reach" approach consists of the eight steps outlined in Table 5-6.

The following "experiences" are offered as examples of how teachers might engage students in meaningful inquiry – within their reach. There are two samples: one plan aimed at second graders and another aimed at fourth/fifth graders. The inquiry problem is the same for both groups. The inquiries differ by depth of study and by levels of cognitive challenge for each group. Naturally, students in the upper grades would be capable of deeper study and higher order thinking. Nonetheless, the process is the same for both groups, and the goals are similar.

Inquiry Project 1: Shoo, Fly, Shoo!
Goal: To engage students in action research.
Suggested Grade Level: Grade 2

■ **Discuss/Arouse Interest**
- Begin by inviting the students to guess the number of flies they saw around the lunch area.
- Record their responses on the board or a flip chart.

■ **Define All Terms**
- Be sure that students understand all relevant terms. Provide comprehensible input when defining, clarifying, explaining.

■ **Pose the Problem/Question**
- Ask the students, "Why are there so many flies?"
- Engage them in further discussion. Record their responses. (Sample responses: They like the cookies. They want our food. They are hungry.)

■ **Investigate the Problem**
- Lead the students on a walking tour of the campus/lunch area during/after lunch time.

■ **Discuss/Analyze Findings**
- Lead the students in discussion of what they saw. (Sample responses: "There were lots of flies." "There was a lot of food on the ground." "The tables were dirty.").

■ **Hypothesize**
- Lead students toward hypothesis (e.g., If there was less food lying around, the flies would go away.).

■ **Test Hypothesis**
- Teacher and students outline a plan to clean up the lunch area daily for one week.

Table 5-6
Inquiry Within Reach
Adapting Classroom Instruction for Students with LLC

■ **Step 1: Identify students' language and learning abilities levels.**
  • Identify students' strengths and interests.

■ **Step 2: Pose Problem or Question.**
  • Engage students actively in discussion. Use peer interpreters as needed.
  • Guide discussion. Use comprehensible language and/or peer interpreters.

■ **Step 3: Define all Key Terms.**
  • Clarify – Use graphics, repetition, comprehensible vocabulary. Peer interpreters.

■ **Step 4: Investigate Problem or Question.**
  • Assign groups and tasks. Balance groups for language and learning abilities levels.
  • Establish guidelines and timeline.
  • Facilitate information-gathering. Give feedback, suggestions, guidance.

■ **Step 5: Analyze Findings**
  • Organize the findings – Assist students.
  • Discuss the findings – Direct discussion using comprehensible vocabulary.
  • Have students formulate a hypothesis.

■ **Step 6: Test the Hypothesis**
  • Have students devise a plan to test their hunch. Encourage input from students with LLC.
  • Implement the plan – Assure that all students participate.

■ **Step 7: Determine Conclusions**
  • Organize findings – Assist students.
  • Discuss findings – What did we discover? Use peer interpreters as needed.

■ **Step 8: Discuss Relevancy of the Inquiry**
  • Relate the study to students' real lives. Use peer interpreters.
  • Use present study to stimulate interest in further inquiries.
  • Record field notes along the way.

- On Friday, lead the class on a follow-up tour of the lunch area. Ask students to observe carefully.
- Record field notes.

■ *Draw Conclusions*
- Lead students in discussion of findings.
- Record findings/observations on the board or a flip chart.
- Lead students in writing up a final statement – a conclusion.

■ *Extension/Invitation to New Inquiry*
- Engage students in discussion of related problems, e.g., bugs or rodents in the classroom.
- Invite them into discussion about new and interesting problems/questions to be pursued.

The sample inquiry that follows focuses on more difficult subject matter, but the approach is similar to that described in the example above.

> **Inquiry Project 2: The Flies Have It**
> *Goal: To engage students in action research.*
> *Suggested Grade Level: Grades 4 and 5*

■ *Discussion/Arousal of Interest*
- Begin by inviting students to guess the number of flies present around the lunch area.
- Record responses on the board or a flip chart. (Responses should vary).

■ *Define All Terms*
- Be sure all students understand all relevant terms. Provide comprehensible input when defining, clarifying, explaining.

■ *Pose the Problem/Question*
- Ask the students, "What could be causing the fly infestation?"
- Engage them in brainstorming. Record responses. (Sample responses: "The lunch area is where the food is." "Students leave food all over the place." "They like the warm weather.").

■ *Investigate the Problem*
- Divide students into investigation teams, complete with team leaders, recorders, and reporters.
- Facilitate field study: Students conduct a study of the lunch area before, during, and after breakfast and lunch periods . They record their findings as field notes.

■ *Discuss/Analyze Findings*
- Investigation teams report their field note findings to the class.
- Lead students in summarizing their findings.

■ *Hypothesize*
- Guide students in formulating a hypothesis (e.g., If we cut off their food supply, the flies would disappear. If we maintain a clean breakfast/lunch area, they will disappear.

■ *Test Hypothesis*
- Facilitate. Students develop a class plan to test their hypotheses. Over the coming month, the class will work in teams to keep the student lunch/breakfast area neat and clean.
- Teams will observe, record field notes, and report to the class weekly.

■ *Draw Conclusions*
- At the end of the month, teams will report their findings to the class (oral and/or written).
- Record key findings on board or flip chart.
- Lead students in writing up a summary of findings and conclusions.

■ *Extensions/Invitation to New Inquiry*
- Engage students in discussion of related problems, e.g., bugs or rodents in the school.
- Invite students into discussions of new and interesting problems/questions to be pursued.

With careful planning and adaptations, second language students with learning disabilities should be able to participate in a variety of inquiry projects. It is important, of course, to know the students' strengths and talents as well as their academic deficits when planning classroom lessons.

Implications for Teachers of Students with LLC
- Inquiry, like whole language and other experiential approaches, engages students in rich language activities in meaningful contexts.

- Comprehensible input is paramount to success. Inquiry is cognitively demanding. Pairing students with LLC with peer interpreters should enhance their chances of success.

- Inquiry requires time and careful planning. Teachers should select projects/inquiry topics that are sure to generate interest and commitment among students.

- Students with LLC may require additional preview-review time.

Creating a Multicultural Curriculum
A "multicultural perspective" should be incorporated into every classroom to meet the diverse needs of students. Most classroom learning experiences can be adapted to make them relevant to students who come from diverse backgrounds. An activity focusing on the topic "climate," for example, might be presented as follows:

1. *Examine climate and weather of various countries.*
   - Countries of students' origins
   - Countries around the world

2. *Develop a word back or word wall.*
   - Geographic features
   - Languages: Vocabulary and Terms
     Examples:
       Linguistic distinctions: typhoon, hurricane, cyclone
       Weather distinctions: tornado, blizzard, storm

3. *Develops maps and mapping skills.*
   - Create maps of countries of students' and/or family origins.
   - Create individual/group maps (countries, continents, world).

4. *Examine how climate/weather is discussed in literature from various countries.*
   - Read literature with "weather-related" themes, e.g., *White Fang*.
   - Read literature from countries in various regions of the world.
   - Read literature from countries of students' origins.

5. *Examine how climate/weather affects lives and lifestyles.*
   - Examine how people dress in various countries.
   - Invite students to share pictures of daily life during different seasons in their homeland.
   - Discuss how weather/climate affects how people dress.
   - Discuss ways in which weather/climate affects the lives of people in other countries.

6. *Examine how climate/weather affects plants and animal life.*
   - Study plants and animals in countries of students' origins.
   - Study plants and animals in various countries, continents, hemispheres.

Examples are presented below of projects that can be adapted quite easily for use with diverse populations. These projects can engage students in creating, constructing, developing, designing, investigating, simulating, performing, and various other activities.

Grade Level - Kindergarten
- *Friends* – Children draw/create pictures of themselves and assemble them into an album.
- *"Picture of Sorts"* – Students create pictures from small items they have sorted into categories (e.g., buttons, popcorn kernels, alphabet macaroni, etc.). The objects are arranged into designs or pictures, then glued.

Grade Level - First
- *Butterflies* – Students construct cardboard butterfly mobiles and write about them.
- *Animal Babies* – Children study likenesses and differences among several animals and create a zoo with pictures.
- *Story Plays* – Students decide upon a favorite story (e.g., *Alexander and the Terrible, Horrible, No Good, Very Bad Day* – a favorite among children) and perform it in the classroom.

Grade Level - Second

- *Tree Houses* - Students design their own tree house dioramas (using shoe boxes).
- *Story Trains* - After reading/hearing several predictable books and stories, it would be an opportune time to introduce students to the concept of story development or plot. Parts of the story are written on cardboard boxes which the students color/paint to look like train cars. Students arrange the story (cars) in order and re-read it aloud chorally.

Grade Level - Third

- *Our Town* - The teacher shares pictures, maps, and other information about the town. Students create a class diorama of the town.
- *Business Center* - Students plan their own city, complete with businesses, government, residential and public places (parks, recreation areas, etc.). Using items brought from home, they set up and simulate business.

Grade Level - Fourth

- *Frontier Life* - While simulating frontier life, students create artifacts and transform the classroom into a log cabin. They explore everything from diet to clothing to daily living conditions.
- *The Gold Rush* - Students simulate life in a mining camp.
- *Inventions* - While studying historical inventions of the 19th century, students are challenged to invent something themselves. Inventions are then demonstrated/shared.

Grade Level - Fifth

- *Ancient Rome* - Students simulate life in ancient Rome by transforming the classroom into a Roman public/government building. Students create a play, complete with their own scripts, and perform it for other classes.
- *Mapping the Globe* - One way to increase student awareness and understanding of world geography is to engage students in creating their own maps of the globe. Using large air-filled balloons, newspaper strips and paste, students create spheres which are then painted to depict continents and other geographical features. This might be accompanied by having students work in groups to investigate and report on life in other countries.

Grade Level - Sixth

- *We, the Legislature* - Students simulate a session of the state/national legislature. They transform the room into a legislative hall, develop their own agenda, assume the roles of congressional members, create and debate laws, and conduct other related business.
- *New Worlds* - Students engage in review of historical ventures into new worlds (e.g., Columbus, moon missions). They are then asked to plan the colonization of a newly discovered planet in the universe.

Implications for Students with LLC

The Project approach provides many opportunities to engage students in meaningful learning and inquiry. Such activities are rich with possibilities for both acquiring and demonstrating knowledge and skills development. However, teachers may need to do the following:

- Provide scaffolding for students with LLC by pairing them with peers.

- Anticipate special needs in planning the projects.

- Match students with LLC to attainable goals and aspects of a project.

- Allow for alternative approaches to problem-solving.

- Provide frequent and positive feedback to students with LLC.

- Plan for alternative assessments of student contributions and products.

- Challenge students with LLC and hold them accountable for what they can do.

Bridging the Paradigms

No single approach to learning works best with all students. Each student is influenced by the experiences he/she has had within his or her culture and learning environment. Although students with special learning needs often require more structure and guidance than their peers, teachers need to challenge them to take on active roles in the learning process. Aspects of whole language, skills-based learning, and other models can be integrated into the classroom curriculum. It is important to bridge the paradigms so that instruction can be adapted to meet the individual needs of children (see Figure 5-2).

When working with students with LLC, it is important to "weave" the curriculum so that topics in mathematics, science, and other subjects are used to help students acquire knowledge of various classroom topics. Figure 5.3, for example, shows how the topic "celebrations" can be woven into various subjects within a multicultural classroom curriculum.

What is critical in all classroom instruction is that the learning materials make sense to the child. Educational professionals must strive to make learning experience relevant to what their students have already learned and experienced. Cultural differences, language proficiency, interests, previous classroom experiences, and a variety of other factors should be considered in developing educational programs for culturally and linguistically diverse students with learning disabilities.

Figure 5-2
Bridging the Paradigms – A Confluence of Models

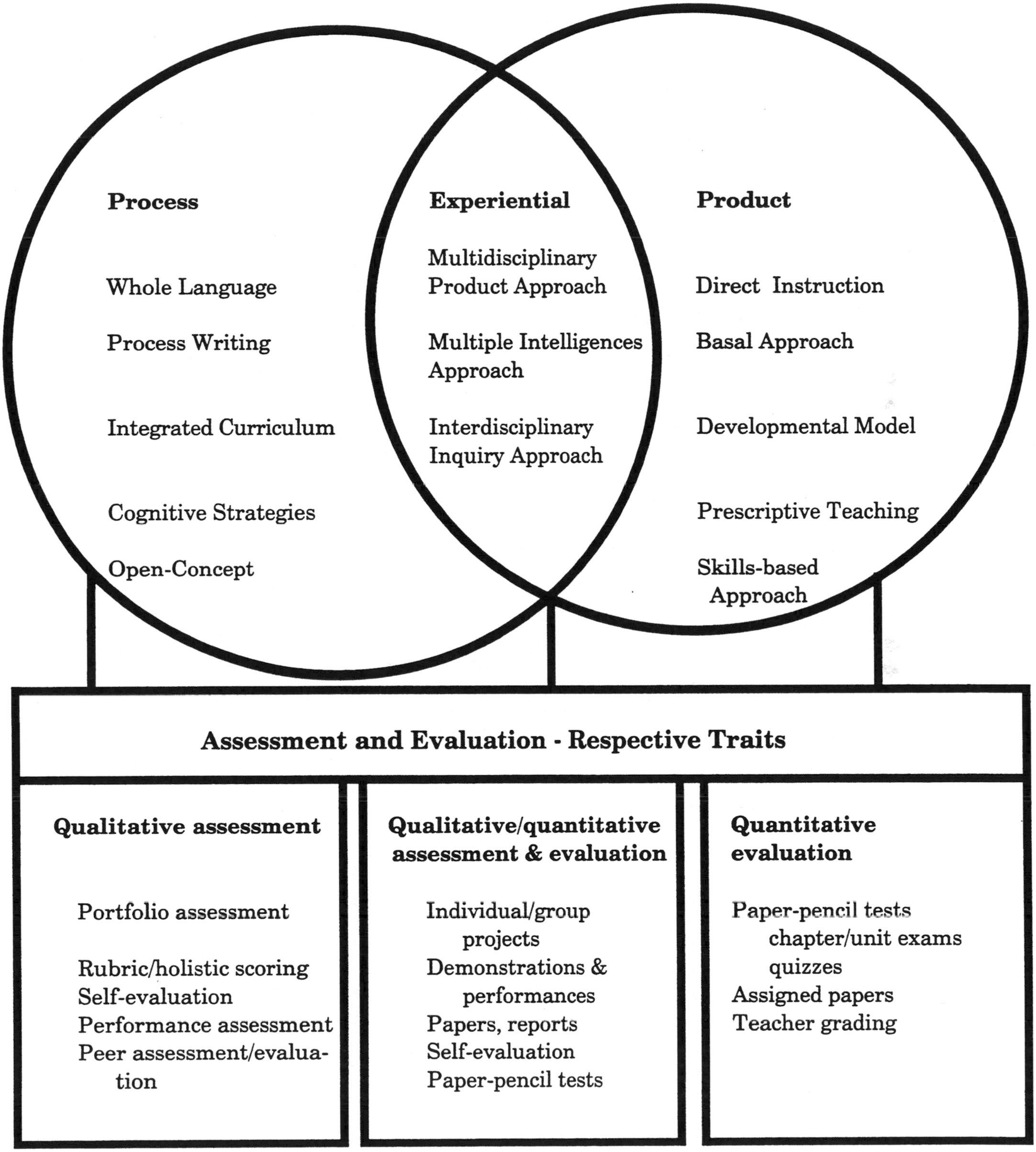

Process

Whole Language

Process Writing

Integrated Curriculum

Cognitive Strategies

Open-Concept

Experiential

Multidisciplinary
Product Approach

Multiple Intelligences
Approach

Interdisciplinary
Inquiry Approach

Product

Direct Instruction

Basal Approach

Developmental Model

Prescriptive Teaching

Skills-based
Approach

Assessment and Evaluation - Respective Traits

Qualitative assessment	**Qualitative/quantitative assessment & evaluation**	**Quantitative evaluation**
Portfolio assessment	Individual/group projects	Paper-pencil tests chapter/unit exams quizzes
Rubric/holistic scoring Self-evaluation Performance assessment Peer assessment/evaluation	Demonstrations & performances Papers, reports Self-evaluation Paper-pencil tests	Assigned papers Teacher grading

Figure 5-3
WEAVING THE CURRICULUM

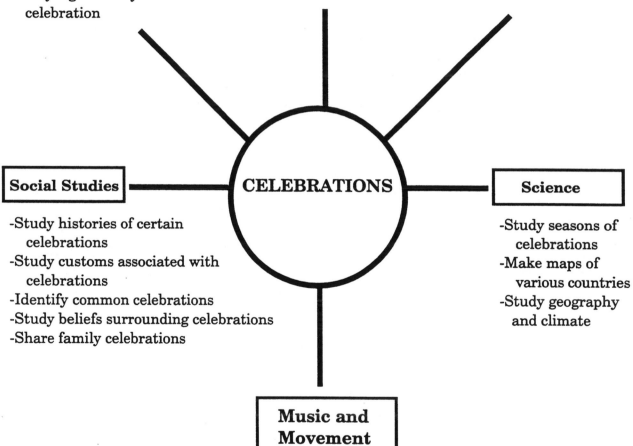

Language Arts

-Read about several cultures
-Write about other cultures
-Make a portfolio of cultures
-Describe a favorite celebration
-Study signs and symbols of
 celebration

Arts

-View paintings, photos of
 celebrations in other cultures
-Create pictures/artwork
-Make costumes, flags, banners

Mathematics

-Study calendars
-Study time zones
-Study timelines

Social Studies

-Study histories of certain
 celebrations
-Study customs associated with
 celebrations
-Identify common celebrations
-Study beliefs surrounding celebrations
-Share family celebrations

CELEBRATIONS

Science

-Study seasons of
 celebrations
-Make maps of
 various countries
-Study geography
 and climate

**Music and
Movement**

-Study music associated
 with celebrations
-Study dance/movement
 associated with celebrations
-Bring/share instruments

Chapter 6
Programs and Practices

The assumption that intelligence can be measured as a single number is just a twentieth century version of craniometry.
Stephen J. Gould

Multiple Intelligences Model

There is a growing body of research and discussion, most notably in Howard Gardner's (1983) work, that strongly suggests the need to revise our views about intelligence and our roles as educators. His theory of multiple intelligences (MI) offers a holistic accounting of individual potential and talents. According to Gardner (1983; 1993) each of us possesses at least eight kinds of intelligence: Linguistic, Logical-Mathematical, Musical, Spatial, Bodily-Kinesthetic, Interpersonal, Intrapersonal, and Naturalistic (see Figure 6-1 and Table 6-1). The degree to which each develops is dependent upon many variables, the most important of which is freedom to pursue development. Because schools are "deficit-driven," they generally devalue or ignore intelligences other than the logical-mathematical and linguistic (Armstrong, 1994; Gardner, 1983, 1991). Hence, students who do not fare well on measures of these intelligences frequently find themselves assigned to remedial or special education programs.

In traditional special programs, educators look for students' deficits in their research, in their diagnoses, in their assessments, and throughout the school day. Once the deficits are found, educators define their roles as remediators of the identified deficits. The students' days are then structured to be filled with activities based on their weaknesses, rather than their strengths. Poor readers, for example, are frequently assigned multiple sessions of reading instruction (e.g., regular class, special class, bilingual class, after school tutoring). In addition, remediation is defined reductionistically, with large and inherently interesting activities, such as reading, broken down into small, often disconnected and uninteresting tasks. Typically, the small reductionistic skills are then selected for instruction. If this sounds familiar to bilingual teachers and/or students, it is because deficit-models have also guided instruction in many bilingual programs. (Rueda, 1989; Poplin, 1993). Although our current diagnosis, assessment, and instructional practices

---

Figure 6-1
Multiple Intelligences Toolbox and Natural Resources

VERBAL/ LINGUISTIC

Reading
Vocabulary
Formal speech
Journal/diary keeping
Creative writing
Poetry
Debate, Impromptu speaking
Humor/jokes
Storytelling

LOGICAL/ MATHEMATICAL

Abstract symbols/formulas
Outlining
Graphic organizers
Number sequences
Calculation
Deciphering code
Showing relationships
Syllogisms, problem-solving
Pattern games

VISUAL/ SPATIAL

Guided imagery
Active imagination
Color schemes
Pattern/designs
Painting, Drawing
Mind-mapping
Pretending
Sculpture, pictures

BODILY/KINESTHETIC

Folk/creative dance
Role playing
Physical gestures/mime
Drama
Martial arts
Body language
Physical exercise
Inventing
Sports/games

MULTIPLE

INTELLIGENCES

TOOLBOX

INTERPERSONAL

Giving feedback
Cooperative learning
Intuiting
Person-to-person
   communication
Empathy practices
Collaboration skills
Sensing others'
   motives
Group projects

MUSICAL/RHYTHMIC

Rhythmic patterns
Singing, vocal sounds/tones
Music composition/creation
Percussion vibrations
Environmental sounds
Instrumental sounds
Music performance

INTRAPERSONAL

Silent reflection
   methods
Thinking strategies
Centering practices
Metacognition
   techniques
Emotional processing

Source: Lazear, D. G. (1992). *Teaching for Multiple Intelligences*. (Fastback No. 342). Phi Delta Kappa Educational Foundation. Adapted with permission.

NATURALIST INTELLIGENCE

Cooking	Forestry	Gardening
Fishing	Animal watching/study	Animal care
Landscaping	Ranching/farming	Plant care
Hunting	Hiking	Nature walks
Recreational areas	Parks	Zoos

Table 6-1
Multiple Intelligences and Language Development

The activities below can be used with students to promote both language development and various types of intellectual abilities. Each activity should engage students in discussion, demonstration, and/or performance. Teachers, aides, or peer interpreters can assist and encourage reluctant students. Try to have bilingual books and materials available for students in the classroom.

Interpersonal

"Introducing" – Students introduce:
  - each other
  - a simple lesson or activity
  - a story, song, or poem

Intrapersonal

Show and Tell – favorite things
Journal writing
Dreams diary or journal
My Life in Pictures (collage)
Write/tell about an imaginary journey
  or a "Perfect World"

Logical-Mathematical

Choral Math – reciting math facts
"Patterns" – identifying/describing patterns
    in nature (layers, lines, sequences, etc.)
Computer literacy
Build, construct – then share, and demonstrate
Create mazes and puzzles – share and discuss

Bodily-Kinesthetic

Rhythmic activities with singing/rapping
"Teach Me That ..." dance, exercise, sport
Mime/acting out scene from a story
Build, construct, create – then discuss
Direct class or group in game/activity

Musical

Pantomime a favorite song
Choral singing, rapping
Discussing different song renditions
Discussing instruments and sounds

Naturalistic

Cooking demonstration
Campus/Neighborhood Walk followed
Planting and tending a small garden
Menu planning
Animal care and/or training
Build a simple ecosystem – discuss it

Linguistic

Choral reading
Rhymes, riddles, songs
Storytelling, retelling
Writing
Letter writing
Act out scenes, stories, plays

Spatial

Mi Vida – painting of my life
"Map of My Room" (neighborhood, etc.)
"My Vision of the Story" – drawn or
    painted interpretation with discussion
Create maps – share with group or class
Build, construct, create – then discuss

remain oriented toward locating and curing deficits rather than capitalizing on talents, our cure rate is extremely low (Coles, 1987; Poplin & Cousin, 1996).

In recent years, however, at least some researchers have directed their interests toward creativity and various non-traditional strengths and talents that have not been well understood or highly valued by the schools. In the second of two studies of computer aptitude among junior high students, Hearne, Poplin, Schoneman, and O'Shaughnessy (1988) found that junior high students with LD had computer aptitudes equivalent to their nondisabled counterparts. Results also indicated that females and males performed equally well on the computer measures. In her studies of divergent thinking and creative talents among bilingual and special education students in an elementary school, Stone (1992) found that students in these categories showed strengths and talents equal to their general education peers.

Such stories are indicators that language-and-learning-challenged students can succeed in many areas not particularly valued by the schools. The kinds of schools advocated by Howard Gardner (1993) exist primarily as pilot programs, such as "Project Spectrum," which is a preschool collaboration between Harvard and Tufts universities; these programs allow students to demonstrate their particular strengths and interests through play, number games, creative movement exercises, and storytelling activities.

Since the early 1980's, Gardner's work has been translated into practical classroom applications that are widely used. Philosophically compatible with whole language and other experiential approaches, MI serves to strengthen curriculum and instruction. (Armstrong, 1994; Lazear, 1991). While many districts across the country have developed MI programs and magnet projects, there is no widely accepted plan at the state or national level for nurturing the multiple intellects.

Approaches based on MI facilitate learning within a multicultural curriculum. Classroom lessons relating to individuals from diverse cultural backgrounds who have demonstrated specific areas of intelligence (e.g., musical) can be used to help students become aware of their own strengths (see Table 6-2). Although literacy skills are important, educators should also motivate students to achieve in other areas in which potential is demonstrated.

Implications for Teachers of Students with LLC

- Nowhere exists a greater need for such planning than in our booming special education programs. An MI approach allows the individualization that may help students with learning problems to reach their potential and achieve success.
- MI provides a strong "organizing center" for curriculum development at both the school and classroom levels. Instruction planned around MI benefits *all* students.
- MI offers educators a broad, holistic approach to assessment.
- Teachers may need training and encouragement to fully realize the aims and benefits of MI approaches.
- Buy-in from parents is crucial. MI might represent a total paradigm shift for parents from "traditional" school backgrounds. These parents should be thoroughly informed about the goals and implications of a multiple intelligences approach, perhaps through open houses, workshops, meetings, etc.
- Students themselves need to fully understand the goals and implications of this model if they are to fully realize its potential for enhancing learning.

Consultation-Collaboration Model

The rapid growth of special education programs across America over the past 30 years has created in its wake the need for an army of specialists in the areas of learning

	Table 6-2 Multiple Intelligences —A Racial/Ethnic Perspective			
	African-American	**Asian-American**	**Latino-American**	**Native American**
MUSICAL	Charlie Pride Carmen McRae Marian Anderson Duke Ellington Dionne Warwick	Yo-Yo Ma Seiji Ozawa T. Akiyoshi	Richie Valens Trini Lopez Linda Ronstadt Joan Baez	Louis Ballard Buffy Ste. Marie
BODILY KINES-THETIC	Willie Mays Jackie Robinson Cheryl Miller Zina Garrison	Kristi Yamaguchi Michelle Kwan Bruce Lee Brandon Lee Jack Soo	Jose A. Limon Pancho Gonzales Evelyn Cisneros	Maria Tallchief Jim Thorpe Billy Mills Jay Silverhills
SPATIAL Visual/Artistic	Matthew Henson Bessie Coleman Paul Cuffe Lorna Simpson Mae C. Jemison	I. M. Pei Maya Lin Ming Cho Lee E. Onizuka I. Noguchi Kang Fa Lee	Ellen Ochoa Marisol Porfiro Salinas Octavio Medellin	Will Sampson Sacajawea W. Richard West Oscar Howe Pablita Velarde
INTER-PERSONAL	M. Luther King Bill Cosby Oprah Winfrey	I. Hayakawa H. L. Fong D. K. Inouye N. Mineta R. Matsuli	Richard Rodriguez Cezar Chavez H. B. Gonzales Lena Guerrero	Larry Echohawk Chief Joseph Ben Reifel LaDonna Harris
INTRA-PERSONAL	Rosa Parks T. Marshall	R. Takaaki B. Hosokawa P. Tajiatsu Nash T. Thien-An N. A. Nga	Dennis Chavez Bishop P. Flores Ruben Salazar	Frank Fools Crow Chief Joseph Buffy Ste. Marie D. Pelotte Black Elk
LINGUISTIC	Marcus Garvey Langston Hughes Toni Morrison Maya Angelou	Yoshiko Uchida Kyoko Mori W. Yamauchi P. K. Gotanda	Carlos Fuentes Carlos Castenada Ruben Salazar Luis Valdes	Sequoyah Simon Ortiz Joy Harjo Louise Erdich
LOGICAL-MATHE-MATICAL	G. W. Carver Clarice D. Reid B. Banneker C. Richard Drew D. Lavon Julian	An Wang H. Yoon Park J. Takemini H. Noguchi	Luis Alvarez Antonia C. Novello M. G. Vallejo Leo Esaki	C. A. Eastman C. L. Tinker
NATURALIST	G. W. Carver Nat Love J. Beckwourth		Louis Fuentes	Ishi Will Rogers George Abrams F. L. Dockstader

disabilities, speech and language, hearing, vision, adapted physical education, occupational therapy, and counseling. However, learning disabilities represents the largest single group served by the schools under Public Law 94-142 and subsequent special education laws. With the number of referrals soaring nationwide, many districts have combined their efforts by creating consortia to meet the varied legal mandates and educational needs of the students being served.

One service delivery model that has emerged from these constraints and has shown promise in mediating growing problems is the *consultation-collaboration model*. In consultation, the specialist in learning disabilities serves as advisor-consultant to a lesser skilled person (teacher). Collaboration, however, refers to a working arrangement between persons of equal skills (Learner, 2000). Coordinated properly, the model can bring together – much like the Child Study Team – a range of voices and expertise to plan for student learning in the *least restrictive environment* (LRE). Generally speaking, the regular classroom is considered to be the least restrictive environment for learners.

In the consultation-collaboration approach, the team is usually headed by a consultant, typically the learning disabilities specialist. Emphasis is given to modification of the program rather than modification of the students (Friend & Bauwens, 1988; Tindal, Shinn, Walz, & Germann, 1987). The team collaborates to establish content, instructional approaches, and assessment procedures for the student. The learning disabilities (LD) specialist and the bilingual specialist (if available) then support the child by consulting with the classroom teacher.

The strengths of the model are rooted in its reliance on *all* team members for support and direction. Decision-making, while generally the province of the classroom teacher, becomes a shared responsibility with specialists, administrators, parents, and other support personnel. Sample responsibilities of the specialist and teacher are listed below. Educators must also recognize the disadvantages and limitations of the consultation-collaboration model, as presented in Table 6-3.

Consultant's Responsibilities (LD Specialist)	**Teacher's Responsibilities**
Assesses abilities	Modifies curriculum
Recommends interventions	Implements interventions
Monitors program	Assesses progress toward school goals
Assesses progress toward I.E.P. goals	Reports student progress
Convenes meetings	

Curriculum-Based Assessment and Instruction (CBA/CBI)

Lerner (1989) described *curriculum-based assessment* as "a procedure designed to strengthen the connection between assessment and instruction by evaluating the student in terms of the curricular requirements of the school or classroom. It is not a new methodology, but is embedded in the broader behavioral approach to teaching special education students systematically and measuring their progress frequently" (p. 71). Curriculum-based assessment (CBA) and instruction (CBI) place the teacher in control of what goes on in the classroom. By assessing student strengths and needs in relation to the classroom curriculum, teachers and special educators can more clearly identify appropriate interventions. Adaptations of classroom instruction and/or content are frequently adequate interventions (Bursuck & Lessen, 1987). By focusing attention on potential problems with curriculum and instruction – rather than looking for deficits within the students – teachers may think twice before making special education referrals. The primary strength of the CBA is that, as teachers develop it, they also formulate the

---

Table 6-3
Points to Consider When Using the
Consultation-Collaboration Model

Consultant Roles

- Coordinates and convenes meetings
- Appropriates special resources (both material and human)
- Supervises instructional planning and implementation
- Monitors progress toward the student's Individualized Education Program (I.E.P.)
- Generally acts as consultant to teachers, parents, and administrators

Strengths of the Model

- Serves students in the general classroom setting
- May result in a fewer inappropriate referrals
- Direct sharing of knowledge and skills in the classroom
- Reduced disruptions in students' schedules
- May lead to a reduction in labeling/stigmatizing

Limitations and Risks

- Misperceptions of the model as a quick fix (Huefner, 1988)
- Inappropriate use of highly trained specialists as tutors or teacher aides
- Over-expectation from administrators, parents, and teachers
- Inadequate support from regular classroom teachers – disproportionate work-load.
- Loss of pull-out programs – the least restrictive environment for some learners
- Sharply reduced individualized instruction
- Possible decline in quality of services provided to students with I.E.P.'s
- Increased caseload, roles, responsibilities – a prescription for burnout

Questions

- Does consulting water down the quality of services provided to students identified as having LD?
- Are peers of students with LD no longer aware of their academic difficulties because they are being served in the general classroom?
- Is the consultation-collaboration model the best approach for all students with LD?

important goals and objectives of the school program. Goal-setting is a natural artifact of this process; as teachers organize the assessment tool, they are also organizing and prioritizing the scope and sequence of the curriculum. Thus, the teachers develop an assessment instrument that reflects what is being taught, in addition to obtaining a clearer and better organized perspective of what will be achieved in the program. CBA can be an adjunct to standardized testing.

Implications for Teachers of Students with LLC

- Using CBA, teachers can focus directly on specific areas of difficulty rather than testing for global patterns of disability.
- This model can allow the teacher, rather than the textbook or curriculum guide, to select the content, instructional materials, and/or methods.
- CBA and curriculum-based instruction provide a means of monitoring the relative effectiveness of specific teachers of students with LLC.

Shared Teaching (Peers/Teams)

Shared teaching is not a new, or even relatively new, idea. The creators of the early academy and university spoke about the need for shared knowledge and instruction. John Dewey knew well the imperative of shared learning and collegiality.

Today, we have institutionalized the approach known as *team teaching* or *peer teaching*. As applied to bilingual and special education, the method brings peers together for the purpose of developing both short-term and long-range plans for students with LLC in the regular classroom. Teachers are encouraged to approach the following tasks as teams, either by grade level or subject area:

Developing the scope and sequence of curricula (Content Selection)
Developing appropriate instructional methods (Strategies, Interventions)
Developing monitoring procedures (Formative Evaluation)
Developing assessment tools and procedures (Evaluation, Summative data)
Developing reporting instruments and procedures (Grade/Progress reporting)

One particularly productive approach engages both parties directly in the actual teaching of lessons as shown in Figure 6-2. Classroom teachers, special educators, and/or bilingual teachers may work side by side or in tandem.

Strategies / Interventions

Cognitive Strategies - Learning Strategies

Cognitive and learning strategies, as they have emerged from the field of learning disabilities, share several common purposes. The primary purpose is that they "enable" students to organize and plan their own learning so that they might be successful both inside and outside of school. A variety of reasons has been offered for teaching cognitive strategies to students with learning problems, among them:

- the usefulness of advance organizers in school studies
- the need for monitoring devices
- the need for initial, medial, and terminal skills enhancers
- the need for memory training
- the need for self-awareness

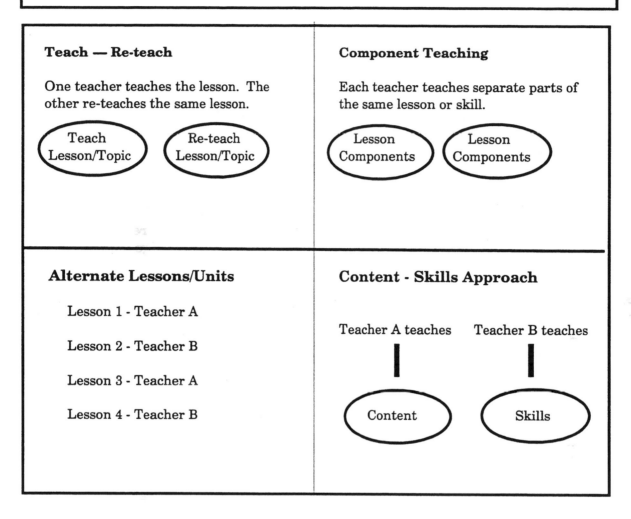

**Figure 6-2
Shared Teaching**

Teach — Re-teach

One teacher teaches the lesson. The other re-teaches the same lesson.

Teach Lesson/Topic   Re-teach Lesson/Topic

Component Teaching

Each teacher teaches separate parts of the same lesson or skill.

Lesson Components   Lesson Components

Alternate Lessons/Units

Lesson 1 - Teacher A

Lesson 2 - Teacher B

Lesson 3 - Teacher A

Lesson 4 - Teacher B

Content - Skills Approach

Teacher A teaches   Teacher B teaches

Content   Skills

- the promotion of independent learning
- the development of self-checking and self-editing skills

Likewise, numerous cognitive and learning strategies have emerged from research over the past 30 years, including:

- ***Graphic/Visual Organizers*** - webbing, mapping, frameworks, etc.
- ***Mnemonic Devices*** - acronyms, rhythmic activities (mental/physical). As applied to:
    - *Reading* - skimming, preview, review, sampling, summarizing
    - *Math* - invented algorithms, procedures
    - *Science/Social Studies* – acronyms to memorize dates, events, lists, word associations
    - *Writing* - acronyms, process approach, invented spelling
    - *Clustering* - words associated with a central idea or concept
    - *Self-Rehearsal* - rapping, singing, repetition of facts/information
    - *Study Skills* - preview, skimming, review, summarizing

Example:
M-ake a Guess (hypothesize)
A-sk Questions (inquiry)
C-heck it Out (read/study)
A-nswer Questions (solve/resolve)
W-rite It Up (document, report)

Though self-management is stressed in the strategy and behavioral models, Poplin and Stone (1993) maintained that it is restricted to learning a pre-chosen set of skills and/or strategies. Individualization becomes a myth, for the only things that are generally individualized are different starting points on the same continuum.

TIP for Students with LLC
Highlight the words you know in a sentence, paragraph, or page. Try to make sense of the reading from only the words you recognize.

TIP for Teachers
Place a marker (dot, X, etc.) by the first letter or number near the point at which the student is expected to begin a writing assignment from the board. Some students have great difficulty deciding which information to record from a board that has several different messages or assignments on it.

Implications for Students with LLC
- As with all interventions, cognitive strategies should aim toward increasing the student's autonomy and sense of self-worth.

- Students with LLC should be allowed to develop mnemonic devices in the primary language.

- For students who have problems remembering, cognitive strategies should be selected on the basis of their broad applications across content areas. A student who has difficulty memorizing facts may also have problems with remembering the mnemonics.

- Students with LLC may need additional time to effectively apply strategies (e.g., visual organizers, mnemonics) in testing and other timed situations.

Preview-Review
As an intervention, this approach begins with a "preview" (in the primary language) of the lesson, concept, or activity. This preview may be presented by the teacher, a bilingual aide, special education teacher, bilingual peer-tutor, or other qualified person. The student then participates as fully as possible in *regular* instruction. Following the instructional session, the student engages in a review of the lesson or activity to check for understanding and/or to reinforce targeted skills and knowledge.

Example:

Preview
- Read the story and/or assignment in the primary language (L1) and/or second language (L2).
- Discuss important and/or confusing vocabulary (words, terms).
- Write key vocabulary words/terms on a Word Wall and in student dictionaries.
- Activate thinking by relating the present activity to prior assignments and experiences.
- Clarify the purpose of the assignment and expectations.
- Check for understanding. Ask for questions and respond to them in a manner that can be understood by the students.

Listening/Reading/Responding. Engage students actively in their learning.
- Encourage active involvement and accept all thoughtful responses.
- Monitor student work. Check for comprehension.
- Assist individuals in L1 and/or L2 as needed.
- Simplify the task as needed.

Review. Reinforce key elements of the lesson/assignment.
- Check again for understanding. Discuss in L1 and/or L2.
- Re-read/repeat key concepts from the reading and/or assignment.
- Reinforce vocabulary – particularly new words and terms.
- Relate the present lesson/assignment to future lessons and learning.

Implications for Students with LLC
- The aims of Preview-Review are clearly to clarify and reinforce language and instruction.
- Both Preview and Review activities should relate the instructional content to real life experiences so that the learning experiences will be comprehensible to students.
- Preview and Review are not inextricable – Students with LLC may not need both components.
- Students with LLC should be encouraged to progress at their own pace.

There should be a clear plan for smooth transition to full instruction in English once it is evident that the student no longer needs the preview component.

Scaffolded Instruction

As early as 1976, the notion of "scaffolding" curriculum and instruction was envisioned as a means of supporting learning-challenged students. In their research, Wood, Bruner, and Ross (1976) noted the need for "a process that enables a child or novice to solve a problem, carry out a task, or achieve a goal which would be beyond his unassisted efforts" (p. 90). Scaffolding refers to both the model and the process for guiding student learning. Curricula are designed around students' present needs. Typically, scaffolding engages the student in a combination of strategies selected on the basis of their applicability to specific tasks (Reid, 1998). In written language, for example, a process model of instruction would provide the student with additional prompts, choices, practice, models (from peers), and time to polish his/her product. If one strategy fails, others are readily in place to bolster the student's confidence and learning.

Simply stated, scaffolding is a process of matching techniques, strategies, and materials to learner needs – enabling devices to both short-range and long-range learning goals. In reading, for example, Graves, Graves, and Braaten (1996) have developed a three-phase approach that they assert to be "particularly appropriate for inclusive classrooms" (p. 14). The "Scaffolded Reading Experience," as it is known, takes learners through successive phases as follows:

- **Prereading activities** – These activities are aimed at relating literature to students' own lives, clarifying concepts, and generally stimulating thinking about the reading topic.

- **During-reading activities** – These activities engage students in a variety of silent and/or oral reading experiences.

- **Post-reading activities.** – These activities are intended to help learners connect the reading to other areas of the curriculum and/or new situations.

Modification is a crucial feature in this approach. It is important for teachers to summarize chapters or portions of books for students who are struggling in their efforts to learn. (For additional information about scaffolding, see Graves & Graves, 1994).

Implications for Students with LLC

- Scaffolded instruction can provide strong supports for reluctant as well as struggling learners.
- Scaffolding, as a practice, can also provide feedback for teachers as to how effective specific interventions/adaptations are with particular subgroups (e.g., second language learners, students with LD, students with other disabilities).
- Over time, students themselves may acquire scaffolding skills that will aid them in their learning.

Cooperative Learning / Group Process Skills

Grouping has served a variety of purposes over the years. Perhaps the most debated has been "ability grouping." Critics argue that such practice unfairly restricts students to homogeneous groups and a narrow curriculum – and precludes opportunities for interactions with students of greater and/or lesser ability. Students with LD have been erroneously tracked into lower ability groups for years, as if problems with reading and writing preclude success in *all* academic pursuits. Cooperative learning groups, on the other hand, are distinguishable by their "purposes" and "arrangements." David and Roger Johnson (1986) identified the following four basic elements that distinguish cooperative learning from other types of group activity:

1. **Positive Interdependence** - marked by a mutuality of interest, concern, and benefit

2. **Individual Accountability** - responsibility of individuals to the group and to themselves

3. **Collaborative Skills** - development/application of individual skills to meet group goals.
4. **Group Processing** - group "self-regulating" skills that enable members/group to succeed.

According to Johnson and Johnson (1986), data obtained from "a meta-analysis of all the available relevant research studies (122 studies from 1924-1981) clearly indicated that cooperative learning experiences result in higher achievement and greater retention of learning than do competitive or individualistic learning" (pg. 556). Since 1981, cooperative learning has become widespread in the nation's schools. Indeed, a small publishing industry has emerged to produce and train educators in cooperative learning philosophy and techniques. As a strategy for working with students with LLC, it holds great promise.

Cooperative learning can be integrated into virtually every aspect of the school curriculum. Teachers themselves must determine when and why groups convene. The teacher assumes a multifaceted role: curriculum coordinator, group monitor, clarifier, advisor, instructor, and evaluator. Teams often work as "jig-saws" to achieve instructional and learning goals – although cooperative groups may be used for social and other non-academic purposes. The primary strength that cooperative grouping brings to second-language learners with LD is "validation." Self-worth and incentive spring from accomplishment and belonging. Learners must be allowed to interact and to test their own ideas and strengths instead of passively accepting those of the teacher, textbook, or peers who do not have language and learning challenges.

"Jigsaw" and Cooperative Learning

Jigsaw is a term closely associated with cooperative learning. It refers to a procedure whereby groups (team members) become interdependent through team interaction and problem-solving. In a typical jigsaw, students are divided into several heterogeneous groups or teams for the purpose of performing tasks. Each student on a team focuses on some aspect of an assigned learning unit and meets with peers from the other teams with the corresponding aspect. After working together to master the material/task, team members return to their original groups to teach their section of the assigned material (Kagan, 1992). In social studies, for example, a group of fifth graders might be assigned the task of preparing a state report. One team member might be responsible for reading about the state's early history. Another might be assigned the task of studying the geography of the state. A third might take charge of recent history and current events, and a fourth might study the state's plant and animal life. Students from different teams who have the same assignments get together to share and to help one another prepare to teach their respective groups what they learned.

Note: Students with LLC can be fully included when they are assigned tasks within their capabilities and paired with at least one bilingual member of a team.

Implications for Students with LLC

Cooperative learning has important implications for students with LLC:

- It encourages understanding and acceptance of L2 learners and students with LD as peers.
- It allows students with LLC to explore their strengths and limitations in a low-risk setting.
- It sharpens perspective-taking and intrapersonal intelligence among group members.
- It promotes self-esteem and a sense of belonging in the general classroom.
- It promotes positive interdependence.
- It encourages mutual respect for individual differences and strengths.
- It promotes sharing/ownership of ideas, better solutions, and improved joint products.
- It encourages sharing of leadership roles and responsibilities.
- It promotes interpersonal and negotiation skills, as well as the value of cooperation.

Other Purposes for Grouping

Groups are convened both formally and informally for a variety of functional purposes. Typically, students rotate from group to group developing and sharing skills along the way. However, some specialized groups may remain relatively permanent. Types and purposes include:

- groups to study different topics/subjects within the same classroom (e.g., North American culture and South American culture)
- groups to study different aspects of the same topic
- groups to study different versions of the same book, story, movie (e.g., myths, legends
- "ad hoc committee" groups (for problem-solving/trouble-shooting)
- planning groups
- groups of "Experts" (e.g., writing center editors, math center tutors)
- "Concierge" groups to offer special assistance to newcomers and second-language learners (e.g., language translation, review of school/classroom rules and responsibilities)

Process Approach (Writing, Reading, Thinking)

> *Writing is not a simple or simplistic linear procedure; instead,*
> *it's a recursive process that takes you back to rethink and redraft.*
> *Bernice Cullinan*

"A process approach is sweeping the land," wrote Bernice Cullinan (1986, p. 494), an approach characterized not by definition but rather by philosophic view. The notion that *process* is more primary than *product* has guided the movement toward integrated approaches to writing over the past 25 years. The movement has been widespread and enormously successful for several reasons: (1) the process approach respects the integrity of the learner; (2) it values and encourages imagination and creativity; and (3) it acknowledges that learners' greatest strengths are most fully realized and best expressed through personal choice. Many children come to school expecting to be able to read and write. Graves (1983) asserted that the urge to write develops early, and that children can learn to take "control of the craft" fairly easily with some guidance. He provided a clear example of this in the following account of a first grade teacher who had invited her students to write by simply giving them each a gold-embossed hardback book.

> They all did. . .in their fashion. They drew pictures, wrote their names, made columns of numbers. Some wrote phrases, made invented spellings, and several wrote in sentences. The important thing is that they all believed they could write. No one said, 'But I don't know how.' Before the year was out these twenty-five first grade children composed 1,300 five-to-six-page booklets and published 400 of the best in hard cover for their classmates to read. A third of these children used quotation marks accurately because they get them when they need them, when someone is talking on their pages. (p. 3)

Reflecting on his observations, Graves lamented, "I struggled with quotation marks when I first taught them to my seventh grade English class" (p. 4). There are lessons in literacy to be learned from children of *all* ages and ability levels.

In recent years, special educators have integrated process approaches widely in learning disabilities programs (Hemming & MacInnis, 1995). Bilingual educators have likewise adopted process models as part of successful whole language instruction among students with limited English proficiency (Ruiz, Rueda, Figueroa, & Boothroyd, 1996). Because many students with LD have significant problems with writing, many researchers have focused their attention on *alternative* strategies and methods. (Hemming & MacInnis, 1996; Lynch & Jones, 1989; Poplin, Gray, Larsen, Banikowski, & Mehring, 1980).

As process approaches began to take hold in the nation's schools, special educators soon took notice of their applicability in learning disabilities classrooms. Kerchner and Kistinger (1984) contributed some of the field's earliest research on the use of the microcomputer as a tool for process writing with students who had been labeled "LD." They found that these students made a positive transfer of writing skills from the computer to hand-written assignments.

Barclay (1990) noted that "an integrative approach to reading instruction offers promising implications for learners with special needs" (pg. 84). In learning disabilities programs, where the school curriculum has been traditionally watered-down and stretched-out, many students are now finding reading success through their own writing (Poplin & Cousin, 1996; Ruiz, 1996). Integrated writing-reading models provide several important incentives for second-language learners who have LD, among them:

- **Voice** – opportunity for input into curriculum (through their own writings)
- **Ownership** – of ideas expressed in the printed word, pictures, and projects
- **Authentic learning** – real and important purposes for writing and reading
- **Self-esteem** – the result of highlighting strengths rather than deficits

For students whose strengths and intelligences mismatch those valued by the school (i.e., skills other than verbal and logical-mathematical skills), whole language, process models, and holistic assessment offer alternative ways to demonstrate learning.

Process Approach in Writing

Cullinan's words (above) capture the *spirit* of the writing process approach. Over the past 30 years, educators have been re-evaluating aspects of language arts instruction in our schools. Along the way, there has also been a refining of alternative views – a "re-vision" of literacy. One important approach that emerged has been process writing. The model may be characterized as a three-stage approach to composition: *prewriting, writing,* and *postwriting*. Though viewed as distinct stages, teachers must keep in mind the *recursive* nature of writing. Thus, writers (students) may move in and out of these stages several times while composing.

Although students engage many or most "levels" of thinking during the writing process, this fact is probably rarely invoked by teachers as evidence of attention to higher order thinking skills and/or "the basics." Figure 6-3 illustrates the mental skills most prevalent at each of the three stages of writing development.

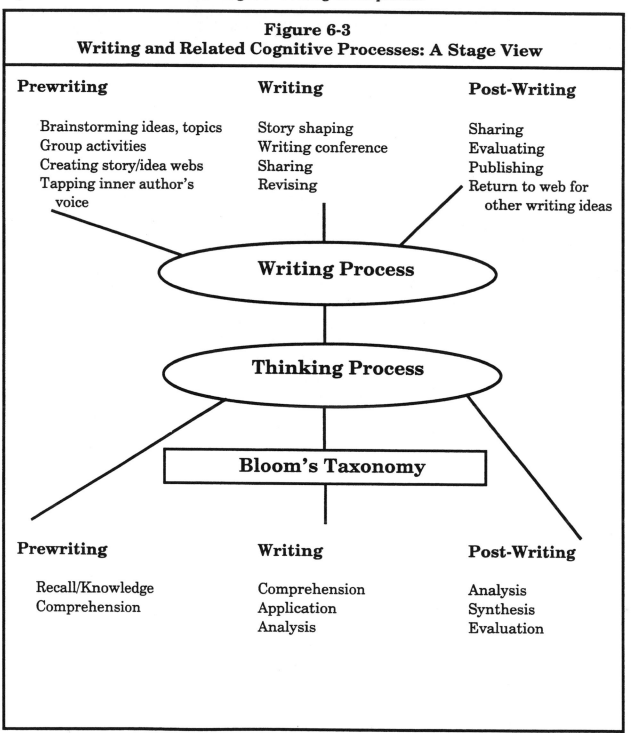

Figure 6-3
Writing and Related Cognitive Processes: A Stage View

Prewriting

Brainstorming ideas, topics
Group activities
Creating story/idea webs
Tapping inner author's
   voice

Writing

Story shaping
Writing conference
Sharing
Revising

Post-Writing

Sharing
Evaluating
Publishing
Return to web for
   other writing ideas

Writing Process

Thinking Process

Bloom's Taxonomy

Prewriting

Recall/Knowledge
Comprehension

Writing

Comprehension
Application
Analysis

Post-Writing

Analysis
Synthesis
Evaluation

Prewriting

In the prewriting stage, students utilize their experiences, observations, and discoveries. At the elementary level, ideas for writing frequently emerge naturally from students' drawings and pictures. "Visual/graphic organizers" have become closely associated with process writing. *Clustering* is an especially popular technique used to stimulate thinking and to explore associations around a nucleus word, concept, or topic (organizing center). Teachers and/or students engage in rapid-fire brainstorming of words associated with the organizing center (see Figure 6-4). The words are quickly recorded for later use in composition. Theoretically, the encircling words (fragments) provide learners with greater and broader understanding of the concept or topic (whole). At other times, student authors imagine, explore, and share ideas. They consider topics and possible forms that a piece might take – a story, a poem, or an essay. Typically some

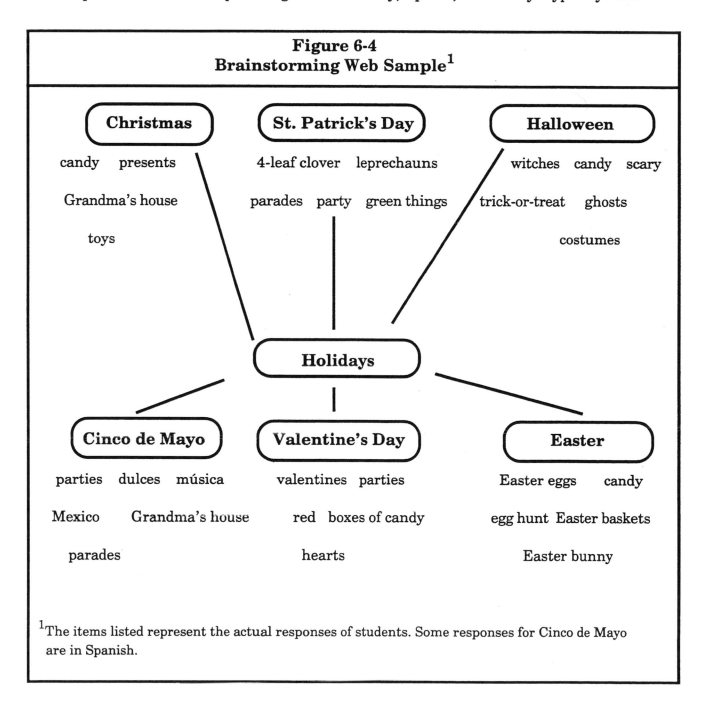

Figure 6-4
Brainstorming Web Sample[1]

Christmas

candy   presents

Grandma's house

toys

St. Patrick's Day

4-leaf clover   leprechauns

parades   party   green things

Halloween

witches   candy   scary

trick-or-treat   ghosts

costumes

Holidays

Cinco de Mayo

parties   dulces   música

Mexico   Grandma's house

parades

Valentine's Day

valentines   parties

red   boxes of candy

hearts

Easter

Easter eggs   candy

egg hunt   Easter baskets

Easter bunny

[1]The items listed represent the actual responses of students. Some responses for Cinco de Mayo are in Spanish.

writing occurs in the form of idea listing or clustering, webbing associations, etc., all intended to help students prepare to begin a written piece. This stage is especially important for students with LLC who frequently require additional prompting and clues, as well as additional time to think through ideas for a story. These activities serve also to promote such concepts as *category, classification,* and *summary.*

Writing

Once ideas have been formulated, students typically move toward the stage of formal writing. They compose a draft of their ideas and concentrate on working the piece through rough draft, revisions, and ultimately to completion. Writers may move back to prewriting if they choose to explore an idea more thoroughly. The writing stage places greater demands on the students; they must begin to think as *authors*. They must determine their audience and what is important to include in their writing. Proett and Gill (1986) stated it this way:

> ... the writing stage needs to be viewed in two very different ways. Seen in one way, it is the flowing of words onto the page, easily, naturally, rapidly. But it is also a time of making decisions, of choosing what to tell and what to leave out, or thinking about who is speaking and who is listening, of determining what order, what structure, what word works best. In some ways these functions even seem contradictory; the first needs to be fluid and fast while the other calls for deliberation and reason. The teaching task is to help the writer coordinate these two functions. (p. 11)

Postwriting

Students at this stage may have finished one draft with some guidance from the teacher. While such input is sometimes necessary, valuable and valid information can come from peer response to the writing. Responses must be *content-focused*. It is important to respond to what is said rather than how it is said. The writer may then wish to revise the text or to keep the text as is. The important thing is that the student seeks feedback and is open to reshaping the piece. Once the text says what the writer desires, he or she can attend to such matters as spelling, punctuation, and usage.

Writing Conference Guidelines

The writing conference is a central feature in the writing process approach. It is an opportunity for the teacher and student to come together for discussion. Conferences may be more numerous with students who are struggling with the many aspects of composing. If we want to promote literacy through writing, then we must nurture those qualities that distinguish authoring from other language activities. If we wish to instill self-confidence with such tasks, then we must demonstrate acceptance, patience, and encouragement. The following points may help guide teachers of students with LLC through writing conferences.

Brainstorming-Composing Phase
- Focus on content, the array of ideas expressed, and story line. Withhold comments about technical qualities (spelling, grammar, mechanics, and usage).
- Present comments/feedback in comprehensible language. Learners new to the process, or those struggling with language problems need encouragement, not judgments.

- Provide prompts for discussion using thoughtful *comments* (e.g., "This looks like it is going to be an interesting story.") and *questions* (e.g., "What else can you tell us about this person?", "What will the girl do next in the story?").

Composing-Revising Phase

- Continue to focus on the composing process and begin to address major story elements, e.g., characters, setting, and plot.
- Question the student about aspects of the story that may need revision, e.g., correcting the sequence of story events.
- Invite questions from the student. Offer suggestions only if they do not change story content.
- Allow/encourage students with LLC to confer with peers.

Revising-Editing Phase

- Assist the writer with technical aspects of the story if necessary – spelling, grammar, mechanics, usage, etc.
- Peer assistance may also be offered, either in pairs or from a designated "Editing Center."
- Work a piece through to its finished form.

Typically, sharing and publishing of students' stories follows the editing phase. Sharing often takes place from an **author's chair**, around which children gather to hear each other read their work aloud. Publishing may take many different forms; there are literally hundreds of ideas to be found in educational and trade books.

Implications for Students with LLC

A process approach allows teachers to weave reading and writing into social studies, science, and other aspects of the curriculum. As with all children, the interests of students with LLC stretch across all disciplines, and their limitations with formal language should not be viewed as insurmountable barriers to success. In mediating learning for students with LLC, teachers should do the following:

- Begin with the assumption that all students can compose.
- Utilize clustering and other simple strategies to help students with LLC visually organize their words and ideas before and during the writing process.
- Do not assume that because students with LLC have heard and seen the directions that they fully comprehend what is expected.
- When appropriate, pair students with LLC with better writers to help model the process.
- Plan frequent conferences. Let the writer lead the discussion as much as possible.
- Keep language simple and comprehensible during writing conferences.
- Focus primarily on the broad or central aspects of writing, i.e., composing, story elements, audience, and author voice.
- Read the stories aloud to/with the students during each conference. Hearing stories read aloud reinforces their perception of themselves as authors.
- Address technical qualities in the latter phases of the process. Technical aspects of writing should not be a deterrent to storytelling.
- Assess work holistically using rubric assessment techniques. As stated by Barclay (1990), "Since the emphasis in reading has shifted from a reproductive to a constructive one, assessment in reading has also undergone major changes. The

current thought in assessment is simple: Assessment must match instruction" (p. 84). Much of what transpires in the process model is creativity and self-instruction. Hence authors' works should not be subjected to deficit scoring.

Alternative Writing Activities

The following alternative literacy development activities are suitable for students with limited reading skills.

- **Cluster Stories**. These stories are told by clustering or webbing words and/or concepts by using pictures and symbols.

- **Ghost Writers**. Students dictate stories in the dominant language. The stories are then translated into English by an aide, peer, teacher, or other competent adult and read aloud to the class.

- **Cloze Technique**. Dictated stories are translated, leaving spaces for words or pictures. The student demonstrates comprehension by filling in the spaces with appropriate words, pictures, or symbols.

- **Rebus Stories**. Students create entire stories using mostly pictures and symbols. They are then transcribed into word stories. Both versions are presented to the teacher and/or class by the student (or peer interpreter). Steps in the process are the following:
  1. Students draw, paint, or locate pictures in magazines to illustrate their stories.
  2. The students then dictate their stories to the teacher, aide, peer, or another adult who leaves spaces beside key words in the stories.
  3. The students cut out the pictures and paste them to the matching key words.
  4. The pages are then assembled into booklets.

- **Parallel Writing**. Students with LLC are paired with English-fluent peers to write a story. They discuss ideas and work out story events and details themselves. Using the same or similar words, both students write down the story on separate sheets of paper. This is an excellent way to encourage language development. Even non-readers who can copy information will be able to participate in "creating" text.

- **Dual Writing**. The student writes portions of a story in English and portions in the dominant language. The story is eventually rewritten in English and read to the class. The activity can be used to provide a bridge between the two languages spoken by the student.

Alternative Reading Approaches and Strategies

There is a continuum of reading approaches to accommodate virtually every learner. Each of the following holds promise for students with LLC:

Into-Through-Beyond Model

The "Into-Through-Beyond" model to literature is an appropriate approach for both second-language learners and students with LD. It has been widely adopted as a systematic, yet broad, approach to reading. The model can engage all students in language-rich discussion and activities. Students must be allowed – even encouraged – to develop their own opinions through discussion, predictions, and reactions to stories. As the teacher directs students with LLC through the process, there should be ample opportunities for the students to respond and to participate as fully as possible. The fact that a student has poor reading skills or vocabulary does not imply that he or she is unable to relate to the situations and characters in a story. The "Into-Through-Beyond" model is outlined in Figure 6-5.

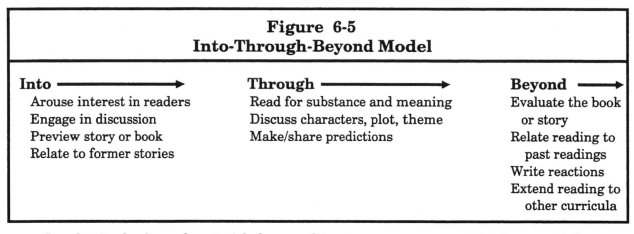

Figure 6-5
Into-Through-Beyond Model

Into ⟶	**Through** ⟶	**Beyond** ⟶
Arouse interest in readers	Read for substance and meaning	Evaluate the book or story
Engage in discussion	Discuss characters, plot, theme	Relate reading to past readings
Preview story or book	Make/share predictions	Write reactions
Relate to former stories		Extend reading to other curricula

In selecting books and materials for your literature program, consider these guidelines:

- Select literature that appeals to a wide range of students' tastes and interests.
- Be sure the books and stories do not negatively portray races, cultures, or persons with mental or physical disabilities.
- Select a balance of high and low-ability reading materials to accommodate all students.
- Look for gender-bias in books and materials.
- Invite parents to contribute books to your classroom library – particularly non-English books.
- Seek help from the school librarian or reading specialist in selecting non-English books.

Reading Recovery (RR)

Reading Recovery was developed by Marie Clay (1985) as a preventative program for use with children in their first year of instruction. It is intended as a short-term intervention (typically 12-15 weeks). Using patterned and predictable books, learners are taught how to use simple strategies in reading. Clay's Diagnostic Survey can be used by reading and/or classroom teachers to identify children who might benefit from Reading Recovery instruction. During the first couple of weeks, the teacher and student simply read and write collaboratively. It is a time for the teacher to observe the child in literacy activities and to build trust and self-confidence. Thereafter, instruction follows a consistent lesson pattern aimed at helping the child both discover and develop strategies for reading. Research on Clay's Reading Recovery program in the United States has been encouraging (Pinnell, DeFord & Lyons, 1988).

Neurological Impress Method (NIM)

The *Neurological Impress Method* (NIM) is a multisensory approach commonly used among teachers of students with reading and learning disabilities. It resembles choral reading, except that it is done on a one-to-one basis. The teacher (reading model) sits beside the student and slightly to the rear so as to speak clearly into the student's ear. The student is instructed to follow the reading passage in the book with his/her finger while reading it out loud with the teacher. This brings the learner's *visual, auditory, tactile,* and *kinesthetic* senses to bear on the act of reading. The approach requires 15-minute daily sessions for a period of six to nine weeks. There is a sizable research base to support this approach with students who are having reading problems (For additional information, see Heckelman, 1978).

Drama – A Multifaceted Literacy Device

In her discussion on building literacy, McMaster (1998) concluded that "drama is an invaluable tool for educators because it is one of the few vehicles of instruction that can support every aspect of literacy development" (p. 575). Drama can be a powerful scaffolding device for all students, but holds perhaps even greater promise for second language learners. Drama is grounded in human experiences and emotions, as well as universal themes and ideas.

Readers Theatre (RT)

According to Regie Routman (1991), *Readers Theatre* involves "creating a script from a narrative text and performing it for an audience" (p. 98). Typically, teachers engage students in RT as an "enrichment" activity. Readers Theatre allows students to participate in ways that silent, choral, or daily oral reading fall short; it allows students to dramatize and animate characters, to play with language, and experiment with voice. Stewart (1997) suggested ways of using Readers Theatre in conjunction with the "writing workshop." She works with her students in selecting *literary devices* that have been used by various authors. These literacy devices are then examined and discussed. For example, E. B. White's mastery of *dialogue*, serves as a wonderful "writing model" for student experimentation. Working through dialogue, students come to recognize the value of punctuation as a "cueing system" for both writer and reader. In Stewart's words, "There are many books at all reading levels that offer rich literature to explore with Readers Theatre" (pg. 175).

Shared Reading

Shared Reading is a formal approach that centers around the repeated reading of a story. Students listen to the initial reading and numerous "rereadings," with ear, eye, and mind toward gaining a greater sense of "story." Modeling is a central element in the process. Selections should clearly reflect all the elements of story (character, plot, setting, theme, style, etc.) and be comprehensible to all listeners. Because the same story is read repeatedly over a period of days or weeks, it is imperative to locate high-interest material. Suggested steps or phases include:

- Introducing the story with simple activities to warm listeners to the subject and/or story.
- Presenting an initial reading that concentrates on story presentation to make the activity a pleasurable experience. The teacher invites student responses to the story.
- Presenting rereadings that expand the experience beyond the words through interaction between students and text (e.g., discussing, predicting, questioning).
- Working on story elements, vocabulary, main idea, context clues, etc.
- Encouraging and reinforcing student actions – rereadings, retellings, etc.

Reader-Repeater

Reader-Repeater engages "paired" students in reading stories and other texts for meaning. The better reader reads the sentences, paragraphs, or passages aloud while the other student listens. The listener then repeats, paraphrases, or summarizes what has just been read. This approach is especially useful in working with students with limited English ability. The approach helps students to focus their attention on the spoken word and promotes the development of listening strategies that are critical for recalling details. For more advanced English language speakers, this approach encourages the development of reading strategies (cueing systems) and cognitive strategies (paraphrasing, summarizing).

Pair Reading

This activity engages paired students in reading either for pleasure or for specific instructional purposes. The object is simply to allow the students to "interact" with the story or text. Students experiment with pronunciation and try to "make meaning" (from illustrations, context, and syntax clues) as they read and discuss stories. Pair reading should be low-stress and low-risk so that English language learners with learning disabilities can hone their skills freely. For non-readers, this activity might be used in combination with the Reader-Repeater approach.

Reading Circles

Reading Circles brings together small and large groups of learners to listen to stories read aloud by the teacher, aide, student, or other competent reader. The main purpose of this activity is to model reading (pronunciation, inflection, pacing, etc.). It is therefore important that the reader possesses the skills to articulate clearly, read well, and show enthusiasm. Modeling is important for *all* children learning to read, especially students with LLC who are struggling with both language and learning problems. Teachers should do the following:

- Select high interest books with illustrations.
- Establish a regular Reading Circle time – daily or weekly.
- Determine the purpose for the reading, i.e., for pleasure or for academic reasons.
- Decide in advance who will read and be sure the student is well-prepared.
- Hook the children's interest by discussing the cover picture, posing questions, predicting story content, etc.
- Engage and direct discussion at appropriate points in a story.
- Bring closure to the reading through discussion and/or summary.

Note: If a story is read for pleasure, simply put the book away once it has been enjoyed. Do not force students to complete activities for every book that they read!

Author's Chair

Author's Chair is closely associated with process writing, although many teachers have adopted it as a permanent feature in whichever reading approach they choose. It provides an opportunity for student authors to share their works aloud and adds to the "authentic" writing experience. If we want children to be writers, then we must help them *think* like writers and *act* like writers. Once they have worked a story through to completion, they should be allowed to share what has been written. All children should have the opportunity to either read or have someone else read their creations. For this brief time, while there is an audience of listeners, they are *authors*. This is a truly rich language experience for all learners.

Reading Tag

Reading Tag engages students in active listening, as well as reading. After reading a sentence, paragraph, or passage aloud from a story or text, the reader tags someone else to read. No student may read twice until all students have been tagged. Since readers don't know who will be called upon next, they must remain engaged and ready. The teacher should record the readers' names on the board or flip chart to keep track of who has and has not read.

Note: Non-readers and/or students with LLC should be paired with peer-pals who are competent readers. Encourage them to follow along and read aloud with the peer-pal to the maximum extent possible.

Choral Reading

Choral reading is perhaps the oldest and most widely-used group approach to teaching reading. Typically, the teacher invites students to read a story or passage aloud in unison. While the benefits are obvious, this approach holds even greater promise for students with LLC, who often cringe at the thought of reading aloud. In choral reading, they are able to "blend in," while consciously monitoring for reading cues (graphophonic, syntactic, semantic, and pragmatic).

Word Recognition - Vocabulary Development

Traditionally, vocabulary development and spelling have been isolated for "drill-and-practice" instruction using workbooks or worksheets. For students with LLC attempting to learn through instruction in English, there are several beneficial strategies, including the following:

- **Word Families.** Present sound, letter, and word patterns (e.g., *cat, sat, fat, rat, mat*). This encourages English language learners to make a guess when they come upon new words (LeBlanc, 1998). The patterns can also be presented graphically. The words listed below, for example, all contain the pattern "at."

  cat   sat   rat   fat   (at)   mat

- **Structural Analysis.** Discuss the components of words (graphemes and morphemes) and how they can be used to facilitate word identification.

- **Attribute Approach.** Vocabulary and concepts can be developed through the study of attributes and/or commonalities. As mentioned previously, clustering is a useful tool in helping the learner to visually organize and mentally categorize information. An example is presented in Figure 6-6.

- **Cognates.** Cognates are words with spellings and meanings in English that are similar to spellings and meanings in another language. For example, the English and Spanish languages share many common spelling patterns. Lists of these similarities can be used to create a word bank from which students may choose when writing or telling stories. The lists can be displayed on a Word Wall in the

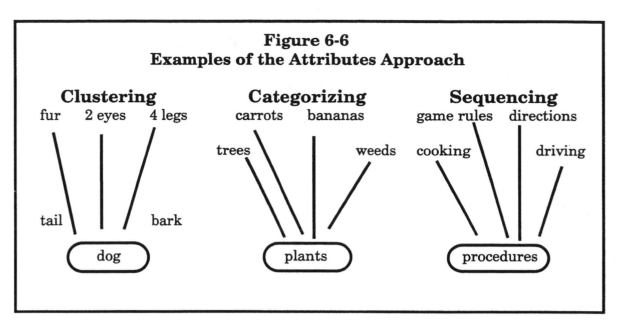

Figure 6-6
Examples of the Attributes Approach

classroom. This is another simple but highly useful tool in building bridges to literacy. Examples of cognates in English and Spanish are presented below:

English	Spanish
accent	acento
accident	accidente
adult	adulto
alphabet	alfabeto
baby	bebe
bank	banco
delicious	delicioso
dentist	dentista
different	diferente
gasoline	gasolina
student	estudiante
tiger	tigre
train	tren

Implications for Teachers of Students with LLC

Regardless of which approach or strategy or *combination* teachers select, decisions should center around students' needs and interests. Books and stories should take learners somewhere. They should entertain, instruct, and challenge. Good books raise as many questions as they answer. Selecting high-interest materials for students requires time, discrimination, and desire. Finding high interest books with comprehensible language for students with LLC can be even more challenging. For a starter list of books and stories appropriate for students with limited reading skills, see Appendix A.

- Teachers should select stories with comprehensible language.
- All of these activities and approaches should actively engage students' linguistic intelligence.
- Reading materials should help students develop a sense of story and story elements (e.g., plot, character, setting theme, and style).

- Teachers should provide varied opportunities and modes of acquiring language skills and opportunities to use reading strategies.
- The activities should increase an awareness of reading cues (graphophonic, syntactic, semantic, pragmatic), as well as context and inference.
- The activities should provide opportunities for varied uses of language, e.g., reading, telling, retelling, discussion, argument, explanation, performances, etc.

Suggestions for literacy programs that promote the development of language and thinking skills are listed in Table 6-4.

Fernald Approach (VAKT)

Grace Fernald (1943, 1988) is cited widely in the literature as a pioneer in reading and language development. In her research, she developed techniques that continue to guide educators today. Specifically, she is noted for her vision of learning as a multisensory process. She reasoned that learners utilize their five senses in combination to gather, organize, and interpret stimuli from the world around them. In essence, they create their own systems of learning and adapting to their environments. The notion of reading as a purely visual task was too simplistic to explain what children do when they read. Fernald noted that when learners were presented with various means of constructing their own meanings through visual, auditory, kinesthetic, and tactile modes, the likelihood of learning was enhanced. Hence, she developed the widely known VAKT approach to teaching and learning. Special educators and bilingual teachers have found this approach to be effective in helping many students with LLC.

The Fernald approach is a four-stage developmental model that takes the learner from a state of teacher-and-context dependency to a state of independent reading. The approach can be adapted for students with LLC beginning at the emergent pre-production stage of language development:

Stage 1 – Visual, Auditory, Tactile, Kinesthetic
- The teacher writes a word.
- The student traces the word with a finger.
- The teacher says the word aloud.
- The student files the word away in a word box.
- The student acquires enough words to write sentences.
- The teacher may type the student's sentences for use in reading activities.

The key aspects of Stage 1 are summarized in Table 6-5. Tracing is considered imperative in this approach. Students trace until they think they can spell a word. Fernald advocated having students start story-writing when they have accumulated enough words to create a simple story. Students continue to trace new words while they write. There is no time limit for the tracing activity.

Stage 2 – Visual, Auditory, Tactile
- The student says words to himself/herself.
- The student writes the words.

Stage 3 – Visual, Kinesthetic
- The student reads words from books.
- The student writes words/sentences.

Table 6-4
Reader Response Activities for
Language and Learning-Challenged Students

- **Oral Responses to a Book or Story**

  - Discussion (in primary and/or second language)
  - How else could the character(s) have solved the problem?
  - What would you have done in his/her place?
  - What would your (father, mother, sister, brother) have done?
  - What was your favorite part of the story?
  - How are you alike/unlike the character(s) in the story?
  - What would you change in the story if you could?

  Ideas
  - Visiting Storytellers – Have students tell stories to other classes.
  - Story retelling – Engage all students over time.
  - Audiotape personal messages to authors.

- **Written Responses to a Book or Story**

  Writing (in primary and/or second language)
  - Rewrite portions, chapters, or entire stories – they may be dictated and copied.
  - Rewrite story endings as you would like them to be.
  - Write notes or letters to favorite characters.
  - Write notes or letters to authors.

  Ideas
  - Rewrite stories as plays.
  - Use stories as sources for Writer's Workshop.
  - Write personal poems as responses to literature. Mail them to authors.

- **Artistic-Creative Responses to a Book or Story**

  - Visual representations – paintings, drawings, three-dimensional designs.
  - Story sets – backdrops, stage properties for performances.
  - Write songs about stories (in primary and/or second language).
  - Create dances to go along with stories.
  - Perform student-written versions of stories for peers (in primary/second language).

Table 6-5
Learning Modalities – Fernald Approach

Characteristics	Instructional Implications
Visual	
Need to see things illustrated Observes others' actions Notices details and changes Learns vocabulary by sight word	Use realia, chalkboard, pictures, color coding, graphics, flip chart, etc. Use appropriate sight word lists from stories/instruction or Brigance, Fry, Dolch, or other appropriate lists. Allow student to respond with graphic representations (drawings, pictures, designs, paintings, etc.). Encourage written language responses.
Auditory	
Need to hear information and instructions Need auditory cues for learning Prefer discussion to independent study	Use comprehensible language in both L1 and L2. Use tape/CD recorders and players. Use cooperative groups. Engage in class discussion.
Kinesthetic-Tactile	
Need direct experiences and concrete examples Physical responses (touches others when talking) Sometimes fidgety/restless during instruction Prefers activities to talk and discussion Frequently out of seat or away from group	Use a hands on approach. Use manipulatives, games, and realia. Ask student to be a teacher helper.

Stage 4 Visual
- Student demonstrates the ability to generalize skills to new reading experiences.

Peer Interpreter/Tutors

Many American schools are seriously understaffed in bilingual and/or special education. In the absence of qualified personnel, the task of instruction is too often relegated to aides and volunteers, many of whom lack the skills that are needed to perform the tasks that they are asked to perform. In recent years, teachers have enlisted the support of their own students to assist them with classroom instruction. Peer interpreters, or "peer pals" as they are sometimes called, perform a variety of helpful acts in the course of a typical school day.

A peer interpreter may be called upon to do the following:

- Act as social liaison between students with LLC and classmates.
- Interpret classroom instruction and discussion.
- Interpret the student's responses to the teacher's questions.
- Explain assignments and expectations.
- Monitor understanding of what is expected.
- Assist the student with LLC in making requests, asking questions, and sharing answers.

In brief, a peer interpreter helps to humanize the pursuit of learning for the child struggling with a foreign language, abstract ideas, and a general disequilibrium brought on by being placed in an unfamiliar, sometimes abrasive environment. They are much more than helpers or management tools, however. The peer interpreter is a lifeline, sometimes the only means of communication available to the student with LLC. For the child who is learning-challenged, school demands might even seem brutal.

While such responsibilities place an added burden on the peer pal, keep in mind that these activities frequently serve also to reinforce learning for the interpreter. The use of peer pals also presents opportunities for the development of leadership and communication skills.

The reproducible form in Table 6-6 can be completed by students who wish to help students with special learning needs. When completing this form, students check off skills that they can teach other students.

Implications for Students with LLC

- Students speak to each other in an idiom probably more comprehensible than the language used by teachers and other adults to express the same ideas.
- The risk factor and "affective filter," which present obstacles to learning, are probably reduced in student-student communications. Concerns about pleasing the teacher or getting the *right* answer are lessened, thus allowing the student to take a chance.
- The mere interactions between and among students can help to build community within the classroom and school.
- Frequent dialogue between peer pals/interpreters and students with LLC can promote the acquisition of English.
- Peer tutor/interpreters may allow the teacher and/or aide to spend more time with students who need special attention.

Table 6-6
I CAN HELP — YOU CAN HELP

I KNOW	I CAN HELP YOU LEARN
_____ Big Letters	_____ Big Letters
_____ Small Letters	_____ Small Letters
_____ Numbers 1-100	_____ Count to 100

I CAN	I CAN HELP YOU
_____ Write all the Big Letters	_____ Write all the Big Letters
_____ Write all the Small Letters	_____ Write all the Small Letters
_____ Write my Name	_____ Write your Name

I CAN	I CAN HELP YOU
_____ Add Numbers to _____	_____ Learn to Add
_____ Subtract Numbers to _____	_____ Learn to Subtract

I CAN	I CAN HELP YOU
_____ Speak English	_____ Learn to speak English
_____ Read my (Book, Story, etc.)	_____ Read your (Book, Story, etc.)
_____ Do my Worksheet	_____ Do your Worksheet
_____ Do my Homework	_____ Do your Homework

****

YOU CAN	YOU CAN HELP ME
_____	_____
_____	_____

- Peer tutor/interpreters, through their modeling, encourage other students (including classmates with LLC) to work cooperatively.

Learning Centers

The notion that students sometimes need to be in "centers" to maximize learning has always presented questions for some educators. Nonetheless, organized properly, learning centers help students "center" on specific ideas, concepts, instruction, and/or expectations. Centers can create "sign systems" that enable students to visualize and imagine themselves in specific roles and endeavors. How do we help learners think like artists? We create an environment that reflects the world of the artist – a studio. How do we inspire students to think scientifically? We direct them through scientific inquiry. How do we encourage students to see themselves as writers, poets, or playwrights? We immerse them in writing, enter them in writing contests, publish their best works, and generally honor their efforts. Such environments can be created within the classroom.

Envision your room as a multipurpose space, confined only by time and imagination. The benefits of such direct and authentic pursuits for students with LLC are incalculable. They immerse the learner in language-rich learning activities that promote the development of interpersonal communication skills and "academic" language proficiency.

Centers that are frequently available to students include the following:

- **Listening Center** – Audiotapes of stories or instructional activities are available in English and/or the primary language to teach or reinforce specific subject matter.

- **Reading Center** – Reading material is available for use in teacher-directed reading with heterogeneous and homogeneous groups of students.

- **Writing Center** – Materials are available to stimulate writing relating to classroom topics or topics of interest to students.

- **Sharing Center** – Materials are displayed so that students can share written work orally and visually with others.

- **Projects Center** – Materials necessary for group projects in science, math, social studies, art, and other areas are available for use as students work together to achieve specific goals (e.g., planning, building, assembling, creating, painting, etc.).

- **Study Center** – Students come to this center to study individually or in small groups.

Implications for Students with LLC

- Learning centers may provide scaffolds for students whose knowledge and/or skills are inadequate to complete assignments independently.
- Centers should not be used to systematically segregate students into ability groups.
- If carefully designed, some learning centers (e.g., those with student-directed activities) require minimal direction from teachers, thus freeing them to help students who cannot complete classroom activities independently.

- Centers often provide opportunities to explore ideas, concepts, skills, or interests in ways that whole class instruction cannot.
- Centers provide an environment that is conducive to active participation in learning experiences and that builds a strong bond between teachers and students.

Graphic/Visual Tools

Instinctively, most teachers utilize whatever means are available to clarify information for their students. The chalkboard has remained the primary instrument used for this purpose, although overhead projectors, television, computers, and variou forms of emerging technology have made their way slowly into mainstream instruction. While various estimates have been offered as to what portion of learning takes place primarily through visual channels, we can assume that it is quite high for fully-sighted persons. Mere *vision,* however, does not control all that goes on in the minds of learners. Each of us constructs knowledge and learning in our own unique ways. We frequently hear educators speak of particular children as "visual learners," meaning, of course, that some children appear to need strong visual cues and examples to make sense of a concept, procedure, or lesson.

In recent years, there has been an explosion of research and development in visual/graphic organizers. They take varied forms, among them:

- **Sentence/Paragraph Frames** – cloze technique, paraphrasing/summary, completions

- **Picture Story Starters** – visual images to stimulate thinking and writing

- **Webbing** – used to illustrate connections among ideas, concepts, components, extensions

- **Mapping** – used to aid students in seeing connections among components, themes, and ideas

- **Clustering** – often used when brainstorming or categorizing

- **Graphs, Charts, Tables, Diagrams** – often used to present information in a concise form

- **Frameworks** – structures and/or outlines intended to aid the learner in constructing or conceptualizing the whole

- **Models** – generally intended as completed samples or examples of what is expected

Graphic organizers satisfy at least three criteria for successful learning in the classroom– they present information in a manner that is *concrete, explicit,* and *concise.* Venn diagrams use intersecting circles to show the interrelationships among items related to a specific topic.

A simple format for a story map is presented in Figure 6-7. Examples of story maps, clusters, and other "graphic organizers" relating to specific topics are presented in Figure 6-8 and 6-9.

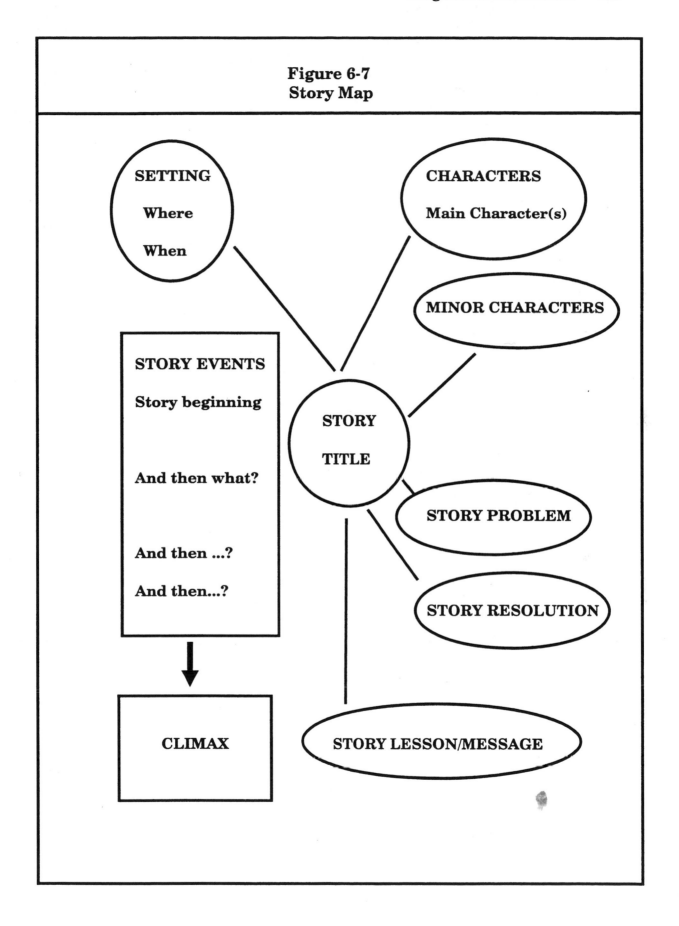

Figure 6-7
Story Map

Figure 6-8
Examples of Graphic Organizers

Example A: Sample Cluster

Teacher writes the word **hot dogs** on the board and asks, "What does this make you think about?" Students share/brainstorm and their responses are recorded on the board.

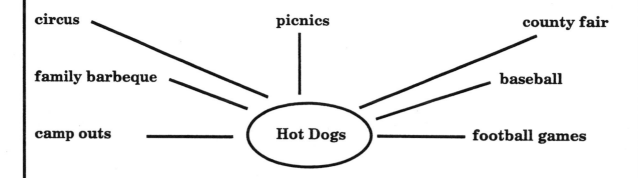

Example B: Sample Web for "Numbers"

The teacher directs students through a discussion about ways in which **numbers** affect them in all areas of life. Students are asked to develop a web illustrating how numbers are connected to the subjects they study in school.

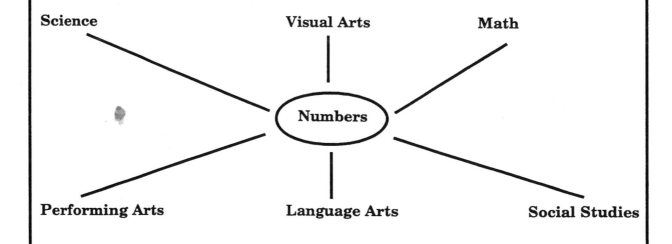

Example C: Story Map for an African Folktale

Based on an African folktale, the following short story presents all the story elements (plot, character, setting, theme, etc.) in a way that is both interesting and comprehensible to young readers. The use of repetition and onomatopoeia attracts the interests of the readers and is best either read or performed aloud. It is a good selection to encourage reluctant readers.

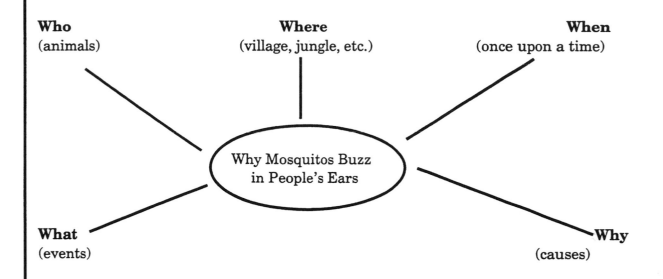

Who
(animals)

Where
(village, jungle, etc.)

When
(once upon a time)

Why Mosquitos Buzz
in People's Ears

What
(events)

Why
(causes)

Example D: Framework for a Social Studies Lesson (Outline)

"Westward Ho"

This framework is provided as an aid to students in their study of the westward movement in the late 19th century. Aside from providing a summary of key events, persons, and ideas, the framework helps learners zero in on the important facts and issues.

It all started when ...
1849 - Discovery of gold in California
Overcrowding in Eastern cities
Immigration

We would get there by ...
Wagon trains
Boats
Horses/mules/oxen
Walking

And we could take...
Food, water, clothing, medicine, tools
Family members
Animals (horses, mules, cows, dogs)

Life along the trail ...
prairie, ocean, desert, storms
   snakes, rodents, coyotes,
      mountain lions, insects, etc.
hard work and little rest
starvation and thirst
illness and death
friendly and hostile tribes
robbers and rustlers

And when we got there ...
search for affordable housing
hard life in mining camps
separation of family members
feast or famine

Example E: Sample Bilingual Web for Spanish Speakers (Grades 3 – 6)

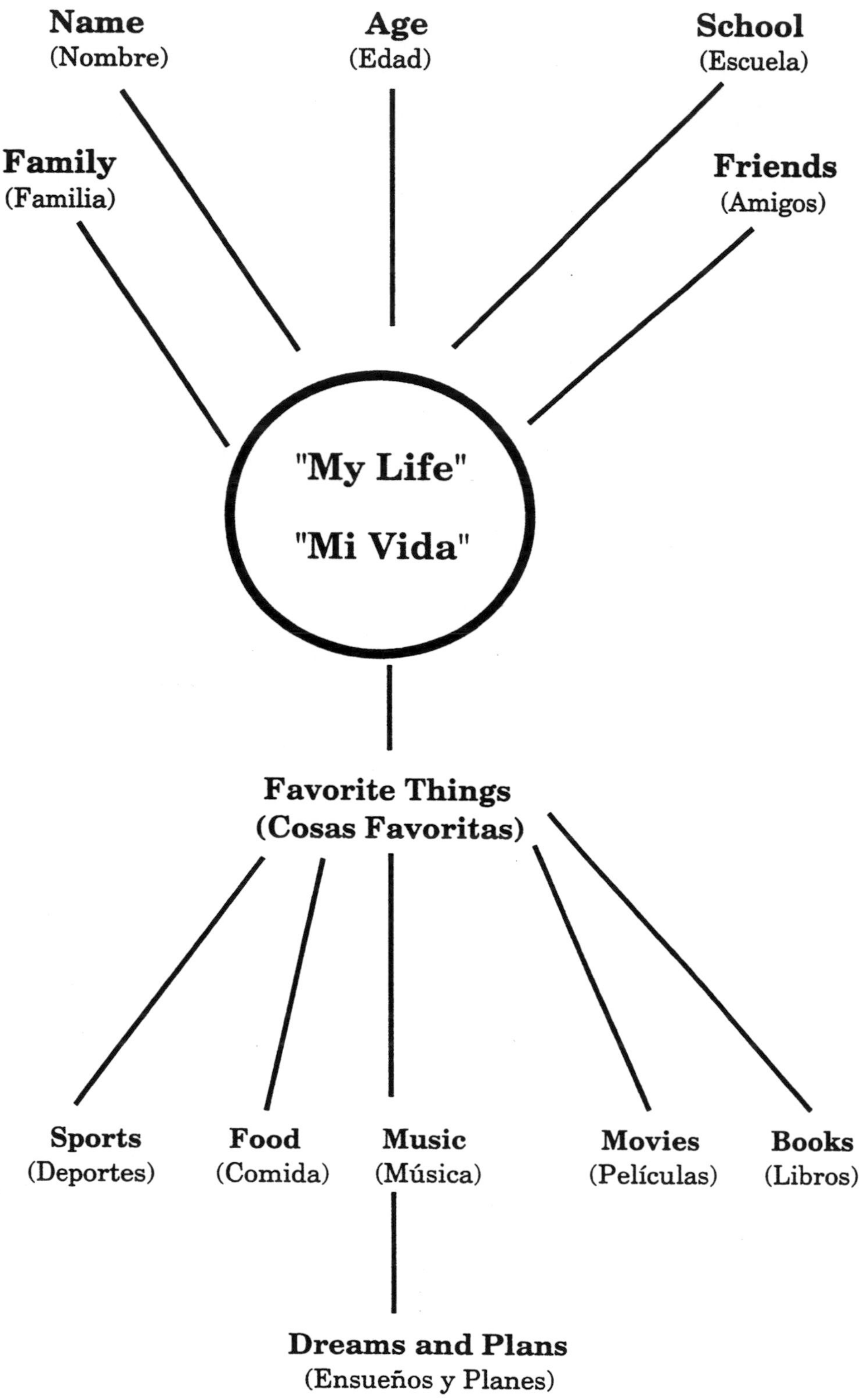

Name
(Nombre)

Age
(Edad)

School
(Escuela)

Family
(Familia)

Friends
(Amigos)

"My Life"

"Mi Vida"

Favorite Things
(Cosas Favoritas)

Sports
(Deportes)

Food
(Comida)

Music
(Música)

Movies
(Películas)

Books
(Libros)

Dreams and Plans
(Ensueños y Planes)

Figure 6-9
Examples of Venn Diagrams

Sample VENN Diagram: Grades 1 – 2
Concept Development

"Cats and Dogs"

Most first and second-graders – regardless of linguistic and/or cultural backgrounds – share many common experiences. One common denominator is "pets". On this topic, students of all ages and ability levels can actively engage in meaningful discussion. The diagram below is a good example of "assimilation - accommodation" theory of learning, in which students encounter *disequilibrium* in their efforts to distinguish *cats* and *dogs*. Generally, learners at this age level can deal only with physical characteristics.

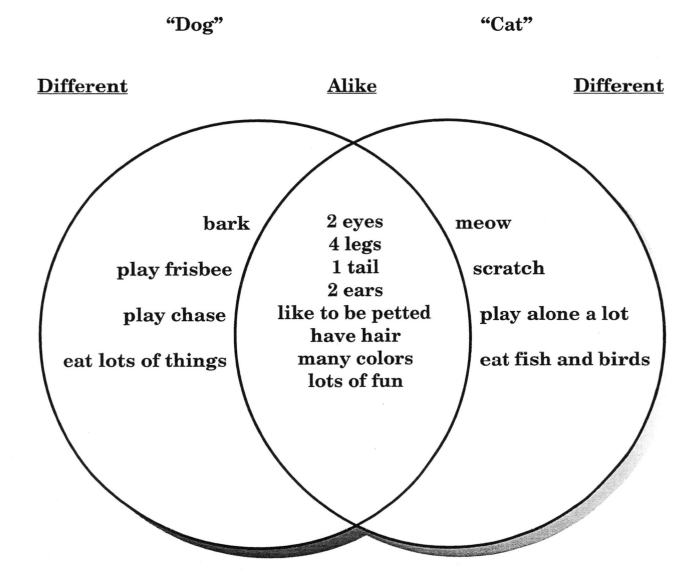

"Dog"   "Cat"

Different   Alike   Different

bark   2 eyes   meow
            4 legs
play frisbee   1 tail   scratch
            2 ears
play chase   like to be petted   play alone a lot
            have hair
eat lots of things   many colors   eat fish and birds
            lots of fun

Sample VENN Diagram: Grades 3 – 4
Concept Development, Classification

This diagram illustrates how the topic "animals" can be adapted for deeper study by third and fourth-graders. Their task is to differentiate farm animals from zoo animals by their physical characteristics and behavior. Students with limited-English ability and/or knowledge of such animals may require additional information and instruction prior to this activity.

"Farm Animals"   **"Zoo Animals"**

Different   **Alike**   **Different**

tame

safe as pets   plant eaters   unsafe as pets

help farmers   meat eaters   not used for work

Sample VENN Diagram: Grades 4 – 5

"Celebrations"

The following VENN diagram illustrates commonalities and differences between celebrations in the United States and Mexico. Students engage in general discussion, and their responses are recorded on the board or flipchart. This is an excellent way to introduce students to the study of foreign countries. It also makes a nice "Welcome" activity for foreign-born students new to the school or classroom.

<u>**United States**</u>   <u>**Both**</u>   <u>**Mexico**</u>

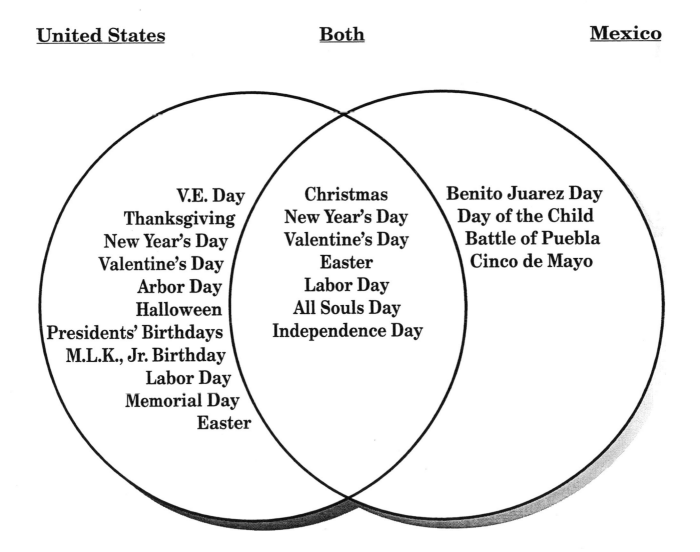

V.E. Day	Christmas	Benito Juarez Day
Thanksgiving	New Year's Day	Day of the Child
New Year's Day	Valentine's Day	Battle of Puebla
Valentine's Day	Easter	Cinco de Mayo
Arbor Day	Labor Day	
Halloween	All Souls Day	
Presidents' Birthdays	Independence Day	
M.L.K., Jr. Birthday		
Labor Day		
Memorial Day		
Easter		

Sample VENN Diagram: Grades 5 – 6
Classification, Analysis, Decision-making

This VENN diagram is based on a unit of study in which fifth and sixth-graders are asked to rank-order animals according to their usefulness and/or harm to humankind. The teacher has produced several lists of different animals for their consideration. The class must determine the criteria themselves. Students will work in cooperative groups. Each group will share its decisions with the class. Students with language and learning challenges should be placed in the cooperative groups – preferably with at least one bilingual peer.

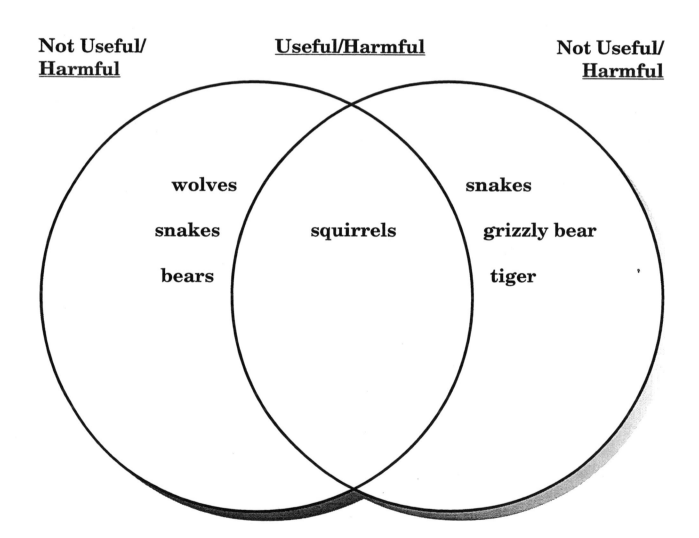

"Animals in the Wild"   **"Zoo Animals"**

Not Useful/   <u>Useful/Harmful</u>   Not Useful/
<u>Harmful</u>   <u>Harmful</u>

wolves   snakes

snakes   squirrels   grizzly bear

bears   tiger

Note: Students are next asked to defend their decisions. After much argument and discussion, they typically arrive at the same revelation – *all* animals are important to world ecology. They each serve a special purpose.

Games and Activities

Games used for the purpose of promoting learning take many forms – from simple guessing games to higher-order problem-solving. Games have been widely used in education primarily because they stimulate interest and active involvement among students of all ages. In recent years, with growing concerns about the need for *cooperation* in solving problems, emphasis has shifted from "individual achievement" to "group accomplishment." While such thinking continues to spark concern among some parents, students, and educators who see competition as natural, healthy, and appropriate, history has documented the benefits of cooperative societies. In his studies of children at play, Jean Piaget (1977) noted that even very young children recognized some need for rules in order for an activity to qualify as a game. When playing with marbles, for example, Piaget noted that while the rules were arbitrary, children came to observe them with little question. As the child grows and matures, this understanding deepens, and eventually, the rules become standards or imperatives.

My purpose here is to suggest to teachers that games guided by rigorous rules sometimes exclude students who are learning or linguistically challenged. Students with LLC, for example, might well display misperceptions or misunderstanding due to a lack of comprehensible information, lack of inclusion in activities, and/or lack of self-confidence. There are many wonderful games – *educational games* – appropriate to the needs and interests of virtually all students. When used with children who have language and learning disabilities, games facilitate interaction and provide a context in which children use language to achieve specific goals. Games challenge students to ask questions, evaluate information, and solve problems. Although games involve competition, they also require cooperation. Games can be used informally or adapted to teach subject matter within specific content areas. For example:

- **Drama** - charades, puppet play, role-playing, simulation games

- **Music** - naming songs, singers, rock bands, etc.

- **Science** - conducting experiments, hypothesis testing, prediction, group investigations

- **Language Arts** - reading/writing games, pair/group story writing, spelling bees, name games

- **Math** - puzzles, knowledge of math facts (+, –, x , etc.), playing Monopoly, counting games

- **P. E.** - team sports and activities

- **Art** - matching artists to the works that they have created

- **Social Studies** - role playing, *wh*-question game (*who, what, where, when, why*)

Even simple games can be formalized to promote academic skills and knowledge. The following sample games demonstrate how game activities can be used constructively to target specific *content areas* and *skills*. These games can be adapted quite easily for use at different grade levels.

Art Smart

Content Areas: Language Arts, Science, Art

Skills: Vocabulary development, classification, fine motor, artistic skills

Description: An activity in which students draw-and-label and/or cut-and-paste body parts, flower parts, tree parts, building parts, etc. in L1 and/or L2.

Bingo Match

Content Areas: Language Arts, Math, Art

Skills: Vocabulary development, number recognition, math operations, visual memory/thinking

Description: Bingo games using pictures, words, and/or numbers. Matching pieces are turned upside down and mixed up. Learners attempt to locate matching parts.

What to Wear?

Content Areas: Social Studies, Art, Math, Language Arts

Skills: Fine motor, artistic, classification, vocabulary development, communication, social skills

Description: Students make or use puppets, paper dolls, etc. to teach vocabulary related to clothing and dress. Students draw, color/paint, cut out, and dress the dolls and puppets. They discuss the clothing they have created or selected with peers and name the articles of clothing in both the first and second languages.

You Don't Say

Content Areas: Language Arts

Skills: Thinking, Listening, Speaking, Reading, Writing

Description: Three ways of playing this game are described below:

Variation 1 - Oral: Teacher leads students in a game in which they must think of synonyms for words in sentences. This activity can be presented in both L1 and L2. Teacher records the synonyms on the board or on a classroom Word Wall for future reference.

Variation 2 - Written: Students work independently or in pairs to complete **Word Search** puzzles. The word searches might be: synonyms, homonyms, antonyms, story characters, etc.

Variation 3 - Oral/Written: Using the **cloze** technique, students complete sentences, paragraphs, and/or stories by filling in missing words/phrases.

Note: Content drawn from current lessons/units can be reinforced with these activities.

In Other Words

Content Areas: Language Arts

Skills: Thinking, Listening, Speaking, Writing

Description: Students are introduced to figurative language. They explore idioms, similies, metaphors, hyperbole, personification, etc. Such literary devices are used in virtually every spoken language. Figurative language activities provide rich opportunities to engage students in both oral and written language experiences. Students can be challenged to create humorous sentences or stories using idioms. Their creations can then be shared aloud. Students with limited proficiency in English may require assistance from an aide or peer when learning figurative language.

Language Lacing

Content Areas: Language Arts

Skills: Thinking, Reading, Speaking, Interpersonal

Description: Students are given packets/envelopes containing long strings and individual words or phrases (on index cards) which have been perforated. Students are asked to lace them together to form sentences, paragraphs, and/or stories. The words and phrases may be taken from a current unit, lesson, or topic. The game serves to reinforce several skills – *Vocabulary development, recall, comprehension, application, speaking*. Encourage students to share their work aloud.

Shape Art

Content Areas: Math, Science, Art, Language Arts

Skills: Math (patterns, estimation, calculation), thinking, artistic, vocabulary development

Description: Students create pictures or objects from geometric shapes made of colorful paper or cardboard. The teacher may select different content areas to target with each activity.

Singing Patterns

Content Areas: Language Arts, Math, Music, Social Studies

Skills: Singing/rhythm, listening, counting, sequencing, vocabulary development

Description: Students sing, rap, and clap to songs with predictable beats and patterns. Examples: Old McDonald had a Farm, Twelve Days of Christmas (Halloween, Cinco de Mayo, Easter, etc.). Students add their own items to the lists.

Where Am I?

Content Areas: Language Arts, Math/Logic

Skills: Listening, thinking, concept development, vocabulary development, logic/thinking

Description: Students try to guess the location of a person after listening to clues. *Example*: I see a floor. I see a chair. I hear water running. I smell soap. I see a plate.

Correct answer: You are in the kitchen.

This game can be adapted to spark the interest of students of all ages. Locations described might include the following: home, beach, desert, island, the mall, farm, circus, Disneyland, school, restaurant, laundromat

The Story Goes

Content Areas: Language Arts, Social Studies, Math/Logic

Skills: Interpersonal, reading/writing, thinking

Description: Students dictate/write individual stories about an event (real or imagined) neatly on paper. The teacher cuts the stories into sections or paragraphs and shuffles them. As a class or in groups, students try to piece the stories back together by reading the sections aloud. This is usually great fun for students.

I'd Rather Be

Content Areas: Language Arts, Art, Math, Social Studies

Skills: Interpersonal, communication, artistic, fine motor, thinking/logic

Description: Students discuss their views of a "perfect day/week" in small groups. They create picture and story maps depicting all the events and activities for that day/week (on poster boards). Students share their projects aloud.

Variation: Teacher can collect the group projects and redistribute them randomly to the groups. The class must then match the group to the project.

If I Had the Money

Content Areas: Math, Social Studies, Language Arts

Skills: Counting/math, interpersonal, intrapersonal, communication, vocabulary development, analytical

Description: Having just received $1,000,000.00, students must decide how they will spend the money. However, they can spend none of the money on themselves. Individually or in small groups, students brainstorm ideas and record them on paper. They then prepare a cost list itemizing how the money will be spent. They must rank-order the items by importance. Individually or in small groups, they will share their plans with the class.

Variation: Students may detail a plan for spending the money on the class itself.

Common Senses

Content Areas: Language Arts, Social Studies, Math/Logic

Skills: Vocabulary development, thinking/logic

Description: A variety of games and experiments can be developed utilizing the five Senses. Here are a few ideas that should stimulate language and academic development for the entire class through several modalities.

1. Ask students to bring things with definite types of "smells" to school. Set guidelines (i.e., Tell students not to bring the pet skunk.). The teacher should bring a variety of things as well, to assure desired results.
2. Place the items around the room and have students smell each item.
3. On the board, record the following categories and list several examples. Then call upon students to "rate" the items brought to class.

Good	Neutral	Not Good	Bad
cookie	book	cabbage	cheese
perfume	rock	boiled eggs	vinegar

4. Students record their individual responses in their Experiment Journal.

Following the procedure described above, activities can be presented related to TASTE, TOUCH (TEXTURES), SIGHT, and SOUND. The examples below show how various items might be rated:

TASTE

Sweet	Salty	Sour	Unpleasant
candy	popcorn	pickle	broccoli
apple	pretzel	sourdough	cabbage
cookie	pepperoni	grapefruit	

TOUCH (TEXTURE)

Soft	Neutral	Hard
silk	jeans	rock
fur	canvas shoe	book
kitten	hair	apple

SOUND

Quiet	Pleasant	Loud	Unpleasant
clocks	talking	arguments	screaming
walking	music	music	music
library	rain	traffic	horns

When talking about sounds, the teacher should ask for examples from everyday life. Students may have different points of view and these differences can be used to spark discussions.

Simulation and Role-Playing

I chose to discuss role-playing and simulation games as distinct categories. These activities can engage students in meaningful thought, inquiry, and self-reflection. They can open our ears to other voices, our eyes to other perceptions, and our minds to other views – indeed powerful opportunities for understanding and growth. Moreover, these activities can be adapted to all language and learning levels.

Simulation Games might be defined as attempts to create or recreate events that simulate reality. Sample simulation experiences follow:

1. An example appropriate for fifth graders might be the transformation of a classroom into an "Old West" town. The teacher and students assume the roles of townspeople and explore vicariously daily life or specific historical events (e.g., discovery of gold, gunfight at the O.K. Corral). Another popular game engages students in a "mission to Mars." What might life be like in a distant galaxy? How will we select who will go? What will the crew take with them? This kind of inquiry can involve even the most reluctant learner. It requires imagination to a greater

degree than knowledge. With some assistance from peer interpreters, students with LLC should be able to participate fully in these activities.

2. Second graders might explore "Life on a Farm" through a simulation activity. Teacher, students, and parents could work together to simulate a farm scene on campus. Many cities have zoo programs that include trips to school sites with certain domestic animals. This presents a firsthand opportunity for children who have never seen farm animals to observe and interact with them. It promotes language, concept, and skills development. Students study feeding habits, characteristics and behaviors of the animals – as well as the roles and responsibilities of farm owners and workers.

Role-playing offers unique opportunities for "perspective-taking." Situations are created to place students in a variety of situations and positions, e.g. role-reversals, stance-taking, playing the role of "devil's advocate," etc. From the *perspectives* of others, students may come to understand, accept, and even appreciate each others' differences, beliefs, values, and opinions, as well as academic abilities and limitations. Language differences are generally more obvious to classmates, and this may present a special challenge to some teachers seeking ways to fully include language-and-learning-challenged students. Here are some ideas that might assist you in creating an inviting and nurturing classroom.

TIPS for Teachers

- Remember that students' commonalities present a strong thread for weaving mutual acceptance.
- Encourage perspective-taking and the sharing of opinions.
- Model acceptance of opinions in your classroom.
- Anticipate conflicting opinions and guide discussion sensitively.
- Invite parents/family members to visit your classroom.
- Create situations that draw students with LLC into the mainstream of learning.
- Create an environment in which students feel "validated" so that they will be motivated to engage actively in the school's agenda.

Visual/Guided Imagery

The use of imagery as a tool for learning has a long and well-documented history (Bagley & Hess, 1982; Galyean, 1983). The maxim that "what can be imagined can be accomplished" has undoubtedly guided persons from all walks of life toward personal success. It is not unusual to see athletes engaged in deep mental play immediately prior to an event, or actors engaged in mental rehearsal before a performance. Some coaches train their athletes in mental imagery techniques. These techniques reportedly serve to relax players and to guide them mentally through perfect performances. Gold medalist Greg Louganis, for example, could be clearly observed in such mental play before a dive.

The use of guided imagery with students with LD is also well-documented in research (Clark, Deschler, Schumaker, Alley & Warner, 1985; McCoy & Weber, 1981; Rasinski, 1985). Clark et al. advocated visual imagery and self-questioning strategies as a means of improving reading comprehension among students with learning disabilities. Weber

(1986) identified three broad areas around which LD research interests have centered:

1. *Imagery and Memory* – typified by the "Cognitive Strategies" movement that has guided much of the research in learning disabilities since the early 1980's. The use of mnemonic devices, verbal rehearsal, and other metacognitive approaches to learning continue to aid language-and-learning-challenged students in the schools. For example, students might visualize the following mnemonic in a test-taking situation:

FROSTY THE SNOWMAN

F ocus on the test.

R ead the words.

O pen your mind.

S elect an answer.

T ime yourself.

Y ou can do it.

2. *Imagery and Vocabulary Development* – aimed at promoting greater accessibility to and proficiency with language. One such approach described by Weber (1986) involves linking together words from different languages that sound *similar*.

   Example: Boat (English) = Boot (German). The learner is asked to *visualize* the objects, *study* their spelling, and *listen* to their pronunciation. They then attempt to create mental images that "link" the two words so that they may be easily recalled. One such *visual image* might be a *boot* shaped like a *boat*. Another student might find that the *sound* of each object is a preferable means of remembering. Others might need to draw or act out the images in order to make the connection.

3. *Imagery to Improve Reading Comprehension* – intended as a means of "animating" story elements and structuring content. One device commonly used by educators that shows strong promise for students with LLC is *semantic mapping*. A graphic depiction of a story, for example, cuts through much of the technical language in order to yield a simplified summary of *plot, character, setting, theme,* and *style*. Often, students – particularly those with language and/or learning problems – have difficulty seeing the whole story or idea because of *too much* information. Clearly, the author's purpose is to communicate with the reader. If the reader needs an interpreter to simplify and explain information presented in a book, the teacher should attempt to accommodate that need. Limited proficiency in English should not be a barrier that makes it impossible for the student to function in the classroom. If the meanings and images in the book are beyond the mental grasp, age, and/or maturity level of the learner, then alternate reading selections or assignments should be provided – in either the first or second language.

Keeping in mind that typical classrooms rely heavily on visual and auditory acuity, it should be noted that other learning styles and modalities – kinesthetic and tactile, for example – might well be more efficient means of learning for students with LLC. I am reminded of images from my own childhood, when, at the age of perhaps four, I learned the names of objects by associating them with things *I already knew*. The neighbor's car, a *Studebaker,* was easy to remember because I saw Mr. Spillers drive away each morning as my family sat down to a breakfast of eggs and <u>bacon</u>. The word "bacon" helped me to remember the "baker" in *Studebaker.* I have frequently heard second-language elementary students engaged in such verbal play – chanting, singing, and using what sounds to some like nonsense to build their own vocabularies. Undoubtedly, countless other second-language learners go through their school day actively trying to link a foreign language to images in their real lives and experiences.

Implications for Using Guided Imagery

- Guided imagery allows learners to tinker with ideas and problems in a world where possibilities exceed limitations.

- Imagery may provide students with a means of quickly accessing visual cues to help them formulate responses.

- Because ideas are shaped greatly by images, perceptions, and analogy, understanding their function in constructing meanings is an imperative for all learners.

- By using guided imagery, students may begin to analyze and clarify feelings that they have about themselves.

- Used as an instructional tool, guided imagery might serve as a catalyst for making leaps of understanding – the conduit through which present knowledge is transformed into a new way of knowing.

Chapter 7
Technology and Learning

Technology is the most subtle and the most effective engineer of enduring social change. Its apparent neutrality is deceptive and often disarming.

Robert MacIver

One goal of technology education in the schools is to develop an awareness of its future implications. We want students to recognize the increasingly important role that technology plays in their daily lives and its link to their own futures. While we cannot expect technology alone to lead our schools to the promised land, the growing need to become both literate and adept in new technologies is self-evident. Despite its growing utility as a creative and self-expressive medium, the computer rarely is accessible for such purposes in most classrooms (Kolich, 1985; Means, Olson, & Singh, 1995; Mergendoller, 1997; Poplin, Drew, & Gable, 1984). The computer has been used more as a teacher than as an expressive medium. The professional literature is replete with evidence that computer-assisted instruction (CAI) is the approach most often used in programs for students with learning disabilities. Typically, students are given drill and practice activities in which information and skills are reduced and segmented, presumably for faster mastery. There is also strong evidence to suggest that students learning English as a second language are subjected to the same CAI approaches. This narrow view of the learner as "receptor" suggests, among other things, that because of their differences, students with LLC possess relatively fewer strengths than their peers and less aptitude for creative tasks such as programming and/or authoring.

Contrary to these notions, Hearne, Poplin, Schoneman, and O'Shaughnessy (1988) found no significant differences between the performances of 56 students with LD and 56 of their non-learning disabled peers on measures of the Computer Aptitude, Literacy, and Interest Profile (CALIP) (1984). Moreover, no significant differences were found between males and females on the CALIP. These findings suggested that students with LD can be equally successful at computer-related tasks as their peers.

Based on a review of recent analyses of educational technology, Mergendoller (1997) reported that computers in schools are used primarily "as an electronic workbook to drill students in basic skills and give practice in solving simple academic problems" (p. 12). In related research, Means, Olson, and Singh (1995) found that schools were referring to their use of computers and technology as evidence of reform and restructuring. In reality, however, related studies suggest that school programs merely adapted the computers to what they were already doing without changing the way in which they were operating (Mergendoller, 1997).

Hypermedia

Hypermedia is an integrated electronic environment that combines text, audio, and video into one large file. Hypermedia makes it possible to explore information relating to various subjects using several technologies at the same time (Wishnietsky, 1992). Training students with LLC to use new technologies facilitates the development of independence in the learning environment. While working on a computer assignment, for example, students are able to go directly to a dictionary or thesaurus without leaving their seats. Information can be collected and compiled from a variety of sources. Through the use of computers, students can access more information than a single teacher or text could possibly provide.

Computer: Both Tool and Creative Medium

As computers play an increasingly vital role in creating and expanding knowledge, the need to examine humanistic implications becomes equally important. Schools should take a "broad view approach" to computer utilization – simulation programs, graphic design, word processing, and programming.

While drill-and-practice may benefit some students, such activities should not fully pre-empt other computer uses. Weston and Ingram (1997) offered several ideas for bringing whole language and technology into harmony. **Whole language** creates a perfect use of computers for:

- discovering and generating ideas
- creating written works and products
- enhancing knowledge and understanding
- extending learning to new situations

Simulation Programs have become so sophisticated that astronauts, pilots, race car drivers, and even Hollywood film-makers now use them in their work. Such programs enable students and teachers to bring realistic worlds into the classroom. With help from peer interpreters, even students with limited language proficiency should be able to fully participate in creating databases. Such activities stimulate the development of a variety of skills, such as classifying/categorizing, organizing, ordering (alphabetical and numerical), and accounting. They also promote the development of personal responsibility.

Graphics

Software provides many visual forms – lines, letters, boxes, designs, borders, etc. Visual information is extremely useful in teaching students with LLC. Computer graphics can be used to:

- stimulate writing and publishing in the classroom
- present design and form to students
- allow students to draw and/or paint pictures

- allow students to illustrate their written stories
- decorate student work (e.g., borders, banners, book covers, title pages, etc.)

Word Processing

Word processing activities motivate poor readers and second-language learners to focus on the letters, word patterns, and other language symbols (punctuation marks, letter case, math symbols, asterisks, etc.) in making meaning from print. It helps students create as well as respond to literary forms. Its usefulness in teaching students with LLC is well documented by research. (Kerchner & Kistinger, 1984). Even lower functioning students can be successful using the delete, backspace, insert, and tab features in producing written work. Word processing further simplifies the writing process approach by allowing students to produce revisions more easily and to edit their creations. Programs that check spelling are particularly useful to those students who have basic knowledge of phonics.

Many programs have been developed in recent years to help school-age children acquire word processing skills. Some school systems have developed or adopted a K-12 computer technology curriculum. Textbooks have even begun to feature computer utilization in their contents.

Programming

Programming is the most sophisticated and creative use of computers, but it is also the application least understood or practiced by teachers. Programming is essentially a step-by-step procedure to create responses and/or actions – much like task analysis. Since all computer programs can be traced to the persons who programmed them, they are limited by the capabilities of their creators. Hence, computer programs with varying levels of sophistication and wide-ranging capabilities are available to educators and students. Teaching programming skills to students, however, has not been a valued pursuit in schools. Does this stem from (1) lack of know how, (2) lack of time, or (3) limited understanding of the potential value that such skills have in the learning environment?

1. **"Lack of know how"** may be a reasonable argument in rural areas and districts where computer access is extremely limited. However, grant money for hardware and software is widely available to teachers and administrators. As for gaining the "know how," consider these possibilities:
   - Attend computer workshops and classes offered by districts and/or local colleges and universities. Some offer college credits, and some are free.
   - Invite computer consultants who are skilled and knowledgeable about classroom applications to conduct hands-on workshops in programming at your school site.
   - Send teachers to workshops and/or classes to learn programming. These teachers can then train other teachers to create programs for students.

2. **"Lack of time"** is probably an equally formidable argument for teachers who feel stretched to the limit already. However, there are ways to integrate programming into the curriculum:
   - Approach programming as a project, one that can be developed over time and expanded.
   - Train a group of students and allow them to train others, until every child in your classroom has mastered the fundamentals of programming.

- Team with a peer to develop a plan whereby academic instruction can be shared and alternated with computer projects and instruction.

3. **"Lack of interest"** is the most difficult hurdle. Teachers must be motivated in order to motivate their students. Becoming aware of the possibilities presented by programming is perhaps the first step. If teachers can find practical use for recent technological innovations, they are generally more receptive to using them. It is therefore imperative to somehow demonstrate both broad and specific applications of programming as it can be used across the curriculum. The "Special Series" Edition on Technology in the *Journal of Learning Disabilities* (1996) includes valuable information for teachers interested in incorporating computers in their classroom. A publication by Morton (1996) about the use of computers in education should also prove to be helpful.

Internet

The internet has the capability to revolutionize the way in which educators conceive of teaching and learning. Information about a variety of topics that was previously difficult to obtain or unavailable can now be obtained almost instantaneously through the internet. The internet offers cooperative research databases, access to online professional conferences, discussion forums, and information resources that have direct relevance to the needs of individuals with disabilities (Masterson, Wynne, Kuster, & Stierwalt, 1999). While some might lament its coming as yet another wedge between human beings themselves in their quest to communicate, the internet is fast becoming a fact of life both inside and outside of the classroom environment. When used to enhance learning, the internet has the power to transform and improve existing structures and systems. Distance learning has become the medium of choice for many educators who are finding it increasingly inconvenient to attend college classes.

The World Wide Web (WWW), or "net," gives its subscribers capabilities to both create and access web sites. Students are able to send and receive "mail" correspondence, engage in discussions through chat rooms, visit private rooms in historic buildings and exotic locales, and participate in a variety of other activities. This is a far cry from traditional letter-writing, face-to-face interchange, or slide presentations.

Unmonitored, however, the internet has already demonstrated its negative capabilities – abusive and/or unlawful uses. Computer files and web site activities must be respected in the same way that we respect student reflection journals and personal diaries. However, the establishment of ground rules and acceptable uses should prevent problems – or, at least make students aware of the dangers of abuse.

Sample Uses of the Internet

Sample uses of the internet in science, math, and other areas of the curriculum are listed below:

— *Science*
- Students use the internet to explore ways to protect the environment.
- Students link with another class in another part of the country to conduct joint science experiments.
- The class develops a directory of web sites that provide information relevant to classroom science projects.

— Math

- Students enter cyberspace to explore the architecture and dimensions of pyramids.
- Students use the internet to access information on math tutoring programs.
- Students engage in chat room discussions of math riddles and exchange student-developed math problems with students in other states.

— Social Studies

- Students use the web to obtain information about historical events that affected their families.
- Students access web sites and use the information obtained to design the "perfect world."
- The class uses the web to study the history of the circus, automobiles, computers, etc.

— Language Arts

- The internet is used by individual students to access story books.
- Students meet and correspond with "net" pals in other countries.
- Students work with "net" pals on writing and reading projects.

— Physical Education/Sports/ Movement

- Students correspond with their favorite athlete or dancer.
- Students study health and fitness through web sites.
- Students works as a team to plan an Olympics Day based on their web site study of the first Olympics games.

— Visual Arts/Performing Arts

- Through the web, students study the lives of their favorite painter, dancer, or actor and write brief biographies.
- Students explore the works of great artists through museum and art web sites.
- Students take art lessons through web sites.

Implications for Internet Use in Programs for Students with LLC

- The internet provides teachers and schools with a tool for monitoring and reporting both group and individual progress.
- Students with LLC can link with peers for tutoring and collaboration on school work in both English and the primary language.
- Students with LLC can access web sites set up especially for English language learners and/or students with learning disabilities.
- The internet allows schools and teachers to develop web sites for tutoring both during and after school.
- The internet provides a way to link parents to schools – from the home, office, or even the car.
- Sources of information available through the internet are inestimable. The internet provides a tool that allows students to delve into a subject of personal interest in ways that are not possible through any other source.

Television and VCR

Television is first and foremost an entertainment medium for children and adults. It has also served as a baby-sitter, teacher, tutor, salesperson, pastor, informer, tour guide, decision-maker, trend-setter, motivator, and even a close friend. It can also be divisive (splintering the atomic family into separate rooms and time schedules) and negative (projecting images of antisocial, violent, and even inhumane behaviors). Teachers have long lamented the negative effects of television viewing on children. Their concerns include:

- Drowsiness and poor attention skills due to television viewing late at night
- The use of vulgar and offensive language learned from television viewing
- Poor quality or lack of appropriate programs for children
- Competition for children's attention and trust (Who should they believe? Who can they trust?)
- Influences on career aspirations and choices (glamorized and/or distorted images by characters on television shows)
- Role-models – positive and negative examples (who they emulate or aspire to become)

How we as educators perceive television and how we choose to use it may have some measurable impact on the way in which our students come to view the medium. Therefore, we must assume rather than avoid responsibility for educating students about the uses and abuses of television. Ways in which television can be used to tutor students and to enhance interaction are summarized in Table 7-1.

Captioned TV

Captioned TV can be a powerful tool for teaching reading to underachieving students, individuals with hearing impairments, and second language learners. Most newer televisions come equipped with caption devices which, when the sound is muted, project the words/dialogue on the screen. The more vivid and interesting the images on the screen, the more engaged learners become. Curiosity and interest will help drive their need to "decode" the printed messages on the screen. Teachers freely select programs to be used by groups or individuals that will promote reading skills. Goldman (1993) suggested that programs be ranked and grouped by language difficulty.

In summary, with each technology comes a new jargon and sometimes an entire "language," replete with foreign-sounding words and odd terms, people conversing in *acronyms*, thinking in *cyberspace*, calculating in *bytes*, and reading from screens rather than from pages of text or books. For teachers who see themselves as "low tech," this can be a frustrating experience. They may feel alienated from their peers – even from their own profession. Imagine for a moment the child who has just arrived from a foreign country, who speaks no English, and who feels alienated from his or her past. Then imagine having the additional burden of a learning problem. Empathy may well help us understand and accept students faced with these conditions.

Brown (1993) offered several ways for schools to balance tools of technology with humanity, such as:

- Identifying technologies that can be mastered and used productively by students in the classroom for real purposes, e.g., publishing, recording, and communication

---

Table 7-1
Educational Uses of Television

Receptive/Tutorial	Expressive/Interactive
Informational Programs -*Nick News* -Professor Gadget -*National Geographic* -Discovery Channel -*Field Trips USA* (History Channel)	*VCR Utilization* -Video games -Classroom dramatic productions, performances -Taped demonstrations -Taped classroom lessons

Instructional Materials
-Supplemental videos to
   reading series
-Taped classroom lessons
	Interactive Television (IATV)
	(Johnson & Tully, 1989)
	-Live instruction and
	   discussion through use of
	   internet from transmitter
	   (teacher) to viewer (student)

Captioned Television
- Programs selected
   to teach reading to
   underachievers
	Video Response Journals
	- Taped reader responses
	- Taped writer responses
	
	Video Conferences
	- Writer's workshop
	- Parent conferences
	- Student conferences

- Utilizing technologies for group purposes as well as individual pursuits
- Viewing technologies as assistants to critical reflection and creativity

The suggestions that follow can be used to "hook" the interest of students with LLC while providing context clues for language development.

— *Previewing* - Select a variety of programs for student viewing.
- Cartoons and comedies are helpful for poor readers because sentences are short and the difficulty level is low.
- Activity and game shows stimulate thinking skills as well as language.
- Sports programs engage many students (Be sure to edit beforehand).

— *Viewing* - Tie instruction to the programs watched. Closely monitor independent viewing.
- Try introducing a story via a television/video and then have students read the rest independently or in pairs.

- Alternate between TV caption reading and reading the story from a book.
- Reinforce language (vocabulary and usage) from the programs. English language learners need to *hear* the words that you wish them to learn.

— *Post-Viewing* - Expand and enrich the literacy experience. Reinforce the effective use of language.
- Create story maps of episodes or stories (pictures and/or words).
- Draw and/or paint scenes from the stories.
- Write about a favorite character in a story.
- Write/tell about a similar incident in your own life.
- Add new vocabulary words from the stories to the classroom Word Wall.
- Write/dictate different story endings.
- Act out scenes from the stories.
- Quiz each other about the stories or programs watched.
- Use story dialogues to teach grammar, mechanics, and usage.
- Have English language learners practice saying words and dialogue from the programs.

Implications for Students with LLC
- Television/VCR viewing presents rich opportunities for modeling the English language to second language learners.
- Video-taped lessons present graphically what is expected, i.e., products, behaviors, responses, etc. These lessons can be used and re-used conveniently by students with LLC both at school and at home.
- Developmental language lessons can be taped and used by students at home to teach English to parents and other family members.
- Students learn to use television/VCR both as entertainment devices and as learning tools.
- Students and/or teachers can be encouraged to video-tape school events to share with parents and family.
- Teachers can video-tape student conferences, announcements, grading procedures, school rules, etc., for parents to view.

Chapter 8
Assessment and Classroom Performance

While standardized tests initially were created to measure student achievement in a simple, quantifiable, and inexpensive way, in practice they have taken on a much more influential role. Tests now are used to measure facts, skills, aptitudes, attitudes, and achievements. Students' scores have been used to fire superintendents, gain merit pay for teachers, and even set property values by using student achievement scores to rate local schools.

Emily Grady

The assessment of student deficits and achievement has become a focal point of heated debate in recent years as reports of declining national test scores have emerged. Evaluation continues to occupy the hearts and minds of parents, educators, and students alike. Engel (1994) suggested that education is undergoing a paradigm shift from *product-driven* to *process-driven* curricula and instruction, a shift that has created a mismatch between process-oriented instruction and inadequate data yielded by standardized testing – a matter of *learning profiles* versus *test scores*. As Tierney (1998) observed, assessment principles "emanate from personal ideals and practice as much as theory and research – a mix of child-centered views of teaching, pluralistic and developmental views of children, constructivist views of knowing, and critical theoretical views of empowerment" (p. 375). In other words, reaching consensus on assessment issues is a formidable task. Tierney outlined 13 "key principles for literacy assessment," most of which redress traditional assessment practices. The first principle emphasized that assessment should originate in the classroom with teachers and students, rather than from the outside by persons or agencies who know neither the teacher nor the students.

The fields of learning disabilities and bilingual education have contributed uniquely to the ongoing dialectic. For decades, special educators have argued that schools need strength and talent-driven curricula (Poplin, 1988; Poplin & Cousin, 1995) and holistic strategies for assessing achievement. The quest for better assessment practices, however, has met with several stumbling blocks. Perhaps the greatest is the demand for quick, positive returns on "educational investments." Bilingual and special education have been targets of criticism in recent years, resulting largely from the *general push* for more accountability in our schools. Calls for "full inclusion" and an end to bilingual education (witness the recent California legislation ending mandated bilingual education) signal a return of locus of control to individual schools and districts. With these measures come a redistribution of responsibility – generally in the direction of the regular classroom teacher. How will a "fully inclusive" classroom meet the needs of second-language learners and students with LD? In *reductionist* classrooms driven by skills-based continua and direct instruction, test scores and other numerical data are readily available to document progress. But do these methods and data fully document student progress? How do we provide objective documentation that learning is taking place in our *constructivist* classrooms? Grady (1992) offered the following reservation:

> A standardized test may show students in the 80th percentile for reading comprehension. The superintendent can look at that score and know that teaching of reading is progressing well in the district. Legislators can look at the numbers and assume that things seem to be under control. Parents can feel secure that the district is educating their children. However these good feelings do nothing to help the children learn to read or help the teachers who are teaching them. Individual strengths and weaknesses are not identified. (p. 13)

Authentic Assessment and the Language-and-Learning Challenged

Priestley (1992) discussed numerous ways of assessing students' "authentic" work, among them the adaptation of evaluation forms for use in portfolio assessment. Priestly suggested three broad categories of criteria: Contents, Attributes, and Other. In keeping with the holistic emphasis in many whole language, bilingual, and learning disabilities classrooms, such forms become useful in documenting actual progress toward I.E.P. goals and objectives. Because the category "Other" remains open for interpretation, it allows bilingual and special educators to adapt the form to their specific needs (Maldonado-Colon, 1993). Teachers of students with LLC, for example, may wish to accumulate samples of "evidence" that students are responding to specific interventions or showing progress in English language development. The inclusion of such evidence in the portfolio will later allow teachers to review student competencies and summarize them on a useful form.

Canales (1992) and Maldonado-Colon (1993) described performance-based assessment as the evaluation of specific competencies and/or authentic products. They proposed the following three categories as criteria for assessing limited English proficient students:

- *Academic competencies* - those skills and knowledge required by the school curriculum
- *Linguistic competencies* - the language skills acquired and applied both inside and outside the school setting

- *Affective competencies* - skills and behavior related to social and emotional development, e.g., motivation, sharing/turn-taking, self-awareness, self-esteem, and social interaction

Each dimension or category relates also to general school goals. Therefore, teachers of students with LLC are able to negotiate instructional and assessment practices.

Balancing Literacy: A Portfolio Approach

On a recent visit to my family home in Louisiana, I was struck by the amount of growth and the number of changes that had occurred in the 15 years of my absence. The fields and woods where I had played ball and run free with boyhood friends are now occupied by fine homes and shopping centers. All this newness and spirit of progress left me with mixed emotions about my own personal connection to the history that had occurred here. I felt like somewhat of a stranger, even as I walked through the home in which I grew up. Rooms filled with family pictures and crowded with momentos stood like a museum showcasing the triumphs and treasures of three generations. Over the years, my mother had compiled a meticulous "portfolio" of each of her three sons' lives, sifting out what she considered the best reflections of who we are – benchmark accomplishments, certificates, awards, diplomas, childhood notes and cards, and even faded programs from graduations. One could observe our personal development over time, to the point of being vicariously acquainted with us. In another, more subtle way, it was an assessment of her own life and accomplishments as well.

I think of this experience each time I enter a classroom now. I look into the faces of my students and imagine who they will become and who will document their journey. No matter what their ages, all learners are entitled to fair and comprehensive assessment, a fuller picture of who they are. Perhaps the single most important trend in evaluating student achievement over the past 20 years has been the "portfolio" movement. In addition to benchmark samples of students' academic achievements, portfolios *can* reflect who they are, what they know, and what they *can* do. Portfolios can also show their interests, strengths, talents and who or what they hope to become. Should we be aiming our teaching efforts solely at school goals? Or, should we include our *students'* goals in our plans?

For students with second-language and/or learning challenges, the answers would seem obvious. We must expand, not *narrow* the range of acceptable proofs of learning. Limited reading skills preclude success with standardized tests for many, if not most, students with LLC. Portfolio and performance assessments represent opportunity for these learners, ways of demonstrating the knowledge and skills that paper-and-pencil tests cannot measure.

Planning a Portfolio Program

Using portfolios across disciplines and school years requires careful planning. Teachers committed to portfolio assessment typically begin by exploring what *they* hope to accomplish in the coming year. Planning for students with LLC requires commitment and collaboration between regular and special educators. Perhaps the following checklist will help.

- Sketch out a general plan for the year – your scope and sequence of the curriculum.
- Rank-order the content and skills you hope to cover during the coming year.

- Decide the number and kinds of portfolios to be developed, e.g., content areas, art, etc.
- Consider language issues. Will the portfolios contain samples in one or both languages?
- Inform administrators and parents about your program. Their "buy in" is imperative.
- Discuss portfolios with students and explain their purposes.
- Share sample portfolios and discuss their contents.
- Make a list of materials and supplies that you may need to accomplish your goals.
- Collect baseline samples of students' work to include in the portfolios.
- Itemize a list of potential contents for each type of portfolio.

Considerations in Using Portfolios

- Many teachers choose to use two separate portfolios for formal assessment purposes– one maintained by the student and the other maintained by the teacher.
- Certain anecdotal notes/records about students with LLC may be considered "confidential."
- For students with LLC, regular and special education teachers may wish to maintain separate folders or joint folders.
- Teachers may wish to pair students with LLC with peer-interpreters. The peer interpreters can provide assistance in the routine handling of portfolios.
- Teachers may wish to invite information from various "specialists" so that this information can be included in the student's portfolio.

Portfolios can be developed for a variety of reasons and uses. In academics, teachers may wish to maintain separate portfolios for each content area, especially language arts and math. Some teachers may encourage students to develop portfolios of artwork. Still others may ask students to compile *group* portfolios containing samples of collaborative work. In general, portfolios contain artifacts of student work and different types of portfolios contain different representations of the student's accomplishments. Items selected for inclusion should represent a range of student efforts and achievements. If the object is to select a representative sampling of the student's work so that specific strengths and weaknesses can be assessed, the portfolio should include devices for communication between the teacher and student. A log for teacher comments and suggestions and a journal for self-assessment and personal reflections are among the devices that might be included. The teacher's log can provide valuable feedback and personal encouragement.

Language Arts Portfolio

Language arts portfolios typically contain samples of work related to reading and written language. These portfolios might include reader response items such as story maps, pictures, drawings, and audiotaped responses, as well as writing samples, published stories, and written tests. Seidel et al. (1997) offer the following list of potential contents for a writing portfolio:

- a satisfying, high quality piece
- a less-than-satisfying, lower quality piece
- a 'free pick' selected by the student

- a 'free pick' selected by the teacher
- student reflections on each major piece
- student logs or journal entries that provide a picture of the development of insight and working process (the choices and discoveries they make, their concerns, resources, frustrations)
- at least one 'biography of a work' that includes all notes, drafts, revisions, and reflections that contributed to the completion of the project (p. 31)

Mathematics Portfolio

Some teachers find math portfolios to be more complicated and burdensome than language arts portfolios. Others, however, find them less burdensome. This difference results largely from differences in how teachers define math. Some find it inextricably linked to science and social studies – and all the projects and paperwork they generate. Others take a narrower view of math – concept of number, math operations, and computation skills. The view taken will dictate the breadth and contents of the portfolio. One is a snapshot and the other is a panorama. Therefore, teachers should predetermine which they favor and why. Just as in language arts, math portfolios should contain the following:

- baseline work samples, including tests
- benchmark samples of growth (tests, oral/written demonstrations)
- artifacts/descriptions of things constructed or developed
- self-evaluation log or journal
- reflection journal
- teacher's comments log

Other items might include:

- goal logs - e.g., addition facts, multiplication facts mastery, long division mastery
- graphics - student-generated tables, figures, designs, etc.
- computer-related items (e.g., logo geometry, keyboard calculation samples)

Note to Teachers: When creating portfolios, the following considerations are important:

- Teachers of students with LLC who decide to maintain a common portfolio must negotiate its scope and contents.
- Regular and special educators should work together to reinforce targeted math skills and knowledge.
- Teachers may wish to use peer-interpreters to assist students with LLC.
- Teachers should allow a range of math products and/or demonstrations as evidence of learning.
- Students should be full participants in their assessment.

Portfolios as Bridges

In schools where portfolio assessment and evaluation have taken root, teachers work together to assure continuity and smooth transition between grade levels. Each school year is viewed as a bridge to the next. Typically, portfolios are passed along to students' new teachers at the end of the year. They provide the new teacher with individual assessments of knowledge and skills levels that are far more comprehensive than report cards or standardized test scores.

Benchmark work samples contained within a child's portfolio can be used as a "baseline" for evaluating future learning. Some schools choose to maintain a K-6 portfolio on each child to document progress across the elementary years. In such cases, teachers must take a long look at what they wish to remain in students' records.

Implications for Teachers of Students with LLC

- Portfolio assessment provides a tool for negotiating the regular classroom curriculum.
- Portfolio assessment aides both special educators and classroom teachers in grading and preparing progress reports.
- Portfolios make it possible to peek inside the private worlds of students so that teachers can see their goals and dreams and better understand their challenges and fears.
- Portfolios open doors for students as well – doors of self-expression and alternative proofs of learning.
- Portfolios encourage students to take charge of their learning and to accept responsibility.
- Portfolios promote development of organizational and decision-making skills.

Holistic-Rubric Assessment

Upon hearing the terms "holistic scoring" or "rubric assessment," most educators probably think immediately of process writing and whole language. However, one does not need to be "wholly" committed to these approaches to take advantage of the assessment techniques associated with them. Models of holistic assessment have been developed for virtually every content area. For example, researchers and teachers have applied whole language principles to mathematics and science – estimation, hypotheses, and even theories are not mathematical laws, but rather the mathematician's "rough drafts." Hence, if we are to encourage math development among students, then we must allow them to tinker with numbers and problems, to "guess" and to "theorize" without penalty. Holistic assessment of any student act or product considers the *process* used by the student. It is far more telling than a mere written response.

The sample rubrics in Table 8-1 are presented to show how assignments can be assessed "holistically" and fairly. Some of our great writers and scientific researchers have reported personal difficulties with the technical aspects of writing (e.g., grammar, mechanics, and spelling). The models presented here can be adapted for use with a wide range of subject areas and situations. The points can be easily converted to letter grades. However, without the rubrics clearly stated to support the grade, there is really no constructive feedback for the student.

Implications for Students with LLC

- Letter grades tell little about the content or specific contexts of learning experiences.
- Rubrics should be developed with diversity in mind. They must fairly assess the group or individual for whom they are intended.
- Rubrics can provide clear and constructive feedback for students with LLC and help them identify their strengths as well as weaknesses.

Table 8-1
Three Examples of Rubrics

Example A: Science Project Rubric (Grade 6)

Excellent Project
>   All components of inquiry present
>   Clear statement of hypothesis
>   Use of computer/internet in research
>   Written report free of errors in grammar, mechanics, usage, and spelling
>   Thorough, well-written report that follows the format

Good Project
>   All components of inquiry present
>   Clear statement of hypothesis
>   Use of at least three sources in research
>   Written report has few errors in grammar, mechanics, usage, and spelling
>   Written report comprehensible and approximates the format

Project Needs Improvement
>   Some components of inquiry missing
>   Hypothesis missing or not clearly stated
>   Sources not stated and/or inappropriate to project focus
>   Report poorly written – many errors in grammar, mechanics, usage, and/or spelling
>   Written report incomprehensible

Example B: Student Essay – Language Arts (Grade 4)

Major Traits	10 Point Scale
Topic sentence clearly stated	10 - 8
Paragraphs well developed, including transition sentences	
Essay supported by adequate facts and details	
Superior clarity in writing – well organized, concise	
Free of grammar, mechanics, usage, and spelling errors	
Topic sentence clearly stated	7 - 5
Paragraphs fairly well developed	
Essay supported by adequate facts and details	
Clarity of writing is fair – comprehensible and concise	
Few errors in grammar, mechanics, usage, and/or spelling	
Topic sentence poorly stated or not stated	4 - 1
Paragraphs poorly developed	
Few supporting facts and details	
Many errors in grammar, mechanics, usage, and/or spelling	

Example C: Student Composition – Language Arts (Grade 2)

Composition Traits	10 Point Scale
A complete paragraph (at least three sentences) Subjects and verbs in all sentences Sentences produced with two or more descriptive words All words spelled correctly Correct punctuation and capitalization	10 - 8
A complete paragraph (at least three sentences) Subjects and verbs in all sentences At least one descriptive word in most sentences Correct spelling on most words Few punctuation and capitalization errors	7 - 5
Incomplete paragraph Sentences/phrases with missing subjects/verbs Few descriptive words Many spelling errors Missing and/or incorrect punctuation and/or capitalization	4 - 1
No attempt to produce written assignment	0

Running Records

"Running records" (see Figure 8-1) is a relatively new term to many educators, although research leading to its development can be traced back to the 1970s. Since that time, many schools across the nation have implemented RR as part of their literacy programs. Running records are intended to aid the teacher in determining two important factors: (1) what cueing systems and strategies readers are drawing upon to help them in their reading, and (2) whether the books or texts are within the reading range of the child.

As most elementary school teachers are aware, readers bring several cueing systems to the task of reading, namely: *graphophonic, syntactic,* and *semantic.*

- *Graphophonic knowledge* – gained through visual clues, i.e., configuration of letters, words patterns (e.g., met, get, set, pet)
- *Syntactic knowledge* – gained by studying word order and the structure of sentences
- *Semantic knowledge* – gained through the use of contextual information. Readers ask themselves, "Does this word make sense?" or "Does this sentence make sense?"
- *Morphemic knowledge* (structural analysis) – gained through study of units contained within words (e.g., prefixes, suffixes, root words, word endings)

Figure 8-1
Running Records Report

Name _____ Developmental Language Stage_____

Book/Story Title _____

Language of Text _____ Source (trade book, basal)

Word Count	Page No.	Errors	Accuracy Rate	Error Rate	Self-Correction Rate	Date

Comments:

When used by proficient readers, these systems work in unison and are self-regulating. For students having difficulty with reading, however, it is important for teachers and special educators to determine ways of engaging the systems.

The Running Records approach is not difficult although it does require time and some training. The process requires "plotting" a reader by using various marks and notations as he or she reads a text or passage (e.g., 100-150 words).

Implications for Teachers of Students with LLC
- Running records allow the teacher to identify individual strengths and weaknesses in the three cueing systems and to determine readability levels.
- Because RR can be used with virtually any printed text, it provides a quick means of reading assessment using everything from comic books to math story problems.
- RR also provides an excellent tool for charting English language development (decoding, vocabulary, fluency) among students with LLC and other second-language learners.

Oral Evaluation/Assessment

An oral evaluation can be used to obtain a comprehensive and accurate assessment of student knowledge and skills. This is obviously true of non-readers, poor readers, and students with limited English ability. The following suggestions are intended to guide teachers through oral evaluations of students with LLC:

- Warm up with discussion to help the student focus on the content of the test and to put the student at ease.

- Speak clearly. Use simple language matched to the student's level of English comprehension.
- Utilize interpreters when necessary.
- Provide sample questions that are similar to the ones you will be asking in the test.
- Include open-ended questions to obtain students' opinions, perceptions, interpretations, etc.
- Allow simple responses to questions, but encourage students to elaborate.
- Repeat student responses to validate them.
- Record student responses on audio or video tape.
- Play back the taped evaluation for the student. Ask if he/she wishes to change any responses.
- Discuss the evaluation experience. Reassure the student.

Anecdotal Records

Anecdotal records have been used for years by professionals in many fields. Their value to educators depends primarily on the *ways* in which they are used. In special education, for example, the uses have ranged from informal kidwatching to formal qualitative research. It is not unusual to find notes, charts, and logs in students' I.E.P. files. Many teachers find such records to be inherently valuable as running commentaries on student behavior and progress. They look for patterns, and then change and record their observations as they are happening. Through observation, teachers are able to note subtleties in attitudes, motivation, and moods. All of these "snapshots" provide a composite picture of student behavior that is difficult to derive from other assessments. There is no one way to develop anecdotal records. However, the following suggestions may prove productive:

- **Make an appointment and keep it** – Designate a time daily or weekly to observe a student.
- **Vary observation time** – Try for a cross-section sampling of the student's school day.
- **Develop individual logs or journals** – Dignify your efforts by maintaining formal records of information that will be shared with peers/parents/administrators, and/or I.E.P team members.
- **Work collaboratively** – Teachers of students with LLC should be able to share their judgments and recommendations from student observations.
- **Determine assessment value** – Decide how the anecdotal records will be used in your overall assessment and student evaluation plans.

Teacher-Developed Tests and Measures

One obvious benefit of teacher-created tests and measures is that the teacher knows the students better than the publishers of such measures. Other important factors worth noting include:

- The teacher is able to select test items, testing format, and time frame.
- The teacher is in control of the test vocabulary and therefore able to customize it.
- Teacher-constructed tests and measures may yield a better and fairer sampling of student knowledge and skills than the publisher's materials.

- Information revealed from teacher measures provides valuable feedback about teaching effectiveness.

Teachers employ a range of personally-developed tests and measures. They include paper-and-pencil tests of content and skills assessment, oral tests and recitations, and criteria for demonstrations, performances, and/or presentations.

Criterion-Referenced Measures

Norman Gronlund (1973), who has written extensively on the use of instructional objectives in classroom teaching, defined criterion-referenced testing as measures of student achievement without reference to the levels of performance of other students within a group. Generally speaking, traditional teacher-made tests may be classified as criterion-referenced. Typically, teachers do not construct norm-referenced tests in an attempt to standardize performance levels within subject areas. They simply want to sample student progress toward curriculum goals. Criterion-referencing has been widely used in special education, where goals and objectives have been reduced, segmented, and individualized. Scales and checklists can often be used as self-evaluation tools (See Figure 8-2). The following examples illustrate the features of criterion-referencing.

Criterion-referenced objective:

Given paper and pencil, Blake will write the correct answers to 80% of the test items within the time allowed.

This statement meets three minimum requirements of criterion-referenced assessment:
- the behavior – *will write the correct answers*
- the conditions under which the task will be performed – *Given paper and pencil, within the time allowed*
- the degree of proficiency or acceptability – *80% of the test items*

Criterion-referenced goal:

By December, Elliott will read aloud 250 basic sight words from a Fry, Brigance, or Dolch basic sight word list with 100% accuracy.

In the second example, the conditions have been stated more generally because the statement is a goal. However, the three minimum requirements – behavior, conditions, and degree of proficiency – are all stated.

Implications for Teachers of Students with LLC
- Criterion-referenced tests describe rather than compare performances. They are useful in documenting progress not obvious from stanines, percentiles, test scores, etc.
- Criterion-referenced measures are a fair and logical tool for use with students with LLC. When these measures are used, students compete only against themselves on I.E.P. goals and objectives.
- Teachers and special educators should predetermine reasonable expectation levels when negotiating I.E.P. goals and objectives for students with LLC.

Figure 8-2
Examples of Self-Evaluation Tools

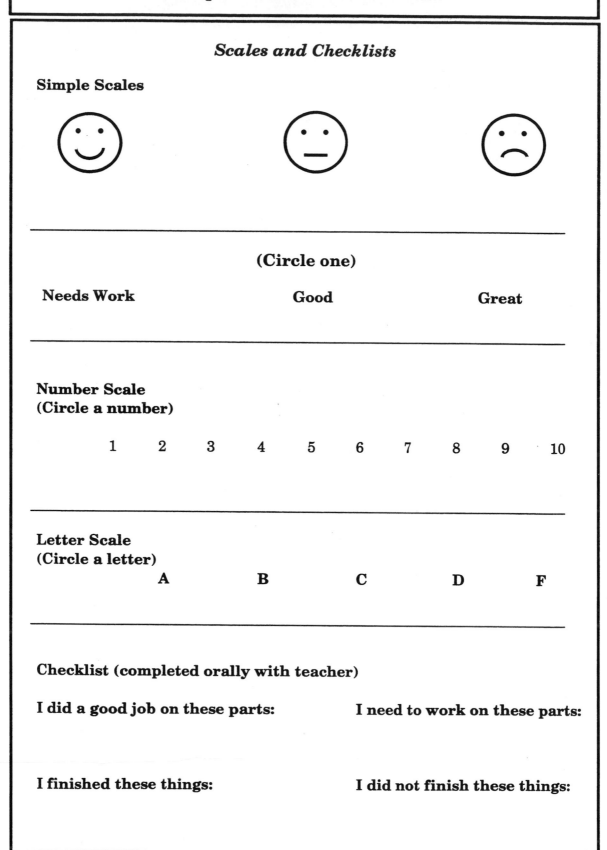

Scales and Checklists

Simple Scales

(Circle one)

Needs Work   Good   Great

Number Scale
(Circle a number)

1   2   3   4   5   6   7   8   9   10

Letter Scale
(Circle a letter)

A   B   C   D   F

Checklist (completed orally with teacher)

I did a good job on these parts: I need to work on these parts:

I finished these things: I did not finish these things:

- Criterion-referenced measures should become *part* of the overall assessment.
- Demanding mastery of specific goals and objectives may sometimes be unreasonable. Failure to master them may be due to a mismatch between the learner's readiness level and the teacher's expectation.
- Cultural differences may sometimes dictate the "conditions" component of criterion-referenced measures and performances. In some cultures, for example, collaborative work is viewed as superior to individual achievement.

Rating Scales

Sometimes educators wish to rate or rank student performances without adherence to strict standardized measures. One common instrument widely used in the nation's schools is the rating scale, used to observe and critique student work and behaviors. It can take many forms – from simple rank-ordering of students by performance on a recent exam to school-wide performance-ratings by teams of teachers. Like other assessments, the purpose determines the measure's complexity, as well as its implications.

Strengths:

- Rating scales provide information about observable behaviors and/or products.
- Scales can be easily constructed and used informally or as part of broader assessments.

Cautions:

- Rating scales are typically subjective and purpose-specific.
- Validity and reliability decrease as the number of persons using the same instrument increases. Each person brings his/her own background and interpretations to the task of rating student work or behaviors.

Inventories

When some teachers hear the word *inventory*, it calls to mind checklists, files, forms, and other chores of accountability. Inventories can provide evidence of student growth. They show at a glance the areas of strength and accomplishment and the areas of need. Sometimes the inventories are imposed on teachers by administrators or state dictates, as measures of teacher effectiveness as much as student achievement. These may yield little information about student progress toward a teacher's goals, and probably even less about students' personal goals. Published inventories are commonly found in reading, writing, and math programs, and to a lesser extent in the arts and social sciences. The "Reading Check" in Figure 8-3 is an example of an inventory. This inventory is divided into three separate levels for use in assessing students at various stages in their development of reading skills.

Teacher-constructed inventories will probably be more useful. The object is not to reinvent the wheel merely in another style. Rather, the object is to carefully select from the school curriculum, by subject area, those items you believe to be the most important. From your list, you should be able to rank order the items by their importance and/or relevancy. Chances are you will keep most of the items on the published inventory, but you will have done some weeding out and rearranging.

If your revised list is not preempted by school or district dictates, you should have a valuable and relevant instrument to gauge the progress of individual students toward classroom goals. It is both a compass and barometer.

**Figure 8-3
Emergent, Early, and Fluent Reading Checklists**

EMERGENT READING CHECK

*Name*_____ *Age*_____

	COMMENT	DATE
Enjoys listening to stories		
Chooses to read from various resources		
Can sit for a time and read a book		
Participates confidently in Shared Reading		
Retells stories and rhymes		
Likes to write		
Understands that writers use letter symbols to construct meaning		
Can show the front cover of a book		
Understands that the print carries the message		
Uses pictures as clues to the story line		
Knows where to start reading the text		
Knows which way to go, L–R, and to return		
Can point and match 1–1 as teacher reads		
Can indicate word		
Can indicate the space between the words		
Can recognize some high-frequency words both in and out of context		
Can write some high-frequency words independently		

Source: Trail, L. (1995). *Highlight My Strengths*. Crystal, IL: Rigby Education. Reprinted with permission.

EARLY READING CHECK

*Name*_____   *Age*_____

	COMMENT	DATE
Enjoys listening to stories		
Chooses to read independently		
Chooses to explore unfamiliar resources		
Beginning to take initiative for responding creatively to books		
Is confident to share feelings about books		
Participates confidently in Shared Reading		
Participates confidently in Shared Writing		
Developing ability to retell longer stories in sequence		
Developing ability to recall facts in informational books		
Writes with confidence and enthusiasm		
Developing ability to identify approximations in personal writing		
Takes responsibility for selecting words for personal writing		
Takes responsibility for selecting words for personal spelling lists		
Less reliant on illustrations as a clue to make meaning		
Beginning to cross-check a number of meaning-making strategies when reading, *e.g.* - checks language predictions by looking at letters		
- rereads, or reruns to check		
- brings own knowledge of oral and written language to reading		
Beginning to check graphophonic detail as a means of confirming predictions		
Expects to get meaning from text		

Source: Trail, L. (1995). *Highlight My Strengths*. Crystal, IL: Rigby Education. Reprinted with permission.

FLUENT READING CHECK

Name_____ Age_____

	COMMENT	DATE
Enjoys listening to longer stories		
Enjoys listening to chapter-book stories as well as picture books		
Reads silently for leisure, pleasure, and information		
Chooses to read independently from an increasing variety of genres for a variety of purposes		
Chooses to explore unfamiliar resources		
Reads chapter books and nonfiction informational texts of particular interest		
Expects to have independent control of first reading of an unseen text and demonstrates confidence when doing so		
Emergent and early reading strategies are secure and habituated		
Integrates and cross checks language cues effectively		
Monitors and checks own reading with confidence		
Becomes more critical and reflective about the messages and information in text		
Expects challenges – demonstrates strategies for handling them		
Is able to summarize information		
Proofreads writing and shows increased knowledge of systems for conventional spellings		
Demonstrates a growing understanding of writing in different registers for different purposes		
Is able to locate information in index		
Contributes effectively in Shared Reading		
Contributes effectively in Shared Writing		
Confident independent reader, ready to go on reading to learn and using reading and writing as tools for learning		

Source: Trail, L. (1995). *Highlight My Strengths*. Crystal, IL: Rigby Education. Reprinted with permission.

Implications for Teachers of Students with LLC

- Inventories are widely used in both bilingual and special education. They help track student progress and deficits.
- Reading inventories should be matched to the language proficiency level of L2 students.
- Informal inventories can be developed for virtually any subject area.
- Teachers of students with LLC may choose to work on the same or separate inventory items. It is important for regular and special educators to coordinate their efforts.
- Inventories can become part of overall assessment.
- Peer tutors and interpreters may be required to reach outcomes stated in the I.E.P.

Part 3
Developing Individualized Programs of Instruction

In my view, there are two aspects to teaching. The first is to put students into contact with phenomena related to the area to be studied – the real thing, not books or lectures about it – and to help them notice what is interesting; to engage them so they will continue to think and wonder about it. The second is to have the students try to explain the sense they are making, and, instead of explaining things to students, to try to understand their sense.
Eleanor Duckworth

Chapter 9
Strategies for Maximizing Learning

The term 'at risk' overlooks the portion of the learner that may well be 'at promise.'

Carol Ann Tomlinson

The ultimate goal of instruction is to enable learners to move as far and as fast as possible toward independence. To achieve this goal, attention must be given to many aspects of their lives in addition to "school learning." We must consider many variables, including learning styles and multiple intelligences, cultural and linguistic backgrounds, and personality. We must examine curricula and instruction in light of individual needs as well as societal needs. We must consider learners' goals and aspirations as well as our own. In short, we must strive to differentiate and personalize learning to the maximum extent possible.

Differentiating Instruction

Differentiating instruction is not a matter of adding more of the same work under the guise of "challenge" to gifted learners. Nor is it reducing the amount of the same work for underachievers. Differentiated instruction is the creation of qualitatively different learning experiences both inside and outside of the classroom. Whereas the traditional classroom marched students through the same lockstep curriculum, differentiated classroom instruction considers individual as well as whole group needs. It recognizes that all students are not naturally interested or fully engaged in every assignment – no matter how well-planned. All students are not at the exact same points in their development – linguistic, intellectual, social, psychological, and/or physical. Differentiated instruction acknowledges that some students are better at reading and language tasks while others excel at technical or mathematical pursuits. Some students with learning disabilities might demonstrate greater computer aptitude than their peers, although they struggle with writing assignments (Hearne, 1987; Hearne & Stone, 1996). Although some gifted students excel in academics, they may exhibit poor social skills, limited musical abilities, lack of physical coordination, or other "deficits" that are not measured by academic achievement measures.

The personal interests of students play a vital role in learning. How do we attend to the varied interests and needs of our students in the classroom? How do we attend to the range of varied abilities? How do we transform a lockstep curriculum into an adaptable learning continuum? We might begin by thinking about and addressing each of the topics that follow:

Topic 1: Thinking About Students

Recognizing and Accepting Differences

Acknowledging cultural and linguistic differences is an imperative of sound pedagogy. However, the typical classroom is marked by several other student variables – ability levels, behavior, creativity, and personality. In order to address these variables, teachers must be willing to provide support at multiple levels and in varied ways. It is becoming increasingly important that teachers develop a wide repertoire of approaches. They might begin by doing the following:

- taking classes, workshops, and/or lessons on wide-ranging topics, particularly as they impact the school lives of students with LLC
- inviting parents and/or other family members to present/participate in classroom lessons
- developing a pool of talents and strengths observed among students and identifying ways to utilize these abilities across various content areas and grade/ability levels
- seeking out district and community resources to enhance learning opportunities for students with LLC
- establishing school/classroom procedures for informally monitoring failure due to individual differences

Capitalizing on Student Interests

As mentioned earlier in this book, learning is influenced greatly by *interest* in the subject matter being taught. Whatever is most interesting to a child at a given time is what he/she determines to be *worth learning*. Imposing "school learning" without considering the general interests of students is a recipe for poor pedagogy at best, and failure at worst. There are many ways to identify and incorporate students' interests, among them:

- oral and/or written interest inventories
- examining samples of students' work
- studying patterns of behavior
- documenting student preferences
- creating forced-choice situations to help students clarify what interests them most
- interviewing/conferencing with parents to gain information and insights
- watching students on the playground and in other situations
- having students develop a list of their personal interests
- helping students develop actual lessons on topics of their choice
- engaging students in inquiry and projects related to specific interests

Adapting to Individual Needs

Infusing the curriculum with student interests is perhaps the easier part. Adapting it to individual needs, regardless of interest level, can be much more challenging. In planning instruction at the individual level, teachers must keep in mind that merely watering down and stretching out the curriculum – even high interest topics – does not necessarily create a curriculum that is suitable for the *needs* of the students. If a text-driven curriculum results in repeated failure, the curriculum and materials used may be the source of the problems being observed. Recognizing such patterns, the skilled teacher would instinctively try qualitatively different approaches and materials – not increased doses of the text. There is a wealth of information, materials, and instructional approaches available to teachers of students with LLC. Aside from the ones discussed in this book, readers are encouraged to contact agencies and organizations listed in Appendix B.

Using Students' Strengths to Facilitate Learning

Many, if not most, teachers report that they entered the profession because of a desire to use their knowledge and skills to help students learn. Others, particularly at the secondary level, enter the field because of a passion for specific subject areas – English, history, math, science, art, movement, etc. In such cases, it is clearly evident that these teachers wish to teach from their own interests and strengths. In culturally diverse classrooms, however, the teachers' interests and strengths often mismatch those of many of their students. Once teachers get beyond this disappointment and are willing to explore students' interests and strengths, they may find many bridges that strengthen the bond between teacher and student. English language learners with LD might present special challenges for teachers unaccustomed to looking for strengths and potential, but they can also be catalysts for change. Once the teacher is introduced to the notion of meeting special needs, the door is potentially open to other differing "views." It cannot be stated too often that learners build best and most efficiently upon their existing knowledge, skills, strengths, and personal interests. To abandon such logic in favor of pre-packaged curricula is counter-productive and often serves only to exacerbate the problems faced by students with LLC.

Independence Versus Learned Helplessness

The phenomenon of learned helplessness has been studied widely in the field of learning disabilities, particularly as it is manifested in the classroom. Stated simply, the learner has come to associate learning with dependency upon teachers, aides, peers, parents, or other persons. It is common to find teachers or parents actually doing the work for the child who is having trouble keeping up with the rest of the class. Sometimes it is simply more time-efficient for a teacher to put the finishing touches on a paper, worksheet, or project than it is to repeat or re-teach the concept, skill, or lesson. What are the cumulative effects of such practice? Over time, such dependency can contribute to feelings of both inadequacy and low self-esteem and, in extreme cases, self-fulfilling prophecy. In the latter condition, the learner has come to expect certain outcomes. The child who frequently makes statements such as, "See, I told you I couldn't do it" or "I never get it right" might well see failure as the only reasonable expectancy. Such ideas are often planted during the child's early years, at home and/or school.

One way that teachers can begin to address such conditions is by identifying where the child is academically, socially, and emotionally. Instruction should begin within the child's zone of comfort in each of these areas. It takes time to move the learner from a level of dependency to one of challenge and growth. However, there are a number of ways to approach the problem:

- Identify the child's strengths, talents, and interests and make these the organizing center for adapting curriculum and instruction.
- Look for or create classroom situations in which the student can experience success and have it validated by classmates.
- Challenge the student to reach just beyond self-perceived "limits." Start small and increase the challenges incrementally within the student's comfort zone.
- Praise progress and success, no matter how small.
- Include the student's work samples in classroom/school displays and discussions.
- Invite the parent/guardian to various events that showcase the child's work, skill, or talent. Validation from parents is critical to the child's self-esteem and sense of accomplishment.
- Pair the student with a peer who challenges but does not overshadow him/her.
- In cooperative grouping, assign the student tasks that are manageable and reinforcing.
- Have the student chart personal progress in academic, linguistic, and/or social skills.

Grouping

As discussed elsewhere in this book, grouping for instruction has become common classroom practice. The value of grouping depends upon its purpose. Cooperative grouping in the general classroom, for example, can be extremely beneficial for students with LLC who are teamed with supportive peers. Cooperative learning may hold multiple purposes, among them:

- team-building
- community-building
- task completion
- academic learning
- communication development
- leadership skill development

Teachers should keep in mind the *real* purposes for grouping. Not all groups need to be formed for academic pursuits. Neither should the teacher feel compelled to "grade" every group activity. Sometimes students simply need to interact and exchange ideas in pairs and small groups without the constriction of academic responsibility. As shown below, groups can be formed for a variety of formal and informal tasks:

Formal Group Tasks
    Process writing assignments
    Group inquiry
    Planning a classroom play
    Problem-solving

Informal Group Tasks
    Planning a class picnic
    "Getting-to-know-you" tasks
    Discussions
    Interest sharing

Topic 2: Thinking About Content

While school systems typically dictate the general content of curricula, individualized education plans can mediate problems that arise for language and learning challenged students. When teachers participate in content selection, however, there are wonderful opportunities to develop classroom activities that more closely match the needs and interests of their students.

Focus of the Curriculum

Curricula, for the most part, are generally dictated by state and local district guidelines. What has come to be known as "core curriculum" refers to the basic content areas: language arts, math, science, social studies, physical education, and often music and the arts. Computer instruction has also made its way into the core curriculum in many school systems across the nation. However, when planning instruction at the individual school and classroom levels, educators will need to determine what represents *core* curriculum – as distinguished from *minimal* and/or *desired* curriculum.

On a curriculum continuum, the *core* sits firmly in the center. As schools and teachers begin to map out their school year around the core curriculum, they will need to decide also what is "minimally" acceptable. This is an important component of planning in today's inclusive classrooms, where students from diverse backgrounds and ability levels work together. The *minimal curriculum* differs from the core curriculum in another important aspect – materials, instruction, and evaluation may differ from student to student, according to individual needs.

At the other end of the continuum, *desired curriculum* reflects what the teacher, school, or district most value and aspire toward – a kind of educational "wish list." While such a curriculum would certainly include accommodations for students with diverse needs, it would probably be designed primarily as an "enrichment" curriculum. Figure 9-1 illustrates how the three designs might compare and contrast. The minimal curriculum engages all students in the same content and similar instruction. However, it has been adapted to accommodate students such as the language-and-learning-challenged.

Scope and Sequence

Efforts to use state, district, or school mandates to determine *what* to teach (scope) and the order in which the information is to be presented (sequence) is often problematic for teachers of students with LLC. Probably few states (and even fewer school systems) have developed K-12 curricula specifically for students with language and learning challenges. In the absence of such models, classroom teachers must become curriculum "developers" much like the LD Specialist, bilingual program specialist, and/or other support personnel. When planning for students with LLC, there are many important factors to consider in deciding the scope and sequence of the curriculum, among them:

- **Learning Profiles** – Relative strengths and weaknesses in each content area are important factors to consider. One common characteristic of students with learning disabilities is uneven development in academic and/or social areas.

- **Performance Patterns** – Student performance patterns and the conditions that possibly contributed to them are paramount to understanding learning behaviors. Fluctuations in performance, for example, might be related more to frequent absences than to learning disabilities or language barriers.

Figure 9-1
The Minimal, Core, and Desired Curriculum

Minimal Curriculum	Core Curriculum	Desired Curriculum

Multiplication

Times facts through 10's
Solution of 5 story
  problems
Peer/Aide/Teacher-
  assisted applications
	Times facts through 20's
	Solution of 20 story
	  problems
	Independent study and
	  applications
		Creation of times games
		Student-created story
		  problems/riddles
		Computer and/or logo
		  applications

Short Story

Read paragraph aloud
  with only 4 miscues.
Identify all characters
  in the story.
Write 2 reasons telling why
  you liked/disliked it.
	Read 500 word passage
	  aloud with only 4 miscues.
	Identify major elements of
	  fiction in the story.
	Write a different story ending.
		Read a short story and
		  discuss with a peer.
		Write a review/critique
		  of the story.
		Write a play based on the
		  short story.

Colonial America

Name the 13 colonies.
Match all colonies to
  drawings on a map
Discuss 2 reasons for the
  Revolutionary War
	Name, spell, and place the 13
	  colonies on a map.
	Draw a map depicting the
	  13 colonies and major cities.
	Write an essay on major
	  reasons for the
	  Revolutionary War.
		Discuss how the 13
		  colonies were settled.
		Create relief map showing
		  terrain and cities.
		Engage in debates
		  about the pros and cons
		  of the Revolutionary
		  War.

- **Approach** – The mode of instruction is intended to match the learner. The sheer volume of content may dictate the instructional approach. In social studies, for example, the time devoted to learning all the important dates and facts may pre-empt altogether highly relevant and stimulating activities such as role-playing and simulation games.

Selecting Books and Materials

In selecting materials for use with diverse populations, teachers should also ask students themselves to preview items. Their input and opinions might prevent mismatches of interest and/or abilities, as well as oversights.

Topic 3: Thinking About Instruction

A recurring theme in this book is the necessity of matching the method to the learner rather than forcing the learner to fit the method. While some knowledge and skills are easily acquired through direct instruction and practice, deeper level learning may derive from hands-on and reflective experiences. A student's learning profile and performance patterns can reveal much about the ways in which he/she approaches learning. In fact, the language and learning challenged student himself may know best the next piece of information or experience needed in a given learning situation. Inviting the learner to participate in curriculum planning is not abdication of responsibility or authority. On the contrary, it conveys trust and respect for the learner.

Building on Prior Knowledge

No matter what the student's background, each child brings to school a wealth of real world experiences upon which to build. Knowledge of these experiences allows the teacher to plan instruction that is individualized and relevant to the student's needs. One might begin by conducting a review of school records, followed by a conference, phone call, or home visit with the parent. By using the information obtained in conjunction with information obtained from various professionals at school, a comprehensive profile of the student's specific strengths and weaknesses can be compiled. Other strategies for gaining insights into students' prior knowledge might include:

- administering interest inventories (oral or written in the primary language)
- assessing performance in specific skill areas
- assessing specific areas of intelligence (i.e., "multiple intelligences" assessment)
- observing behavior in various situations
- interviewing the student
- interviewing siblings and friends of the student

Once the teacher has gathered this information, there is a stronger "data base" from which to plan instructional programs. However, instructional approaches may be:

- **Student-selected** – The student chooses how lessons and information will be presented (e.g., orally, visually, physically, written, etc.).

- **Negotiated** – The student, teacher, and/or specialist negotiate content and instruction (either or both).

- **Teacher-selected** – The general classroom teacher makes all decisions about pedagogy, based upon knowledge of student's background and experiences.

- **Specialist-selected** – The LD specialist, speech-language pathologist, and/or other specialists collaborate to determine the appropriate instructional approach, based upon the student's background.

- **Team-selected** – A team consisting of the teacher, specialists, and parents/guardians select the methods that will be used in classroom instruction.

Regardless of the approach selected, each must begin where the learner is, using prior knowledge to build bridges to new learning.

Teaching and Learning in Context

Attempting to teach a child how to swim by showing drawings or pictures of the body (arms, hands, legs, feet) in proper positions is a fairly futile approach. What students (or adults for that matter) would be interested in learning the latest dance if they first had to study hundreds of pictures or drawings of the feet in various positions before they were allowed to dance? Probably few, if any. Learning new skills is best accomplished through direct experience in contexts where these skills are actually being used. Equally important is an understanding of how to apply acquired skills to new situations.

In reading, for example, students in kindergarten and first grade begin to learn the rudiments of literacy: alphabet letters, sound-symbol relationship, decoding skills, word recognition, etc. This is generally accomplished through a combination of drill-and-practice and story book reading. Students are likely to hear hundreds of narratives during the first few years of school, all of which require the same kind of reading skills. However, as students progress through the grades, they are introduced to other forms of print, "textbooks," which require different and/or additional kinds of reading skills. In social studies, for example, students learn to read maps and charts. In math, they must learn to read graphs, figures, and other numerical formats. This reading differs from narrative reading in several ways. First of all, it is *technical* reading, which engages the student in levels of critical thinking not necessary for the interpretation or understanding of story books or other narratives. For many readers, information in textbooks can be "decontextualized" to the point of frustration. For instance, map-reading and mathematical charts presented in isolation, without a "story context" may have little meaning to students. Math teachers are frequently concerned about the number of students who have difficulty with word/story problems. Perhaps the story problems themselves lack adequate context or comprehensible language. Simply stated, reading is not a generic skill or ability that transfers readily to all areas of the curriculum or all new situations. For this reason, all teachers need to be involved in the teaching of reading.

Students for whom language and academic learning are a challenge are frequently the first to experience frustration when called upon to apply their present skills to new situations. For this reason, teachers must plan ahead to "scaffold" new experiences for students with LLC. In other words, teachers must identify and/or create contexts that will enhance opportunities for learning.

Engaging Students as Both Learners and Teachers

The adage that "To teach is to learn twice," is particularly relevant here, not merely for its implications of reinforced knowledge and skills, but also for its heuristic value. When students are encouraged to think like *teachers*, they must consider how others might learn differently from themselves. In the process, they are allowed to re-frame questions and issues, take others' perspectives, and generally "think" in other ways. These are not activities that should be used exclusively in gifted and talented programs, but rather applied liberally throughout the general school curriculum. Critical thinking skills are equally important to students with LLC as they are to their peers. There are many ways to engage learners with LLC in teaching roles, among them:

- **Job Fairs** (upper elementary) – Students explore interesting occupations and teach what they learn to a peer, group, or class.
- **Special skills** – Students identify at least one skill at which they are particularly adept and develop lessons to teach other students who are struggling with that skill.
- **Cross-age teaching** – Students are paired/placed with students at another age/grade level to teach specific skills and convey new information.
- **Co-teaching** – Students identify a concept or skill around which they develop a lesson collaboratively with the teacher or aide.
- **Peer-teaching** – Students with LLC work collaboratively with peers who are functioning at "grade level" to develop a lesson and present it to the class.
- **Tutoring** – Students engage in ongoing tutorials with peers and students at other age/grade levels.
- **Demonstrations/Performances** – Students select a scene, act, process, dance, or other behavior to demonstrate to the class.

Core Curriculum – Simplify and Complicate

Instructional approaches like learners themselves should be viewed as a continuum. No one instructional model or approach fits every child, and yet the typical core curriculum and accompanying textbooks are aimed at *all* students. In order to best serve the needs and interests of all students along the continuum of "individual differences," teachers must devise ways of adapting the core curriculum.

One model, advocated by LeBlanc (1998), suggests that teachers envision all classroom instruction as a continuum, with the core curriculum goals at its midpoint. In planning instruction for students with disabilities or learning problems, the teacher would "simplify" content and instruction. Students beyond the midpoint might need more challenge than the core curriculum provides. The teacher would create ways to "complicate" the core curriculum to more closely match the ability levels of these students. Complication, in this case, implies *challenge*. This might seem like an oversimplification of the process. There are, however, many ways for teachers to infuse curriculum and instruction for individuals all along the continuum. In the example presented in Figure 9-2, one major area of study from the California core curriculum is used to illustrate how California Mission History can be adapted for diverse populations.

Topic 4: Thinking About Assessment and Evaluation

Use Authentic Assessment Techniques

In a previous chapter of this book, readers were introduced to a wide range of tools and procedures for evaluating student achievement and progress. *Authentic* and *holistic* assessment should be the guiding principles in educational evaluation. Students do not *all* learn best in a single modality or at the same speed. Students also differ in the types of experiences that they need to acquire new information. Students create learning and meaning *individually* and *personally* – in their own ways.

**Figure 9-2
Example of Curriculum Adaptations**

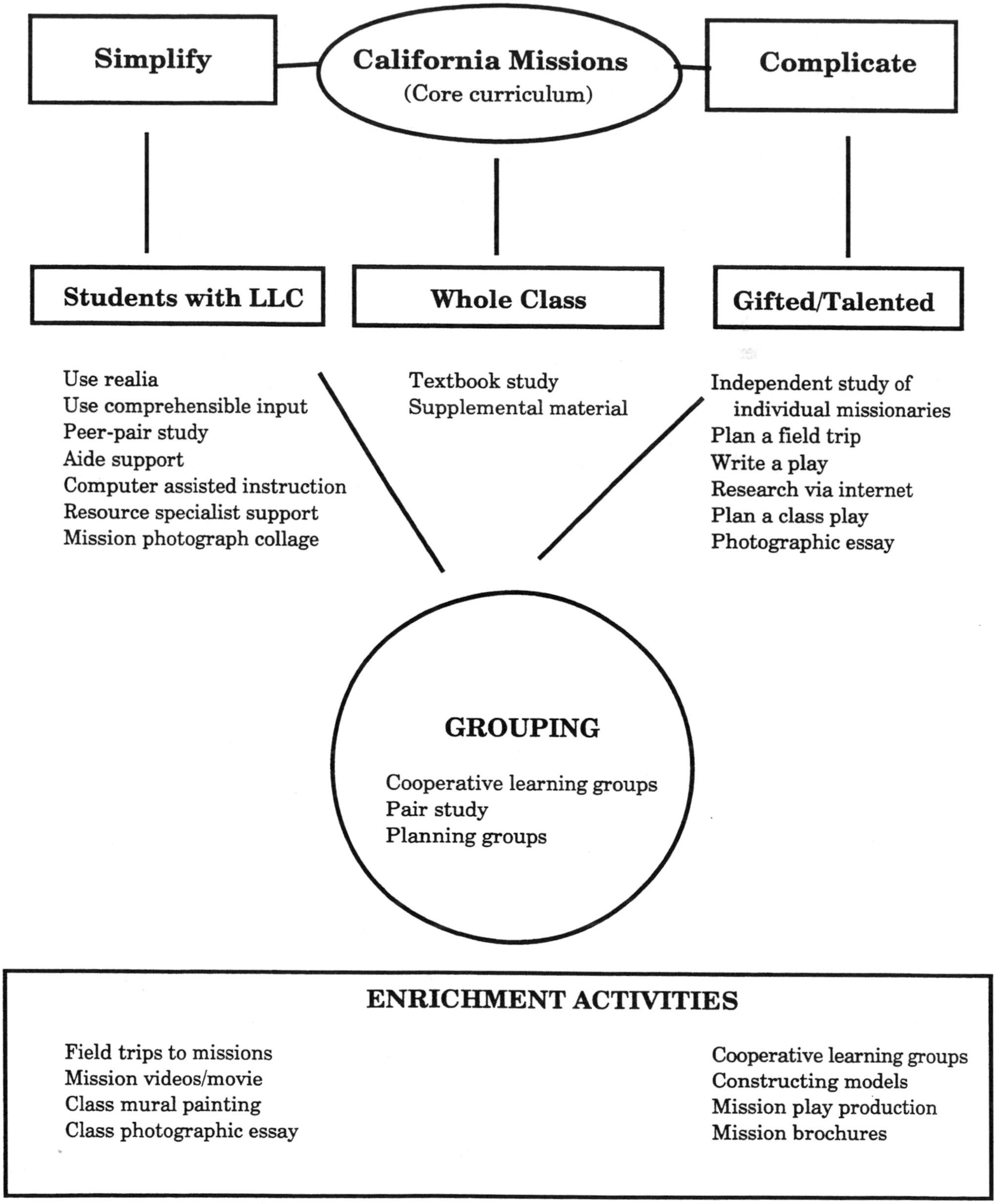

Simplify — **California Missions**
(Core curriculum) — **Complicate**

Students with LLC	**Whole Class**	**Gifted/Talented**

Students with LLC

Use realia
Use comprehensible input
Peer-pair study
Aide support
Computer assisted instruction
Resource specialist support
Mission photograph collage

Whole Class

Textbook study
Supplemental material

Gifted/Talented

Independent study of
    individual missionaries
Plan a field trip
Write a play
Research via internet
Plan a class play
Photographic essay

GROUPING

Cooperative learning groups
Pair study
Planning groups

ENRICHMENT ACTIVITIES

Field trips to missions   Cooperative learning groups
Mission videos/movie   Constructing models
Class mural painting   Mission play production
Class photographic essay   Mission brochures

Why then, other than for reasons of efficiency, do we insist upon assessing student growth with narrow measures? How can the "basics" be assessed without teaching to the paper and pencil tests that measure them? Of what true value and long-range significance are results of standardized tests? A partial response to these questions, as they relate to language and learning challenged students, would include the following points:

- Assessment should measure growth – not merely mastery. Instruments and procedures must therefore yield both breadth and depth of *learning* and *learner* behaviors.
- Authentic assessment can include paper-and-pencil tests, as well as consider performance on standardized tests – as parts of the whole picture.
- While there is still widespread debate as to what constitutes the "basics," reading, writing, and arithmetic are all arguably at the center. Although skills continua and hierarchies typically serve as the organizing models for curriculum development, assessment typically consists of verbal and logical-mathematical measures – written and/or oral. However, the rapid growth of the learning disabilities field in the last 30 years provides strong evidence that such approaches have failed many students in our schools.
- Assessment measures that fail to take into account cultural and linguistic backgrounds and experiences produce flawed and discouraging pictures of student knowledge and behaviors.

Topic 5: Thinking About Management

Classroom management is a top priority in classrooms with diverse populations. Teachers must orchestrate a range of learning activities appropriate to individual and group needs. However, there are some general suggestions that teachers might find helpful. For openers, start with an open mind – and proceed gradually. The task is neither to *save* them all nor to *change* them all. You make a difference simply be being there – and trying. In your quest to become "Teacher on the Mount," however, the following sources can provide fine guidance and inspiration.

> *The Quality School* (1990) by William Glasser
> *The Quality School Teacher* (1994) by William Glasser
> *Managing Classrooms to Facilitate Learning* (1991) by A. Bauer
>   and R. Sapona
> *Conflict Resolution for Kids: A Group Facilitator's Guide* (1995) by P. Lane

Taking a Gradual Approach
Students do not need to learn everything TODAY. Teachers might begin their planning by simply previewing what they hope to accomplish in the coming year.

- Sit down and prioritize the curriculum.
- Include personal priorities.
- Establish year-end aims.
- Anticipate long-range needs.
- Plan extracurricular activities well in advance (e.g., field trips, classroom visitors, etc.).

- Contemplate ways to adapt instruction for students with language and learning challenges.
- Plan strategies of assessing general progress.
- Think of ways for students with LLC to take leadership and/or special responsibility roles.
- Plan ways to accommodate and/or challenge other students with special needs.

Beginning with Whole Group Instruction

Despite what might be stated in individualized education plans (I.E.P.), students with LLC frequently surprise their teachers with leaps of insight and/or knowledge on certain topics. Rather than working from their *deficits* to their *strengths*, these children should participate in general classroom instruction until they have demonstrated a *need* for assistance. By beginning instruction as a whole group activity, the teacher is able to study classroom dynamics – student interactions and behaviors. Careful observation will provide insights into student personalities and abilities, and how grouping might best work.

Once the class is engaged in meaningful learning, the teacher and/or aide can work with individuals and small groups that need additional help or alternative materials and instruction. By planning ahead, the teacher might be able to anticipate the needs of students with language and learning challenges. It is often productive to team with another teacher so that both large and small group instruction can be presented.

Instituting Self-Management

Students who are held accountable for their own learning and behavior are likely to acquire responsibility and self-management traits. Although many students with learning disabilities reportedly have problems with organization and responsibility, teachers must keep in mind that frequently the intervening problem prevents them from assuming the same levels of responsibility as their non-LD peers. Teachers who become frustrated with students who lose papers, lose their place in reading, lose their place in line, or lose their pencils, paper and books, must realize that the underlying cause might be a *memory* problem – not a disorganization problem, per se. Hence, holding these students accountable for the same level of "organization" skills as their non-LD peers is perhaps unrealistic. This is not to suggest that the development of such skills is a low priority. Rather, it simply implies that these students might need an approach in which they can be reinforced in other ways. Consider, for example, the child who is constantly losing a pen or pencil. One intervention is to simply tie the pencil or pen with a long string and attach it to the desk with strong tape. Teachers might then provide these students with other organizational tips whereby they can better manage their materials and themselves. Other management tips are included in the list below. The matrix in Figure 9-3 can be used to monitor learning.

Record Keeping

- Consider assigning numbers to students. This works great for tracking textbooks and other instructional materials.
- Have students distribute and collect materials.
- Develop a filing system simple enough for students to maintain portfolios/records.
- Set aside time daily to score, check, record, and/or respond to student work.

Figure 9-3
Monitoring Learning and Language Development

Use this matrix to monitor the amount of time students with LLC are engaged in various activities. Select a block of time daily to "kidwatch" – say, from 8:30 - 9:30 a.m. or intermittently during the school day. Over time, a pattern of information about learning and instruction will emerge. If, for example, you find after an eight-week period that a student is engaging more in independent activities, it may well indicate the student's readiness for more complex tasks and content. The patterns should assist you in decision-making regarding students' needs.

	Independent	Peer-Pair	Small Group	Large Group
Reading				
Writing				
Math				
Science				
Social Studies				
Art				
Music				
Sports				

Instruction

- Assess students periodically and utilize the information for instructional planning.
- Prioritize district/school "essential learnings." Map out a sensible plan.
- Use strategies for second language learning discussed in this book and elsewhere.
- Record important instructions. Let both L1 and L2 learners use the tapes.
- Utilize aides and bilingual students as peer interpreter-teachers.
- Use cooperative learning as a teaching aide – pair/group with a purpose in mind.
- Incorporate student-led class discussions and instruction.
- Seek out suggestions and materials from peers, administrators, and district personnel.

Grading/Evaluation

- Portfolios. Hold students responsible for contents.
- Authentic Assessment. Use holistic/rubric scoring where appropriate.
- Complete the most important assignments early. Score and record them.

Reporting

- Utilize bilingual personnel to prepare reports in the parent's primary language.
- Develop graphs, checklists, etc. to illustrate progress and areas of difficulty.
- Work on progress reports along the way – since you did the important things first!

Topic 6: Thinking About Learning Styles

Research and development in the areas of learning and teaching styles have contributed positively to classroom instruction. "Learning styles" has become an especially hot topic among special educators who continue to search for answers and responses to student underachievement. But what do we mean by learning styles? How does it impact learning inside and outside the classroom? How do we identify our students' learning styles? How do we best use this knowledge?

Dunn (1995) defined learning styles as, "how children learn. They develop through interactions of biology and experience" (p. 7). Each person learns differently – even within families, although some learning patterns become obvious to teachers who know what to look for. First, we must distinguish learning "modality" from learning style. We often speak of learning modalities or learning "preferences" when referring to sensory channels (visual, auditory, tactile, kinesthetic). We might hear, "Blake is a *visual learner*. But Juan, on the other hand, is an *auditory learner* who needs to hear the story read aloud." We also hear frequently that many learners have to write things down in order to remember them. Such statements hold the *senses* as referents. However, there are probably few extreme examples of such dependence on a single sense or *modality*. We must realize that learners use all senses and integrate them in proportion to need or applicability in given situations. A chef relies as much upon smell and taste in cooking and meal-planning as he/she does upon vision and touch (tactile/kinesthetic modes). Likewise, it would be absurd to suggest that Juan's other senses are of no particular value to him since he is an *auditory learner*.

When we speak of learning *styles*, on the other hand, we are referring to the larger constructs – *analytical* and *global* thinking and response. All learners think differently. They construct their own meanings and learning, and they interpret situations uniquely. All students do not use the same strategies to learn, despite traditionalist efforts to make them more uniform. Where some prefer to approach new learning through independent reading and study, others might need group activity or teacher feedback in order to assure learning. Dunn (1995) reported that "about 28% of students are peer-oriented" and show greater achievement when working with classmates than when working with the teacher or alone. An additional 28% "prefer learning with an adult" (pp. 15-16).

Some children tend to be global thinkers while others tend to be analytical thinkers. Difference can often be observed among these two groups in many aspects of behavior, as shown in Table 9-1.

Effects on Classroom Learning

Traditional classrooms have been characterized by structure, desks in rows, direct instruction, basal-centered content, and a prevailing passivity. In such classrooms, students who cannot sit still, jump from one idea or activity to another, or need to see finished product samples in order to know what is expected may be at risk of being perceived as underachievers or "difficult." Conversely, students whose thinking and learning styles match those of the teacher and/or textbook may be perceived as high achievers, even "gifted." Mismatch between teaching and learning styles is widespread (Dunn, 1995). The effects on student achievement are sometimes obvious, and, at other times, they are unknown. As educators, we should seek out these keys to success – both in our students and in ourselves. By understanding our own learning and teaching styles we might better adapt to those of our students.

Implications and Adaptation for Students with LLC

Over the years, several "inventories" to assess learning styles have been developed. Dunn and Dunn (1992) offered a comprehensive analysis in their *Individual Learning Styles approach*. They suggested that teachers do the following:

- **Ask students how they think they learn best**. This is an obvious and productive place to begin. In any language, school-age students should be able to provide information about what and *how* they like to learn. For kindergartners and first-graders, a teacher might begin with a simple *question-explanation-demonstration* approach. For example:

    Question - What is your favorite game?
    Explanation - How did you learn how to play that game?
    Demonstration - Please teach me (or another student) how to play it.

    Question - What do you like to learn about at school?
    Explanation - What is the most "fun way" to learn about it?
    Demonstration - Please teach me about (one thing) you learned at school.

> **TIP**: Have a peer interpreter pose the questions to the student. Students present information and questions in their own idiom. It is often more easily understood, and the responses are more natural and revealing.

- **Watch students to see how they respond and problem-solve**. The language of problem-solving is the language of learning. As mentioned throughout this

Table 9-1
Analytical Thinking vs. Global Thinking

When It comes to	Analytical thinkers tend to prefer	Global thinkers tend to prefer
1. Sound	Silence for concentrating	Some sound for concentrating
2. Light	Bright light for reading/studying	Very low light for reading/studying
3. Room temperature	Turning thermostat warmer, wearing heavy clothing	Turning thermostat cooler, wearing lightweight clothing (even in winter)
4. Furniture	Studying at a desk and chair	Studying on a bed or floor
5. Mobility	Sitting still for long periods of time	Moving around constantly
6. Time of day	Learning early in morning Going to bed early	Learning later in the day; staying up late
7. Eating	Eating breakfast and regular meals	Skipping breakfast; snacking
8. Learning	Working alone or under the direction of another person; being self-directed	Working in a group or peer learning; discovering rather than being told
9. Tasks	Working on one job at a time until done; being somewhat compulsive	Starting more jobs than they complete; procrastinating
10. Planning	Making lists for everything; planning far ahead; putting tasks on a calendar; avoiding risk-taking	Doing things when they feel like it; not planning ahead, but rather going with the flow; experimenting
11. Deciding	Taking a long time to make decisions; second-guessing decisions	Being spontaneous in making decisions; doing what feels right
12. Time	Punctuality; wearing watches with large numbers	Running late; wearing fashion watches with few or no numbers
13. Neatness	Neat, well organized appearance; outfits that go together	Disorganized appearance; clothes may not match
14. Perceiving	Seeing things as they are at the moment; noticing details	Seeing things as they might be; perceiving the whole, ignoring details
15. Assembling	Following directions step-by-step; starting over if they get stuck	Studying the picture/diagram, then assembling it their own way
16. Thinking	Logically, analytically, sequentially; seeing cause-effect; perceiving differences; understanding symbolic codes	Intuitively and randomly; seeing similarities and connections; working from whole to parts, from concrete to symbolic
17. Learning	Sequential tasks and concrete, logical steps	Learning through open-ended tasks, creating new ideas; learning through simile and metaphor
18. Remembering	Remembering what has been spoken	Remembering images of what has been seen and experienced
19. Taking tests	Predictable test formats (multiple choice, true-false, essay)	Opportunities to express themselves in ways other than writing

book, kidwatching is the most direct means of gaining clues to children's language and literacy development. Jean Piaget devoted a large portion of his professional life to the observation of children, both at play and in structured learning situations. From his observations, he was able to make certain judgments about the ways in which children constructed their own learning and solved their own problems – that is, their *learning styles*, as they have come to be known today.

- **Make changes and observe how it affects students.** As classroom teaching becomes routinized, students may come to accept learning as the act of doing things the teacher's way or the text's way. When the routine is disrupted by posing another way of framing a problem or finding a solution, students are forced to ask questions and consider other solutions. Making changes purely for the sake of variety is probably not beneficial for students with LLC.

- **Ask parents for information.** Parents can be strong allies in planning individualized instruction for students with LLC. They bring background knowledge of the student's social, developmental, and academic history. They can often provide insights about motivation and the aspirations of the student with LLC. It also dignifies the educational process to include parents as fully as possible – like their children, they are primary stakeholders in public education. Acquiring information from parents can be accomplished in several ways:

  - **Interviews/Conferences** – Set up informal conferences with parents before or after school.
  - **Written Survey** – Develop a simple questionnaire/opinionnaire (in the parents' primary language) to send home. Reward students for returning the questionnaire.
  - **Telephone Survey** – Set aside time to contact parents/guardians of students with LLC. The discussion might relate to items on the written survey.
  - **Letters/Notes** – Ask parents/guardians of students with LLC to share information and insights through written notes or letters.
  - **Home Visits** – Contact parents/guardians and arrange to meet with them in the convenience of their own homes. Such visits can provide insights into the students' life outside of school – in the neighborhood and in the home.
  - **Meetings of Parent-Teacher Groups** – Encourage parents to participate in group functions that involve both parents and teachers. Teachers may be able to meet with parents/guardians informally before or after meetings.
  - **Parent Workshops/Classes** – Teacher-led workshops on relevant topics may provide incentives for parents to visit the school or classroom. Teachers may be able to team by grade level to present information, engage parents in discussion, or to help parents/guardians in acquiring various skills.

Program Development Guidelines

The development of individualized instructional programs requires close cooperation between school specialists, teachers, and parents in all aspects of assessment and program planning. Although test results can be helpful, they generally fail to provide information about the student's interests, needs, and goals. They also fail to provide information about areas of "strength" that can be used to facilitate learning. The guidelines for program development below can be used as a checklist of "things to do" in the assessment and program planning process:

1. Determine the student's present levels of oral language proficiency (primary language and English).

2. Determine the student's present levels of written language proficiency (primary language and English).

3. Examine background information:
   - Student's support systems – family, community
   - Student's school records/history

4. Identify/review the student's strengths, interests, and talents. Use appropriate instruments.

5. Identify delivery models that are relevant to the student's needs.
   - Full inclusion in regular classroom with adaptations
   - Full inclusion in general classroom with support services
        Learning Disabilities Specialist and/or Bilingual Specialist
        Speech-Language Pathologist
        Adaptive Physical Education
        Counselor
        Instructional aide, peer tutor, volunteer

   - Pull-out program for a portion of the school day plus other support services
   - Special program placement (e.g., Special Day Class) for most or all of the school day

6. Determine monitoring procedures:
   - Meetings with parents/teachers and other team members
   - Periodic adjustments in curriculum and instruction

7. Review general classroom curriculum – academic and linguistic requirements

8. Develop a plan for adapting curriculum and instruction to student's needs
   - Identify material/resources needed
   - Select appropriate interventions/strategies/techniques
   - Select or develop evaluation tools and procedures
   - Create goals and objectives that target the student's interests, strengths, and talents

Using the "Let Them" Approach to Language Development and Literacy

In our good intentions to mediate learning for students who are language-and-learning challenged, we sometimes underestimate their abilities and thereby exclude them from rich learning experiences. The following points should be considered when developing programs for these students:

- Much important learning arises in its own time and frequently under *uncontrolled* conditions. Do not over-structure learning experiences.

- There is no *correct* order for the presentation of literary or artistic genres. Let students explore literary genres concurrently. Some will gravitate toward poetry and others will prefer stories.

- Let students experiment with *authoring* in the many genres. Some will excel with poetry, others with storytelling, and still others with drama. Students sell their own preferences to one another in ways that teachers cannot.

- Sometimes pictures, drawings, and other artwork speak more powerfully than the printed word. Link writing, art, and imagination together – let them illustrate.

- Students need to know that literary knowledge and skills are broadly applicable and valuable. Take them to libraries, movies, and literary events. *Create* literary events at school.

- Imagination and creativity cut across all cultures and languages. Read about imaginative people and their creations, discoveries, and/or ideas.

- Encourage students to be apprentices. Bring writers into the classrooms to share and model their talents.

- Encourage all students to explore their ideas both inside and outside the classroom. Students need to connect what happens in the classroom to other aspects of their lives.

- Encourage students to involve their parents and families in their learning and creative endeavors.

- Provide *students* with opportunities on some occasions to determine which direction the day's curriculum will take *you*. The courses they choose often result in those "teachable moments" that we as educators pray for.

Chapter 10
The Adaptive Instructional Model (AIM)

The *Adaptive Instructional Model* (AIM) is a multidimensional approach to teaching and learning that I developed based on my experiences in working with students from diverse cultural backgrounds. The approach is especially valuable in programs for students with language and learning challenges. The five components – Discussion, Instruction, Development, Performance, and Evaluation – are designed to create a classroom learning environment in which Multiple Intelligences (MI), skill development, and higher order thinking processes are woven together within the curriculum. AIM is a highly adaptable approach to planning for students with special needs. The plans presented in this section were developed with the student with LLC in mind. A *description* and *rationale* for each component follows.

1. **Discussion** – Discussion is an essential activity for both second language learners and students with learning disabilities. The major purposes of discussion include the following:

    *   It is a cueing system and model for second language learners.
    *   It encourages vocabulary and language development in all learners.
    *   It is the most immediate means of clarifying information and instruction.
    *   It encourages interaction among all students and the development of social skills.

2. **Instruction** – Instruction, whether direct or guided, requires careful planning. To accommodate the needs of second language learners requires school personnel to obtain information about language development in both languages, cultural experiences, and various other factors that may influence learning. In planning

sound curriculum and instruction for the student with LLC, one must do the following:

- Address the student's strengths and abilities – as well as deficits and disabilities.
- Provide for the development of "multiple intelligences."
- Engage in on-going *assessment* of student progress and *adjustment* to student needs.
- Provide adequate instruction and information in the primary language.
- Develop materials and lessons appropriate to student needs.
- Provide a safe and secure learning environment.
- Provide experiences rich in opportunities for social development.

3. **Development** – Creation and experimentation are natural to children. In the real world, children explore their interests, acquire a multitude of practical skills, and polish their emerging talents. So, too, should school abound with opportunities for growth and development. For students with LLC, controlled projects and activities that allow them to become immersed in creating and experimenting are excellent means of:

- stimulating interest and commitment to task
- immersing students in concrete and language-rich pursuits
- developing skills in most/all subject areas concurrently (listening, speaking, reading, writing, math, social studies, science, art, music, physical development)
- exploring interrelationships and connections
- testing "hunches" and hypotheses
- assessing developmental strengths and weaknesses
- promoting cooperation and mutual respect
- encouraging independence and self-esteem

4. **Performance** – Students who have been allowed to experiment and create often want to share their discoveries and creations. For the student with LLC who struggles with writing, reading, or math, there are many ways of demonstrating knowledge and/or skill development. Performances can be presented by showing, oral sharing, computer demonstrations, signing (e.g., American Sign Language), singing, acting out dramatic skits, displaying drawings, etc. Such activities:

- encourage development of skills undervalued or overlooked in the school curriculum
- allow students to express their knowledge and skills in "their own way"
- allow students to more fully assess their own strengths and talents
- stimulate an appreciation of individual differences among the students
- provide the teacher with a fuller, more enhanced picture of the learner
- allow the teacher to assess and evaluate a wide range of skills
- promote the development of positive self-image

5. **Evaluation** – Evaluation has always been a hotly debated topic. Whether to apply norm-referenced or criterion-referenced measures in the assessment of individuals is an on-going challenge to special educators who *must* assess student progress toward I.E.P. goals. Moreover, it is often necessary to conduct assessments in both

the primary language and English. A student who speaks Spanish more fluently than English, for example, may demonstrate better writing skills in English if instruction has not been available in Spanish. To make appropriate decisions relating to the student's capabilities and learning needs, it is important to examine skill mastery in relation to the learning opportunities that have been made available. The following factors need to be kept in mind:

- Learning disabilities may preclude "paper-and-pencil" assessment tasks as a fair measure of knowledge or capabilities.
- Limited proficiency in the language used in assessment may preclude paper-and-pencil assessment tasks as fair measures of understanding.
- Assessment may need to be conducted in *both* the primary language and English.
- Assessment of students with LLC should include some/all of the following:
  - Conferences with the student
  - Portfolios of benchmark samples in each subject area (reading, written language, math, science, social studies, art, computer utilization)
  - Audio/visual (tapes) of oral tests/activities, interviews, performances, etc.
  - Anecdotal records and information
  - Self-evaluation – student comments, statements, self-perceptions
  - Log of accomplishments – linguistic, academic, social, artistic, physical, etc.
  - Log of goals – developed by both student and teacher

Planning Classroom Lessons

Effective implementation of the AIM model begins with careful planning. The sample "lesson form" in Figure 10-1 may be reproduced to guide the planning process. The first step is to list specific goals for the lesson. A brief description of the task may be included in the goal statement. The specific skills and "intelligences" that will be tapped during the lesson should be listed. Skills from Bloom's Taxonomy (Bloom, Krathwohl, & Masia, 1956) have been used by the author when planning lessons for students with LLC:

1. Knowledge/recall
2. Comprehension
3. Application
4. Analysis
5. Synthesis
6. Evaluation

The comprehension skills emphasized in school reading programs are often based on Bloom's taxonomy, although the terms used to describe these "thinking skills" may differ somewhat from those listed above. Therefore, teachers may wish to use the terminology contained within the school reading curriculum when listing the skills being taught.

Space is included at the bottom of the form for listing modifications and adaptations identified as necessary to implement the lesson effectively.

Implementing the AIM Model

Examples are presented in this section to show how the AIM Model might be implemented in the classroom environment with students who demonstrate language and learning challenges in first grade, fourth grade, and sixth grade classrooms.

Figure 10-1
AIM Instructional Model
Sample Unit/Lesson Form

Unit/Lesson _____ Grade/Age _____

Language of Instruction _____ Date _____

Goals _____

_____

_____

_____

_____

Target Skills/Intelligences:

Bloom's Taxonomy _____

_____

_____

Multiple Intelligences _____

_____

_____

_____

Modifications/Adaptations

Discussion _____

_____

_____

_____

Instruction _____

_____

_____

_____

Development _____

_____

_____

_____

Performance _____

_____

_____

_____

Evaluation _____

_____

_____

_____

AIM Model – Grade 1

Curriculum Area: Reading (Core Literature)

Materials: *Chica Chica Boom Boom*, a book published by Houghton-Mifflin. The audiotape will also be used. A matrix showing how the target skills/intelligences can be targeted using this book is presented in Table 10-1. A sample web for the activities is presented in Figure 10-2.

Phase 1: DISCUSSION

Target Skills/Intelligences:
- Bloom's Taxonomy: Recall, Comprehension
- Multiple Intelligences: Verbal, Bodily-Kinesthetic, Musical, Interpersonal

Activities:
- Teacher introduces the lesson by leading the students in singing and/or reciting the "Alphabet Song."
- Listening: The teacher reads the story aloud with the students in a reading circle.
- Several copies of the book are passed among the students to allow them to view the illustrations.
- Listening: Students listen to the audiotaped reading of the story.
- Discussion: Teacher and students discuss the following:

> Coconut trees
> Rhyming
> Alphabet letters

Modifications/Adaptations for students with LLC
- Preview the activity with the students with LLC in the dominant language.
- Clarify/explain new words, concepts (e.g., rhyme).
- Read the story to the student in L1 if possible.
- Sing the Alphabet song in both English and L1 if possible.
- Record the Alphabet song in both English and L1 if possible.
- Discuss any similarities between alphabets, e.g., English and Spanish.
- Encourage the students to recite the alphabet in both languages.

Phase 2: INSTRUCTION

Target Skills/Intelligences:
- Bloom's Taxonomy: Recall, Comprehension, Application
- Multiple Intelligences: Verbal, Logical-Mathematical, Interpersonal, Spatial/Artistic

Table 10-1

Matrix for: CHICA CHICA BOOM BOOM
(Core Literature)

	KNOWLEDGE/ RECALL	COMPREHENSION	APPLICATION	ANALYSIS	SYNTHESIS
VERBAL/ LINGUISTIC	-Recalls story details -Knows alphabet	-Tells what happens in the story -Understands directions	-Can share/tell directions -Participates in singing	-Can tell why the tree bent -Able to line up alphabetically	Helps make up a new alphabet song
LOGICAL/ MATHEMATICAL	-Knows number of ABC letters -Can count to 30	-Knows what to do -Knows how to place in order	-Participates in *Alphabet Number* game -Lines up properly	-Can tell why the tree bent -Can figure out solution	Can think of ways to solve the problem
VISUAL-SPATIAL	Recalls colors and shape of coconut tree	Understands what to paint and sing	-Paints a coconut tree -Joins in *rapping*	Can see likeness in songs, trees	Creates a better tree for the ABCs
INTERPERSONAL	Knows what cooperative groups are	Knows how to cooperate and share	Works on projects with teacher, peers	Understands the importance of cooperation	Helps create a new group game
INTRAPERSONAL	Reinforces present knowledge and skills	Recognizes his/her role	-Performs to best of his/her ability -Shares ideas	Recognizes/thinks about personal strengths and talents	-Shares solutions -Shares opinions
BODILY-KINESTHETIC	-Knows how to line up in ABC order -Knows rhythm	Knows what is expected and when	Participates in ABC games and songs/clapping	-Can help unscramble ABC line -Recognizes rhythm differences	Helps create new activity, game
MUSICAL	-Knows alphabet song -Knows what rhythm is	Comprehends the music directions	Participates in singing, clapping, chanting, rapping	Can recognize patterns and differences in music & rapping	Creates a new *Rap* or clapping pattern

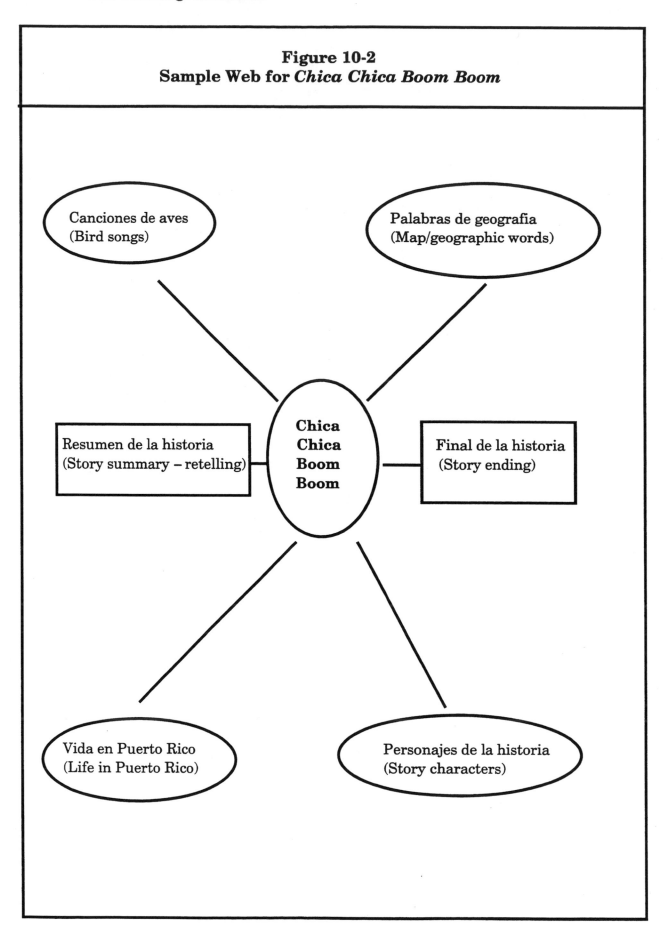

Figure 10-2
Sample Web for *Chica Chica Boom Boom*

Activities:
- Teacher reviews the alphabet and records it on the board.
- Students practice reciting the alphabet in pairs (in L1 and/or L2).
- "Counting Letters" sequencing activity follows: Teacher leads students in "counting" the letters *in order*. Students guess the name of the next letter (e.g., 1,2,3,4? The answer is E.)
- Teacher reviews the story.
- Teacher models painting of a coconut tree on construction paper.

Modifications/Adaptations for Students with LLC:
- Preview instructions for the activities in both languages.
- Pre-practice the "Counting Letters" activity with the students.
- Pair peer interpreter or instructional aide with the student when practicing the alphabet.

Phase 3: DEVELOPMENT

Target Skills/Intelligences:
- Bloom's Taxonomy: Comprehension, Application, Analysis, Synthesis
- Multiple Intelligences: Verbal, Logical-Mathematical, Spatial/Artistic, Interpersonal, Bodily-Kinesthetic, Musical

Activities:
- Teacher leads students in "Alphabet Line" game. Students are each given at least one large letter of the alphabet. Teacher "scrambles" the students, and the students have to unscramble themselves by lining up in alphabetical order. This activity should be repeated several times.
- Independent work:
  - Painting – coconut tree on construction paper
  - Cutting – large alphabet letters from magazines (upper and lower)
  - Pasting – upper case alphabet letters *climbing up* one side of their painted coconut tree trunk and fronds. Lower case letters are pasted *climbing down* the other side.
- Teacher assembles and binds paintings of "alphabet trees" into large booklets.

Modifications/Adaptations for Students with LLC
- Pair students with LLC for the "Alphabet Line" game.
- Begin with letters that students recognize.
- Practice "lining up" in alphabetical order.
- Simplify instructions for the project.
- Allow additional time for completion.
- Allow students with LLC to work in pairs.

Phase 4: PERFORMANCE

Target Skills/Intelligences:
- Bloom's Taxonomy: Recall, Comprehension, Application
- Multiple Intelligences: Musical, Verbal, Bodily-Kinesthetic, Interpersonal

Activities:

- Students listen to "Rapping the Alphabet" audiotape. Group engages in singing, chanting, and clapping along with the tape.
- Teacher records the students' performance (audio/videotape) for playback.
- Oral sharing: Individuals share their finished alphabet trees.

Modifications/Adaptations for Students with LLC

- Teacher leads students with LLC in *pre-practice* singing, chanting, clapping, and rapping.
- Teacher, aide, or bilingual peer may translate for students with LLC.
- Rapping is permitted in both languages.

Additional Suggestions:

- Invite bilingual parents and/or volunteers to help out.
- Use a variety of alphabet songs in both languages.

Phase 5: EVALUATION

Criteria for Evaluation (all students)

- Completion of the project
- Degree of participation in the activities
- Quality of the work (e.g., letter-cutting, correctness of paste-up, correct letter order and direction, neatness)

AIM Model – Grade 4

Curriculum Area: Reading (Core Literature)

Materials: *Ramon and the Pirate Gull,* a book published by Houghton-Mifflin. A matrix showing how the target skills/intelligences can be targeted using this book is presented in Table 10-2.

Note: This plan is designed to include the student with LLC whose learning disabilities are in the areas of language arts and mathematics.

Phase 1: DISCUSSION

Target Skills/Intelligences:
- Bloom's Taxonomy: Recall, Comprehension
- Multiple Intelligences: Verbal, Interpersonal, Intrapersonal

Activities:
- Students share personal knowledge about birds, particularly gulls.
- Students respond to the following probing questions:
  - Where do birds live?
  - Why do you think that birds are different colors?
  - What do sea gulls eat?
  - How would you care for a sick or injured bird?
  - How do you care for your pets?

Phase 2: INSTRUCTION

Target Skills/Intelligences:
- Bloom's Taxonomy: Comprehension, Analysis
- Multiple Intelligences: Verbal, Logical-Mathematical, Interpersonal, Intrapersonal, Bodily-Kinesthetic, Musical

Activities:
- Students read the short story aloud.
- Students create a "story map" on the chalkboard depicting story elements.
- Students discuss story elements:
  - Characters
  - Setting
  - Plot – story development (actions, events, story ending)
  - Lesson or message in the story
- Discussion of Puerto Rican culture (language, lifestyles, etc.).
- Music – Students listen to a variety of Puerto Rican/Caribbean music while they work.
  - "Yellow Bird" is an excellent choice, as it is authentic Caribbean music.
  - Others: "Flamingo," "Poinciana," contemporary Puerto Rican music

**Table 10-2
Matrix for: RAMON AND THE PIRATE GULL
(Core Literature)**

	KNOWLEDGE/ RECALL	COMPREHENSION	APPLICATION	ANALYSIS	SYNTHESIS
VERBAL/ LINGUISTIC	Recalls details from story	Understands the story problem	Creates a story map	Can explain Ramon's dilemma	Can offer a solution to the problem
LOGICAL/ MATHEMATICAL	Knows the following map, island	Knows how to complete the map Follows directions	Creates a map with several land features	Can compare/contrast tow islands	Can apply new knowledge to future task
VISUAL- SPATIAL	Recalls details of island from picture	Understands the tasks: map and mini-mural	Creates a collage picture of island life	Can discuss differences in pictures and maps	Can apply skills to new task
INTERPERSONAL	Recalls rules of cooperative groups	Understands his/her role in group	Works with group on mini-mural	Helps group solve Ramon's problem	Offers suggestions for <u>caring</u> for bird
INTRAPERSONAL	Can recall feelings of helping others	Can understand how Ramon might feel	Shares personal thoughts/feelings	Can imagine living in Puerto Rico	Makes up his/her own story about <u>caring</u>
BODILY- KINESTHETIC	Knows how to draw/cut/ paste/sing	Understands directions- how/what/when to perform	Participates in all activities	Demonstrates understanding of patterns in movement	Creates a different clapping, movement pattern
MUSICAL	Recalls words to *Yellow Bird*	Comprehends the lyrics and music directions	Participates in all musical activities	Recognizes differences in rhythm, tempo, and/or clapping pattern	Creates a different song

- Cooperative groups:
  - Identify jobs and daily living patterns from pictures (e.g., National Geographic)
  - Paste pictures on large posters with labels such as, "Daily Life," "Jobs," "Dress," "Food," "Animals."
  - Practice reciting/singing words to "Yellow Bird" (very simple words).
  - Study simple maps of the Caribbean and Puerto Rico.

Modifications/Accommodations for Students with LLC:
- Preview the instructions in the primary language (teacher, aide, peer interpreter).
- Simplify instructions and complex words and terms (e.g., plot, setting) as needed.
- Record the story (or excerpts) in both languages for listening activities.
- Allow students with LLC to read with a fluent bilingual peer (re-reading as needed).
- Allow oral responses in the primary language.
- Assign at least one bilingual student to each cooperative group.
- Ask the group chairperson to encourage students with LLC to participate actively.

Phase 3: DEVELOPMENT

Target Skills/Intelligences:
- Bloom's Taxonomy: Comprehension, Application, Analysis, Synthesis
- Multiple Intelligences: Verbal, Logical-Mathematical, Bodily-Kinesthetic, Artistic, Musical, Interpersonal

Activities:
- Students create maps of Puerto Rico (from pictures samples).
- Cooperative Groups create "mini murals" of daily life (drawing, painting).
- Cooperative Groups develop a "Caring for Birds" poster, describing ways to care for wild and pet birds (feeding, housing, protecting).
- Journal Writing: Students write three things they have learned in their journal.

Modifications/Accommodations for Students with LLC:
- Assign at least one bilingual student to each cooperative group.
- Ask the group chairperson to encourage students with LLC to participate actively.
- Preview instructions and plans in the primary language (teacher, aide, peer interpreter).
- Simplify complex instructions, words, and terms.
- Assign individual tasks to students with LLC that can be accomplished with little or no help (e.g., tasks that do not require complex language skills).

Phase 4: PERFORMANCE

Target Skills/Intelligences:
- Bloom's Taxonomy: Comprehension, Application, Analysis, Synthesis
- Multiple Intelligences: Verbal, Logical-Mathematical, Artistic, Bodily-Kinesthetic, Musical, Interpersonal

Activities:
- Cooperative groups share orally their "Mini Mural of Daily Life."
- Individuals share aloud at least one personal contribution made to the group.
- "Story Retelling" - Volunteers retell the story of *Ramon and the Pirate Gull.*
- Choral singing of "Yellow Bird."
- Volunteers share three things they have learned.
- Cooperative groups share their maps of Puerto Rico.

Modifications/Accommodations for Students with LLC:
- Allow students with LLC to learn the words to Yellow Bird in the primary language.
- Allow students to practice singing with a peer interpreter, aide, or teacher.
- Allow students to retell the story of *Ramon* in their primary language.
- If writing is difficult for the student, the teacher, aide, or peer should write down what the student says.
- Provide students with various means of demonstrating their understanding.
- Adapt the assignments to language and/or ability levels.
- Provide parents with clear, simple information about assignments. Encourage their support.

Phase 5: EVALUATION

Criteria for Evaluation - Holistic/Rubric Assessment
- Level of participation
- Completion of picture posters, journal writing, maps of Puerto Rico, mini mural, etc.)
- Quality of work (e.g., correctness, neatness)

AIM Model – Grade 6

Curriculum Area: Language Arts

Project Topic: Hollywood

Materials: See individual activities. A matrix showing how the target skills/intelligences can be targeted using this book is presented in Table 10-3.

Phase 1: DISCUSSION

Target Skills/Intelligences:
- Bloom's Taxonomy: Recall, Comprehension, Analysis
- Multiple Intelligences: Verbal, Logical-Mathematical, Interpersonal

Activities:
- Teacher probes students' present knowledge about the topic.
- Cluster/Web the information and ideas on the board or flip chart for all to see.
- Teacher poses general probing questions:

  How did nineteenth-century settlers arrive in southern California?
  What problems did they face in their travels?
  What problems did they face once they arrived?
  Why did movie producers come to southern California?
  Who were the movie pioneers and early actors/actresses?
  What were their cultural and language backgrounds?
  Why did the movie industry flourish in present day Hollywood?
  How were/are movies made?
  Who are some present-day actors and directors, and what are their cultural and language backgrounds?

- Information obtained during "brainstorming" is recorded on the board.
- Small group work: Groups are assigned specific questions from the above list. The group develops a "web" of information to share with the class.

Modification/Adaptations for Students with LLC:
- Preview information with students in their primary language.
- Clarify/simplify all unfamiliar terms, idioms, vocabulary.
- Allow students to respond through peer interpreters in each group.
- Present appropriate challenges.
- Use visual cues as much as possible (pictures, charts, graphs, maps, etc.).

**Table 10-3
Matrix for: "Hollywood"
(Social Studies Project)**

	KNOWLEDGE/ RECALL	COMPREHENSION	APPLICATION	ANALYSIS	SYNTHESIS
VERBAL/ LINGUISTIC	Recalls names of Latino/Latina actors	Understands how to write a travel journal	Writes a travel journal Co-writes a one-act play	Can explain why producers came to Hollywood	Works on an original one-act play
LOGICAL/ MATHEMATICAL	Knows facts about distance, geography of U.S.A.	Discusses difficulty of early travels to Hollywood	Creates a relief map of the U.S.A.	Understands roles of climate and geography in movie making	Develops alternative land routes to Hollywood
VISUAL- SPATIAL	Recalls facts from movies and videos made in Hollywood	Can read a map	Creates a relief map Play production	Can determine needs for a play production	Co-produces a one-act play
INTERPERSONAL	Knows how to work in cooperative groups	Understands what it was like to travel west	Participates in play production group tasks	Can help identify/decide roles for play production	Offers unique skills/ideas to play production
BODILY- KINESTHETIC	Can operate a video camera	Demonstrates understanding by doing	Engages in play productions	Can explain how activity stimulates self-growth	Performance of original work
MUSICAL	Recalls some movie music themes	Understands how music is used to enhance movies	Participates in music selection/performance	Can compare/contrast music genres	Co-select/perform music for one-act play

Phase 2: INSTRUCTION

Target Skills/Intelligences:
- Bloom's Taxonomy: Comprehension, Application, Analysis
- Multiple Intelligences: Verbal, Logical-Mathematical, Interpersonal, Artistic, Bodily-Kinesthetic

Activities:
Teacher provides instruction aimed at the development of multiple skills.
- Students examine early photographs, maps, artwork, pictures, etc.
- Students view silent movies (available on videotapes).
- **Reading** – books/excerpts about 19th and early 20th century history of southern California and Hollywood.
  - silent reading
  - choral reading (simple scripts/scenes in Spanish/English).
  - partner reading
- **Writing** – "scriptwriting" simple One-Act plays (L1 and/or L2). These scripts may be dictated to an aide, parent-volunteer, or other adult.
- **Science** – climate and geography of southern California.
- **Math** – mapping (distance, mileage, direction, time, etc.).
- **Social Studies** – study of settlement patterns in southern California, cultural and linguistic differences, impact of multiculturalism on movie industry today.
- **Art** – creating painted contour/relief maps, set design, costumes, etc. for student-written and produced play.

Modifications/Adaptations for students with LLC:
- Preview objectives in both languages (teacher, bilingual aide, peer, volunteer).
- Implement whole-class choral reading whenever possible.
- Models skills through oral reading.
- Audio-record lessons so that students can hear the lessons several times.
- Select "writing partners" so that students with LLC work with peers who have adequate skills in both languages.
- Allow student to dictate information for the teacher or aide to write down.
- Present computer activities to encourage students with LLC to see the computer as an expressive medium.

Phase 3: DEVELOPMENT

Target Skills/Intelligences:
- Bloom's Taxonomy: Application, Analysis, Synthesis
- Multiple Intelligences: Verbal, Logical-Mathematical, Artistic, Bodily-Kinesthetic, Interpersonal, Intrapersonal, Musical

At the Development stage, students are expected to pull from the foregoing Discussion and Instruction to expand their knowledge, polish skills, and discover connections among school disciplines.

The following activities are suggested for individuals, cooperative groups, or partners:

- **Oral and/or Written Summaries** – Information is presented or discussed by the teacher.
- **Map-making** – An imaginary trip is taken from "East Coast to California," including trails, rivers, mountains, Indian territories, etc.
- **"Journal of My Trip West"** – Students describe imaginary experiences along the way.
- **Researching and Writing** – Students write brief biographical sketches of favorite actors/actresses/directors.
- **Scriptwriting** – Students work in small groups or pairs to produce one-act plays in English, Spanish, or other languages.
- **Planning a Play** – The following project requires the participation of a group of students or an entire classroom.
  - One-act plays are read by their writers (groups, pairs, or individuals).
  - Class selects a student/group-written play to produce.
  - Students assign roles and responsibilities to every classmate.
  - Students devise plan for acquiring materials and resources.
  - Students develop a timeline and schedules (construction, rehearsals, performance).

Modifications/Adaptations for students with LLC:

- Allow students to produce oral summaries in L1 - through an interpreter.
- Allow dictation and transcription from the primary language.
- Vary the roles of students with LLC to increase the "breadth" of their experiences.
- Capitalize on the students' strengths and talents.
- Utilize the computer as appropriate for writing assignments.
- Simplify assignments that require complex language skills.
- Present non-threatening challenges.

Phase 4: PERFORMANCE

Target Skills/Intelligences:
- Bloom's Taxonomy: Application, Analysis, Synthesis, Evaluation
- Multiple Intelligences: Verbal, Logical-Mathematical, Artistic, Interpersonal, Intrapersonal, Musical, Bodily-Kinesthetic

Activities:
- Oral sharing of imaginary trip
- Oral presentations of relief map projects
- Oral presentations/readings of research papers (e.g., My Favorite Actor/Actress/Director)
- Play production – Students assume all responsibilities of producing a student-written one-act play for the school (i.e., writers, artists, set designers, properties manager, wardrobe, stage manager, directors, choreographers, camera crew, advertising, etc.).

Modifications/Adaptations for Students with LLC:
- Allow "Journals" to be shared by aide, teacher, or peer interpreter.
- Allow the student with LLC to work with a peer interpreter, group, or an aide as needed to complete the written portion of the map project.

- Identify the students' strengths and assist the class in the casting and job assignments for the play. Encourage students with LLC to assume challenging roles.
- Simplify language in assignments as necessary to ensure comprehension.

Phase 5: EVALUATION

Evaluation should take into account the breadth of the project and the wide range of skills and knowledge required to complete it. For these reasons, holistic assessment and teacher-devised rubrics seem appropriate.

- Rubric scoring of each written assignment by the teacher
- Rubric scoring for all oral presentations (group, pair, individual) by the teacher
- Individual assessment of student contributions to the play production by the teacher
- Individual student conferences with the teacher
- Self-evaluations using criteria that are negotiated with the teacher

Promoting Behaviors that Facilitate Learning

If students are to experience success in the classroom, they must feel comfortable in the learning environment. Does the student feel that his or her participation in the classroom in valued? Does the student feel that success is possible? Does the student see the value of the information that is being taught?

It is often difficult to determine what is going on inside the student's mind. Many students are good at covering up feelings of inadequacy that impact their functioning in the school environment. Students who act as if they don't care about learning to read are, in many cases, covering up feelings of shame and embarrassment caused by their lack of success in the classroom.

Four "Behavior Charts" are presented in Appendix C that may be helpful in changing behaviors that often affect students functioning in the classroom. The suggested interventions on these charts are designed to help students overcome a variety of negative feelings that often impede learning.

Language Development and the Instructional Curriculum

The AIM model can be used when presenting instruction in either the home language or English. Opportunities for reading instruction in the native language help children to develop competencies that will transfer to English. If instruction is available only in English, it is critical that comprehensible input be provided. If learning is to occur, the student must be able to relate what is being taught to his or her previous knowledge. We cannot expect children to learn if the instruction makes no sense to them. Teachers must tune in to what the child knows so that they can create instructional activities that are relevant to these experiences.

The activities described in the AIM model can be adapted quite easily to meet the needs of students at different levels of language development. When developing instructional objectives for individual students, the "stages" listed in Table 10-4 can be used as a guide. Examples of instructional goals and objectives for each of these stages of language development are listed on pages 210-217 for a student named "Juanita." These sample goals and objectives should prove to be helpful in generating I.E.P. objectives for individual students with a variety of needs. When selecting instructional objectives from this list, the measurement criteria should be adjusted based on an assessment of the student's specific needs and abilities. Special education teachers, specialists in bilingual education, speech-language pathologists, and other professionals should work as a team to ensure that the instructional objectives are appropriate for the student's language level. If the language level of the instructional activities is too advanced, the student will have difficulty making sense of the instruction.

Table 10-4
Matching Instruction to Stages of Language Development

Pre-Production Stage

Visual/Written Responses
- drawings, paintings, graphic designs
- written response – copying

Oral Responses
- yes/no responses in English
- dictated stories, responses in
    primary language

Physical Responses
- matching objects
- choosing among things
- circling or pointing
- mime/acting out responses

Early Production Stage

Visual Written Responses
- drawing, painting, graphic designs
- grouping and labeling
- copying
- simple Rebus responses

Oral Responses
- one/two word responses
- naming, saying
- choral responses

Physical Responses
- gestures - pointing, selecting, matching
- constructing
- mime and /or acting out responses

Speech Emergence Stage

Visual/Written Responses
- written responses
- drawings, paintings, graphics

Oral Responses
- recalling, answering
- telling, retelling
- describing, explaining

Physical Responses
- role-playing, acting out
- cooperative group tasks
- constructing, creating
- demonstrating

Intermediate Fluency Stage

Visual Written Responses
- essays, summaries
- written tests
- painting, drawing, graphics
- creative writing, e.g., stories

Oral Responses
- explanations, descriptions
- summaries and opinions
- debating and/or defending

Physical Responses
- demonstrating
- constructing creating
- videotaped presentations

Pre-Production: Stage I

At the Pre-Production stage, students are highly dependent upon *visual* clues in making meaning. They infer and intuit from gestures and signals, pictures and graphics, and intonation and inflection. Emphasis is given to receptive vocabulary development and simple responses.

Goals

■ *Linguistic*

By March, Juanita will demonstrate progress in English language development (both oral and written).

■ *Academic*

By March, Juanita will demonstrate improvement in reading skills (phonemic awareness/decoding, vocabulary, and comprehension).

■ *Social*

By March, Juanita will demonstrate improved social skills in the classroom and on the playground.

■ *Talents/Strengths*

By March, Juanita will demonstrate improvement in at least one area of particular strength or talent.

■ *Tools and Technology*

By March, Juanita will use accessible tools and technology to promote language development and learning.

Objectives

By March, Juanita, when asked, will point to 20 objects in the classroom or in pictures with 90% accuracy.

By March, Juanita will respond to 20 Yes/No questions in English with 90% accuracy.

By March, Juanita will correctly identify 20 objects in pictures by pointing to them as the teacher says the words in English and/or the primary language.

By March, Juanita will respond correctly to 10 commands presented by the classroom teacher (e.g., Stand, Sit down, Point to, Line up, etc.).

By March, Juanita will copy information from the chalkboard with 95% accuracy.

By March, Juanita will write all letters of the English alphabet (upper and lower cases).

By March, Juanita will point to all letters of the English alphabet when asked.

By March, Juanita will demonstrate improvement in social skills by sharing, turn-taking, cooperating, and/or helping others.

By March, Juanita will demonstrate improvement in self-confidence and motivation by volunteering and/or accepting responsibility.

By March, Juanita will demonstrate improvement in artistic ability by creating drawings and/or paintings of 3 different subjects.

Early Production: Stage II

Goals

■ *Linguistic*

By March, Juanita will demonstrate improvement in oral communication skills in English.

By March, Juanita will use grammatically correct sentences and/or phrases to respond to questions, convey ideas and information, and/or make requests.

By March, Juanita will demonstrate increased comprehension of English vocabulary.

■ *Academic*

By March, Juanita will demonstrate improvement in written language skills in English.

By March, Juanita will learn simple rules of English grammar, mechanics, and usage.

By March, Juanita will show evidence of understanding instruction in each academic area.

■ *Social*

By March, Juanita will increase her level of participation in cooperative groups.

By March, Juanita will increase her social skills by tutoring/helping classmates.

By March, Juanita will demonstrate respect for others.

■ *Talents/Strengths*

By March, Juanita will show improvement in areas of particular strength, talent and/or interest.

■ *Tools and Technology*

By March, Juanita will increase her knowledge of learning tools and technology.

Objectives

By March, Juanita will respond correctly to English greetings from the teacher and/or classmates 90% of the time.

By March, Juanita will use grammatically correct sentences and/or phrases to answer 10 of 12 comprehension questions from a story read aloud to her.

By March, Juanita will increase spoken vocabulary by 10 words in each of the following areas: reading/literature, math, social studies, science, art, music, and physical education.

By March, Juanita will orally describe a scene from a story the class has read using the English vocabulary she has acquired.

By March, Juanita will select the correct words from a list to complete a (fill-in-the-blank) worksheet for a story read aloud to/with her.

By March, Juanita will write 10 simple sentences in English, using at least one adjective to describe the subject.

By March, Juanita will respond to 5 one-word sentence completion items in each of the following areas with 90% accuracy: reading, math, social studies.

By March, Juanita will, using a story frame, write 3 additional words/phrases about the story.

By March, Juanita will increase level of participation in cooperative group tasks, as demonstrated by contributions to discussion, decision-making, and /or written products.

By March, Juanita will demonstrate an improvement in social skills by working cooperatively and playing fairly with peers 90% of the time.

By March, Juanita will demonstrate improvement in fine motor skills in each of the following areas, as measured by:

- printing/cursive writing – letter formation, spacing, size, level of difficulty
- cutting – accuracy, speed, use of scissors, level of difficulty
- pasting – accuracy, neatness, speed, level of difficulty
- art – proper use of tools/materials
- tools/technology – proper use of computer keyboards, audiotape player/recorders

By March, Juanita will use the student *Picture Dictionary* in completing writing/spelling assignments 90% of the time.

By March, Juanita will demonstrate computer knowledge by responding correctly to 8 of 10 simple commands using the keyboard.

By March, Juanita will demonstrate improvement in her artistic ability (or other talent) by creating and displaying pictures from a portfolio.

Speech Emergence: Stage III

Goals

■ *Linguistic*

By March, Juanita will demonstrate progress in oral language development in English.

By March, Juanita will demonstrate progress in written language development in English.

■ *Academic*

By March, Juanita will increase vocabulary development in all subject areas.

By March, Juanita will increase use of the English language in both formal and informal discussions.

By March, Juanita will demonstrate increased knowledge of English grammar, mechanics, and usage.

■ *Social*

By March, Juanita will demonstrate improvement in social skills related to leadership and responsibility.

■ *Talents/Strengths*

By March, Juanita will demonstrate growth in her artistic talent and abilities.

■ *Tools/Technology*

By March, Juanita will increase her use of classroom tools and technology to complete assignments.

Objectives

By March, Juanita will respond correctly to 10 of 12 oral test questions using English phrases/sentences.

By March, Juanita will recite a brief passage from a literature selection with correct pronunciation.

By March, Juanita will use English to successfully direct a peer to the office/lunch room in 4 of 5 attempts.

By March, Juanita will use correct verb forms in completing 18 of 20 test items.

By March, Juanita will choose correct English words/phrases to complete 10 fill-in-the-blank questions on a (reading, social studies, science) test.

By March, Juanita will select 10 nouns, 10 verbs, and 10 adjectives from three lists to create 10 grammatically-correct sentences.

By March, Juanita will match 5 synonyms, 5 antonyms, and 5 homonyms in a list of words to the correct words in a second list.

By March, Juanita will use her English vocabulary to develop a simple story map (characters, place, key events) from a literature selection read aloud to/with her.

By March, Juanita will demonstrate understanding of homework assignments by returning attempted/completed assignments within the time allowed 90% of the time.

By March, Juanita will average 90% on periodic spelling tests over a 12-week reporting period.

By March, Juanita will read aloud 50 of 250 basic sight words when presented with a printed word list.

By March, Juanita will increase her level of involvement in classroom assignments by initiating discussions, helping to clarify instructions, and assisting less capable peers.

By March, Juanita will demonstrate improved social skills by initiating conversations, games, and other social activities with English-speaking peers.

By March, Juanita will demonstrate her artistic talent by directing a small group (four students) in a drawing/painting/coloring exercise.

By March, Juanita will use the dictionary to complete independent written assignments 90% of the time.

By March, Juanita will demonstrate knowledge of the classroom computer program by successfully completing 9 of 10 assignments independently.

Intermediate Fluency: Stage IV

Goals

■ *Linguistic*

By March, Juanita will demonstrate adequate skills and knowledge to transition into all day English instruction.

By March, Juanita will use acquired language skills to develop high levels of proficiency in writing (i.e., composing, revising, and self-editing).

■ *Academic*

By March, Juanita will demonstrate improved performance in all subject areas.

By March, Juanita will demonstrate improvement in problem-solving and decision-making skills related to classroom learning.

■ *Social*

By March, Juanita will increase her degree of participation in class/group tasks.

By March, Juanita will demonstrate increased social awareness and responsibility.

■ *Talents/Strengths*

By March, Juanita will demonstrate growth in her artistic abilities.

■ *Tools/Technology*

By March, Juanita will demonstrate improved computer skills and knowledge.

By March, Juanita will use reference books correctly to assist learning.

Objectives

By March, Juanita will read aloud a teacher-selected short story with no more than 5 miscues.

By March, Juanita will retell/paraphrase a short story read aloud by/with her.

By March, Juanita will create and write a new story ending to a short story read by/with her.

By March, Juanita will correctly solve 10 of 12 math story problems in which she must determine the correct operation from context clues.

By March, Juanita will write a three-paragraph composition on a topic of her choice, with correct punctuation and capitalization and 90% correct spelling.

By March, Juanita will orally compare and contrast English and Spanish versions of a children's short story read aloud by/with her.

By March, Juanita will demonstrate knowledge of reference books (encyclopedia, dictionary, thesaurus) by using them successfully to complete five science and/or social studies assignments.

By March, Juanita will demonstrate understanding of testing language by averaging 90% on tests containing the following items: true/false, fill-in-the-blank, sentence completion, yes/no, short answer, matching, and essay.

By March, Juanita will demonstrate increased awareness of social conventions and rules by sharing/writing opinions on local issues and/or current events.

By March, Juanita will demonstrate increased artistic ability by completing two art projects using different mediums (e.g., drawing, painting, sculpting, etc.).

By March, Juanita will demonstrate increased understanding of computer applications by utilizing the computer to complete assignments in various subject areas.

Working With Parents of Students with LLC

Effective teachers of language-and-learning challenged students never work with just the child – they work with the parents as well. Parents should always be an integral part of the child's education. The child is an extension of the home, and special educators must recognize the impact of background and home environment on educational planning.

Parents hold both entitlements and responsibilities with regard to their child's education. Their children are entitled to fair and equitable education practices, and parents are responsible for supporting the goals of the schools – so far as the goals do not infringe upon their civil rights. This agreement is well rooted in American schools, although many immigrants do not know their roles in this agreement. Hence it becomes the responsibility of the schools to educate parents in their respective rights and responsibilities (Roseberry-McKibbin, 1995). How we go about doing this has been a topic of much discussion, as minority populations in the schools have increased dramatically in recent years. The following points seem especially relevant:

- **Communication and Trust** – Clearly, the first order of business is to establish open lines of communication with parents and families. They need to know that they are welcome at the schools, and that their children are safe from mistreatment and prejudice.

- **Role Clarification** – Parents must be invited into educational planning. Frequently, parents of minority students do not attend meetings or attempt to participate in their child's education because of feelings of inadequacy, inferiority, or lack of English ability. Others may feel that education is the province of the school – not the home. In either case, parents are often alienated from their child's "school world." There are many ways to build bridges successfully between school and home.

  - Institute Parent-Family Nights at school.
  - Invite parents to multicultural festivals, parades, and events.
  - Start after-school programs and classes for parents and families.
  - Make home visitations to interact with parents and learn from them.
  - Open the school library to parents so that they can select books.
  - Present "Welcome Days" in which community leaders, merchants, etc. are on hand to interact with parents.

- **Responsibility** – Once parents are aware of their roles, they can begin to address the school's expectations and concerns. Although parents of many minority students do not speak English, they may be competent readers and writers in the native language. Moreover, students who come to school with high levels of development in a language other than English typically make the transition to English much faster. (Cummins, 1989; Krashen, 1983). Parents of students with LLC, regardless of English ability, should be expected to work with their children at home, if only in areas such as math, which does not require complex language skills. The "guidelines" in Table 10-5 should be reviewed with parents. These guidelines may be adapted or translated into the home language for distribution to parents.

Table 10-5
Guidelines for Parents of Students with LLC

- Be sure your child has periodic medical, dental, and vision check-ups.
- Set aside time to discuss your child's day at school.
- Attend parent conferences and other important school meetings.
- Consult with your child's teachers frequently.
- Request modified or alternate assignments if the work is too difficult.
- Arrange an area in the home for study and homework.
- Check for daily homework assignments and review the instructions with your child.
- Maintain a schedule for homework and help your child when necessary.
- Read with your child daily (in the primary language or English).
- Write notes, letters, and cards to each other.
- Display your child's work prominently in the home.
- Record your child's stories, books, etc. on tape.
- Request a list of age-and-ability-appropriate literature from your child's school.
- Cook with your child. Math lessons abound in the kitchen.
- Play with your child. Games and recreation activities provide rich opportunities for bonding.
- Provide encouragement and praise daily.
- Help your child identify his/her strengths and talents and nurture them at home.
- Enroll in classes to improve your primary and/or English language skills.
- Become a parent volunteer for your child's classroom and/or school.
- Chaperone school field trips when possible.
- Visit the library (school or public) with your child.
- Visit a zoo, museum, festival, or other cultural attractions and discuss these visits with your child.

Do not do the following:

- Do not criticize your child for learning problems over which he/she has no control.
- Do not compare your child with special needs to his/her siblings, friends, or other people.
- Do not confuse the child with too much information or alternate approaches to homework.
- Do not finish or let others finish homework assignments for your special needs child because he/she forgot or failed to do them. (This may lead to learned helplessness and/or feelings of inadequacy.)
- Do not place pressure on the child to complete assignments obviously beyond his/her reach.
- Do not disrupt or pre-empt homework schedules with other activities (e.g. TV, shopping, baby-sitting, errands, etc.).

When working with parents from diverse cultural backgrounds, it is important to remember that their perceptions of "disabilities" may be very different from those of school professionals. Cultural issues that are important to consider when working with Hispanic and Asian families are presented in Tables 10-6 and 10-7 respectively.

Although cultural differences are important to consider, it is also important to remember that there is diversity within any culture. By studying different cultures, educational professionals become aware of cultural "tendencies" that may be relevant in the classroom learning environment. Each child is unique, however, and interacts with the culture in unique ways. To meet the needs of students with LLC, professionals must look at each child in relation to what he or she has experienced and learned in school, at home, and in the community. In this way, we do not "stereotype" students and are able to develop individualized programs of instruction relevant to their experiences and learning needs.

Table 10-6
Working With Hispanic Parents:
Implications for Professionals

- Professionals will more readily gain the trust of parents/family members if they have a humanistic orientation rather than a task orientation. Informal friendly chatting can set the stage for work to be done.

- Professionals should attempt to communicate with both parents in meetings. It is important to understand that the father is often the decision-maker for the family.

- Professionals should use formal titles with Hispanic adults to show respect. Adults should be addressed with the formal *you* (*Usted*) rather than the less formal *you* (*tu*).

- Choose interpreters with care, as the use of friends and family members may violate family privacy.

- Families may appear to be passive about accepting treatment for conditions they believe are the result of external forces. Professionals must work to foster confidence and trust.

- Because of their respect for professionals, parents may not openly disagree with them. However, they may only pretend to follow suggestions. Professionals should always follow up when suggestions are given.

- Professionals need to remember that there may be child-rearing norms among some Hispanic families that do not fit the mainstream timeline for developmental milestones.

- Latino parents may not wish to be actively involved in making decisions concerning their children's schooling, and may defer to professionals to make the right decisions.

- Some parents may believe that an all-English program is superior to bilingual programs that enhance Spanish skills.

- Professionals should define terms such as learning disability clearly for parents to ensure that their meaning is understood. Otherwise, parents may mistakenly associate the term with mental illness or mental retardation.

- Professionals may need to assist families so that they can be assertive in obtaining needed services (e.g., educational, medical).

- Professionals should state their expectations and should explain the importance of maintaining schedules. Parents may be late for or miss appointments due to different perspectives about time and/or lack of understanding about the importance of schedules.

Source: Roseberry-McKibbin, C. (1995). *Multicultural students with special language needs*. Oceanside, CA: Academic Communication Associates, Inc., pp. 69-70. Adapted with permission.

Table 10-7
Working with Asian Parents:
Implications for Professionals

- Asians generally prefer to be referred to as Asians rather than Orientals.

- Shaking hands with someone of the opposite sex may be considered unacceptable.

- Parents may not disagree openly with or question professionals. When parents say "yes," they may mean "I hear you" rather than "I agree." Professionals need to be sure that parents truly understand the information that is being presented.

- It is best to establish rapport before venturing into frank discussions about specific problems that the child is encountering in school.

- Direct eye contact may be considered an open show of rudeness or challenge between individuals who are conversing.

- Much information is conveyed nonverbally through subtle gestures, postures, positioning, facial expressions, eye contact, and silence.

- It may be considered disloyal or disgraceful to the family for parents to openly discuss a child or family-related problem such as a disability. Professionals need to be sensitive when asking personal questions and may need to be indirect when discussing areas of concern.

- Many groups believe that caring for the handicapped is the responsibility of the family rather than the school.

- Some families believe that birth defects and disabilities result from sins committed by parents and even remote ancestors.

- Some parents may believe that ESL or bilingual classes are inferior to classes without these programs. Professionals should provide parents with information about bilingual programs of instruction.

- Asian parents often expect students to bring home large amounts of homework. Professionals may be asked to account for too little homework.

- Some Asian families may offer gifts in exchange for professional services, and may feel offended if professionals turn these gifts away.

- Use of the left hand to touch someone or to hand something to someone may be frowned upon. Some Asians consider the left hand to be unclean.

- Professionals should dress formally when making home visits. Some Asians view informal dress on such a visit as a sign of disrespect.

Source: Roseberry-McKibbin, C. (1995). *Multicultural students With special language needs*. Oceanside, CA: Academic Communication Associates, Inc., pp. 80, 83. Adapted with permission.

References

Armstrong, T. (1994). *Multiple intelligences in the classroom*. Alexandria, VA: Association for Supervision and Curriculum Development.

Astman, J. A. (1986). Reading and the role of imagination: Observations on meaning, skills, and the nature of knowing. In M. P. Douglass (Ed.), *Claremont Reading Conference: 50th Yearbook* (pp. 28-42). Claremont, CA: Claremont Reading Conference.

Au, K. (1993). *Literacy instruction in multicultural settings*. New York: Harcourt Brace Jovanovich.

Baca, L. M. & Cervantes, H. T. (1989). *The bilingual special education interface*. St. Louis, MO: Times Mirror/Mosby.

Bagley, M. & Hess, K. (1982). *200 Ways of using imagery in the classroom*. NJ: New Dimensions of the 80's Publications.

Barclay, K. D. (1990). Constructing meaning: An integrated approach to teaching reading. *Intervention in School and Clinic, 26 (2)*, 84-91.

Beaumont, C. & Langdon, H. W. Speech-language services for Hispanics with communication disorders: A framework. In Langdon, H. W. & Cheng, L. L. (Eds.) *Hispanic children and adults with communication disorders: Assessment and intervention*. Gaithersburg, MD: Aspen.

Benesch, R. (1988). *Ending remediation: Linking ESL and content in higher education*. Alexandria, VA: Teachers of English Speakers.

Bloom, B. S. Krathwohl, C. R., & Masia (1956). *Taxonomy of educational objectives. Handbook 1: Cognitive domain*. New York: David McKay Co.

Brown, K. (1993). Balancing the tools of technology with our own humanity: The use of technology in building partnerships and communities. In J. Tinajero & A. F. Ada (Eds.), *The power of two languages: Literacy and biliteracy for Spanish-speaking students* (pp. 178-198). New York: Macmillan/McGraw-Hill.

Bursuck, W. D. & Lessen, E. (1987). A classroom-based model for assessing students with learning disabilities. *Learning Disabilities Focus, 3*, 17-29.

Cambourne, B. (1988). *The whole story: Natural learning and the acquisition of literacy in the classroom*. Ontario, Canada: Scholastic-TAB, Ltd.

Campbell, D. (1999). Ethical issues in ESL. *Advance for Speech-Language Pathologists and Audiologists, 8 (46)*, 6-9.

Cartwright, G. P., Cartwright, C. A., & Ward, M. E. (1984). Educating special learners (2nd ed.). Belmont, CA: Wadsworth.

Cheng, L. L. (1991). *Assessing Asian language performance*. Oceanside, CA: Academic Communication Associates.

Clark, F. L., Deshler, D. D., Schumaker, J. B., Alley, G. R., & Warner, M. M. Visual imagery and self-questioning: Strategies to improve comprehension of written material. *Journal of Learning Disabilities, 1*, 145-149.

Clay, M. M. (1985). *The early detection of reading difficulties*. (3rd ed.), New York: Heinemann.

Coles, G. (1987). *The learning mystique: A critical look at learning disabilities*. New York: Fawcett Columbine.

Compton, C. (1997). *A guide to 100 tests in special education*. Belmont, CA: Fearon.

Cowles, R. V. (1991). Learning disabilities: A religious matter too. Unpublished master's thesis. School of Theology at Claremont, Claremont, CA.

Cullinan, B. E. (1986). Books in the classroom. *The Horn Book, 62,* 494-496.

Cummins, J. (1984). *Bilingualism and special education: Issues in assessment and pedagogy.* Austin, TX: PRO-ED.

Cummins, J. (1989). *Empowering minority students.* Sacramento, CA: California Association for Bilingual Education.

Cummins, J. (1991). Interdependence of first- and second- language proficiency in bilingual children. In Bialystok, E. (Ed.), *Language processing in bilingual children.* New York: Cambridge University Press.

Cummins, J. (1993). Empowerment through biliteracy. In Tinajero, J. V. & Ada, A. F. (Eds.). *The power of two languages: Literacy and biliteracy for Spanish-speaking students* (pp. 9-25). New York: Macmillan/McGraw-Hill.

Cummins, J. (1997). The role of primary language development in promoting educational success for language minority students. In *Schooling and language minority students: A theoretical framework* (pp. 3-50). Los Angeles: Evaluation, Dissemination, and Assessment Center, California State University.

Darling-Hammond, L. (1994). Setting standards for students: The case for authentic assessment. *The Educational Forum, 59,* 14-21.

Dewey, J. (1964). The child and the curriculum. In R. Archaumbault (Ed.), *John Dewey on education* (pp. 339-358). Chicago: University of Chicago Press.

Drecktrah, M. E. & Chiang, B. (1997). Instructional strategies used by general educators and teachers of students with learning disabilities. *Remedial and Special Education, 18 (3),* 174-181.

Dunn, R. (1995). Strategies for educating diverse learners. *Fastback No. 384.* Bloomington, IN: Phi Delta Kappa Educational Foundation.

Dunn, R. & Dunn, K. (1992). *Teaching elementary students through their individual learning styles: Practical approaches for grades 3-6.* Boston: Allyn & Bacon.

Echevarria, J. & McDonough, R. (1993). Instructional conversations in special education settings: Issues and accomodations (Education Practice Report 7). Santa Cruz: University of California at Santa Cruz, National Center for Research on Cultural Diversity and Second Language Learning.

Engel, B. S. (1994). Portfolio assessment and the new paradigm: New instruments and new places. *The Educational Forum, 59,* 22-27.

Fernald, Grace (1988). *Remedial techniques in basic school subjects.* Austin, TX: PRO-ED.

Flippo, R. (1997, December). Sensationalism, politics, and literacy: What's going on? *Phi Delta Kappan,* 301-304.

Flores, B., Cousin, P. & Diaz, E. (1991). Transforming deficit myths about learning, language, and culture. *Language Arts, 68,* 369-379.

Freeman, D. E. & Freeman, Y. S. (1994). *Between worlds: Access to second language acquisition.* Portsmouth, NH: Heinemann.

Freire, P. (1970). *Pedagogy of the oppressed.* New York: Seabury.

Friend, M. & Bauwens, J. (1988). Managing resistance: An essential consulting skill of learning disabilities teachers. *Journal of Learning Disabilities, 21 (9),* 556-561.

Galyean, B. (1983). Guided imagery in the curriculum. *Educational Leadership, 40 (6),* 54-58.

Gardner, H. (1982). *Art, mind and brain: A cognitive approach to creativity.* New York: Basic Books.

Gardner, H. (1983). *Frames of mind.* New York: Basic Books.

Gardner, H. (1991). *The unschooled mind: How children think & how schools should teach.* New York: Basic Books.

Gearheart, B. R., & C. J. (1989). *Learning disabilities: Educational strategies.* Columbus, OH: Merrill Publishing Company.

Goldman, M. E. (1993). Using captioned TV for teaching reading. *Fastback No. 359.* Bloomington, IN: Phi Delta Kappa Educational Foundation.

Goldman, S. R. & Rueda, R. (1988). Developing writing skills in bilingual exceptional children. *Exceptional Children, 54,* 543-551.

Goodrich, H. (1997). Understanding rubrics. *Educational Leadership, (December/January),* 14-17.

Grady, E. (1992). The portfolio approach to assessment. *Fastback No. 384.* Bloomington, IN: Phi Delta Kappa Educational Foundation.

Graham, S. & Harris, K. R. (1994). Implications of constructivism for teaching writing to students with special needs. *The Journal of Special Education, 28 (3),* 275-289.

Graves, M. F., Graves, B. B., & Braaten, S. (1996). Scaffolded reading experiences. *Educational Leadership, February, 1996,* 14-16.

Gredler, M. E. (1997). *Learning and instruction: Theory into practice* (3rd ed.). Upper Saddle River, NJ: Prentice-Hall, Inc.

Gronlund, N. E. (1973). Preparing criterion-referenced tests for classroom instruction. New York: Macmillan.

Hammill, D. D. (1993). A brief look at the learning disabilities movement in the United States. *Journal of Learning Disabilities, 26 (5),* 295-310.

Hammill, D. D. & Larson, S. C. (1974). The relationship of selected auditory perceptual skills and reading disability. *Journal of Learning Disabilities, 7,* 41-47.

Harry, B. (1992). *Cultural diversity, families, and the special education system: Communication and empowerment.* New York: Teachers College Press.

Hearne, J. D. (1987). Computer aptitude: New measures for new directions. *Counterpoint. May 1987,* 9.

Hearne, J. D. (1989). Learning disabilities: Models, trends and implications for secondary education. *American Secondary Education, 17 (3),* 20-23.

Hearne, J. D. & LeBlanc, L. (1991). Reading as inquiry: Using literature in the social studies. In P. Dreyer (Ed.), *Claremont Reading Conference 55th Yearbook.* Claremont, CA: Claremont Reading Conference.

Hearne, J. D., Poplin, M. S., Schoneman, C. & O'Shaughnessy, E. (1987). Computer aptitude: An investigation of differences among junior high students with learning disabilities and their non-learning-disabled peers. *Journal of Learning Disabilities, 21 (8),* 489-492.

Hearne, J. D. & Stone, S. (1996). Multiple intelligences and underachievement: Lessons from individuals with learning disabilities. In Poplin, M. S. & Cousin, P. (Eds.). *Alternative views of learning disabilities: Issues for the 21st century* (pp. 103-120). Austin, TX: PRO-ED.

Heckelman, R. G. (1978). *Using the neurological impress reading technique; Solutions to reading problems.* Novato, CA: Academic Therapy Publications, 28-32.

Heshusius, L. (1991). Curriculum-based assessment and direct instruction: Critical reflections on fundamental assumptions. *Exceptional Children, 57,* 315-329.

Hodgkinson, H. (1993). American education: The good, the bad, and the task. In S. Elam (Ed.), *The state of the nation's public schools: A conference report,* (12-23). Bloomington, IN: Phi Delta Kappa.

Huefner, D. S. (1988). The consulting teacher model: Risks and opportunities. *Exceptional Children, 54 (5),* 403-414.

Hunter, M. (1989). Knowing, teaching, and supervising. In P. Hosford (Ed.), *Using what we know about teaching.* Alexandria, VA: Association for Supervision and Curriculum Development.

Idol, L., Nevin, A., & Paolucci-Whitcomb, P. (1996). *Models of curriculum-based assessment.* Austin, TX: PRO-ED.

Johns, K. M. & Espinoza, C. (1992). Mainstreaming language minority children in reading and writing. *Fastback, No. 340.* Bloomington, IN: Phi Delta Kappa Foundation.

Johnson, D. W. & Johnson, R. T. (1986). Mainstreaming and cooperative learning strategies. *Exceptional Children, 52 (6)*, 553-561.

Joyce, B. & Weil, M. (1986). *Models of teaching (3rd ed.)*. Englewood Cliffs, NJ: Prentice-Hall.

Kagan, S. (1992). *Cooperative learning.* San Juan Capistrano, CA: Kagan Cooperative Learning/Resources for Teachers.

Keefe, C. H. & Keefe, D. R. (1993). Instruction for students with LD: A whole language model. *Intervention in School and Clinic. 28 (3)*, 172.

Kirk, S. A. (1963). Behavioral diagnoses and remediation of learning disabilities. *In Proceedings of the Annual Meeting of the Conference on Exploration into the Problems of the Perceptually Handicapped Child.*

Kohlberg, L. (1983). *The psychology of moral development.* San Francisco: Harper & Row.

Krashen, S. (1983). *Second language acquisition and second language learning.* Hayward, CA: Alemany Press.

Krashen, S. (1982). *Principles and practices in second language acquisition.* Oxford: Pergamon Press.

Krathwohl, D. R., Bloom, B. S., & Masia, B. B. (1964). *Taxonomy of educational objectives, Handbook II: The affective domain.* New York: David McKay Co.

Kugelmass, J. W. (1996). Educating children with learning disabilities in Foxfire classrooms. In M. S. Poplin & P. T. Cousin (Eds.), *Alternative views of learning disabilities: Issues for the 21st century* (pp. 251-268). Austin, TX: PRO-ED.

Langdon, H. W. & Merino, B. J. (1992). Acquisition and development of a second language in the Spanish Speaker. In Langdon, H. W. & Cheng, L. L. (Eds.) *Hispanic children and adults with communication disorders: Assessment and intervention.* Gaithersburg, MD: Aspen.

Larson, S. C. & Hammill, D. D. (1975). The relationship of selected visual-perceptual abilities to school learning. *Journal of Special Education, 9*, 281-291.

LeBlanc, L. (1998). From discipline-specific knowledge to interdisciplinary knowing. Unpublished manuscript.

Lerner, J. (1988). *Learning disabilities: Theories, diagnosis, and teaching strategies* (5th ed.). New York: Houghton Mifflin Company.

Lerner, J. (2000). *Learning disabilities: Theories, diagnosis, and teaching strategies* (8th ed.). New York: Houghton Mifflin Company.

Loesch, P. (1998). (personal communication).

MacInnis, C. & Hemming, H. (1995). Linking the needs of students with learning disabilities to a whole language curriculum. *Journal of Learning Disabilities, 28*, 535-544.

Maldonado-Colon, E. (1993). Cultural integration of children's literature. In J. V. Tinajero & A. F. Ada (eds.), *The power of two languages: Literacy and biliteracy for Spanish-speaking students* (pp. 100-106). New York: Macmillan/McGraw-Hill.

Masterson, J. J., Wynne, M. K., Kuster, J. M. & Stierwalk, A. G. (1999). New and emerging technologies: Going where we've never gone before. *Asha, 41 (3)*, 16-20.

Mattes, L. J. & Omark, D. R. (1991). *Speech and language assessment for the bilingual handicapped.* Oceanside, CA: Academic Communication Associates.

McCoy, K., & Weber, R. (1981). Image and perceptual representation of words in learning disabled and normal children. *Learning Disabilities Quarterly, 4*, 76-81.

McGee, L. M. & Lomax, R. G. (1990). On combining apples and oranges: A response to Stahl and Miller. *Review of Educational Research, 60*, 133-140.

McMaster, J. C. (1998). Doing literacy: Using drama to build literacy. *The Reading Teacher, 51 (7)*, 574-584.

Means, B., Olson, K., & Singh, R. (1995). Transforming with technology: No silver bullet. *Phi Delta Kappan, 77*, 69-72.

Mehan, H., Hertweck, K. & Meihls, J. (1986). *Handicapping the handicapped.* Palo Alto, CA: Stanford University Press.

Meltzer, L. & Reid, K. K. (1994). New directions in the assessment of students with special needs: The shift toward a constructivist perspective. *The Journal of Special Education, 28*, 338-355.

Mercer, C. D. (1987). *Students with learning disabilities*. Columbus, OH: Merrill Publishing Co.

Mergendoller, J. R. (1997). Technology and learning: The research. *Principal, 76*, 12-14.

Moreno, B. D. (1993). Listening to children's voices: Opening the door through fairy tales. In J. V. Tinajero & A. F. Ada (Eds.), *The power of two languages: Literacy and biliteracy for Spanish-speaking students*. (pp. 71-83). NY: Macmillan-McGraw-Hill.

National Joint Committee on Learning Disabilities. (1988). (Letter to NJCLD member organizations).

Newman, J. M. & Church, S. M. (1991). 19 Ways to misread whole language. *Education Digest (April)*, 25-29.

Ortiz, A. (1997). Learning disabilities occurring concomitantly with linguistic differences. *Journal of Learning Disabilities, 30 (3)*, 321-332.

Piaget, J. (1955). *Language and thought of the child*. New York: New American Library.

Piajet, J. (1977). (H. E. Gruber & J. Voneche, Trans.). *The essential Piaget*. New York: Basic Books.

Pinnell, G.S., DeFord, D. E., & Lyons, C. A. (1988). *Reading Recovery: Early intervention for at-risk first graders*. Arlington,VA: Educational Research Service.

Poplin, M. S. (1984). Toward a holistic view of persons with learning disabilities. *Learning Disabilities Quarterly, 7*, 290-294.

Poplin, M. S. (1986). The quest for meaning. In M. P. Douglass (Ed.), *Claremont Reading Conference: 50th Yearbook* (pp. 1-27). Claremont, CA: Claremont Reading Conference.

Poplin, M. S. (1988). The reductionist fallacy in learning disabilities: Replicating the past by reducing the present. *Journal of Learning Disabilities, 21*, 389-400.

Poplin, M. S. (1993). Multiple intelligences and the learning disabled. Unpublished manuscript. The Claremont Graduate School, Claremont, CA.

Poplin, M. S. (1996). Looking through other lenses and listening to other voices: Issues for the 21st century. In M. S. Poplin & P. T. Cousin (Eds.), *Alternative views of learning disabilities: Issues for the 21st century*. Austin, TX: PRO-ED.

Poplin, M. S. & Cousin, P. T. (1996). *Alternative views of learning disabilities: Issues for the 21st century*. Austin, TX: PRO-ED.

Poplin, M. S. & Stone, S. (1992). Paradigm shifts in instructional strategies: From reductionism to holistic/constructivism. In W. Stainback & S. Stainback (Eds.), *Controversial issues confronting special education* (pp. 153-179). Boston, MA: Allyn and Bacon.

Rasinski, T. V. (1985). Picture this: Using imagery as a reading comprehension strategy. *Reading Horizons, 25*, 280-288.

Reid, D. K. (1998). Scaffolding: A broader view. *Journal of Learning Disabilities, 31, 4*, 386-396.

Reyes, M. de la luz. (1992). Challenging venerable assumptions: Literacy instruction for linguistically different students. *Harvard Educational Review, 62 (4)*, 427-446.

Reynolds, M., Wang, M., & Walberg, H., (1987). The necessary restructuring of special and regular education. *Exceptional Children, 14*, 5-29.

Roseberry-McKibbin, C. (1995). *Multicultural students with special language needs*. Oceanside, CA: Academic Communication Associates.

Routman, R. (1991). *Invitations: Changing as teachers and learners K-12*. Portsmouth, NH: Heinemann.

Rueda, R. (1989). Defining mild disabilities with language-minority students. *Exceptional Children, 56*, 121-128.

Ruiz, N. (1989). An optimal learning environment for Rosemary. *Exceptional Children, 56*, 130-144.

Ruiz, N. T., Rueda, R., Figueroa, R. A., & Boothroyd, M. (1996). Bilingual special education teachers' shifting paradigms: Complex responses to educational reform. In M. S. Poplin and P. T. Cousin (Eds.), *Alternative views of learning disabilities: Issues for the 21st century*. Austin, TX: PRO-ED.

Salend, S. J. & Fradd, S. (1986). Nationwide availability of services for limited English-proficient handicapped students. *The Journal of Special Education, 20*, 127-135.

Seidel, S., Walters, J. , Kirby, E., Olff, N., Powell, K., Scripp, L. & Veenema, S. (1997). Portfolio practices: Thinking through the assessment of children's work. In R. M. McClure (Ed.), *NEA School Restructuring Series*, Washington D. C.: National Educational Association.

Shepard, L. A. (1987). The new push for excellence: Widening the schism between regular and special education. *Exceptional Children, 53*, 327-329.

Shuy, R. (1984). Language as a foundation for education: The school context. *Theory into Practice, 23*, 167-174.

Sleeter, C. E. (1986). Learning disabilities: A social construction of a special education category. *Exceptional Children, 53 (1)*, 46-54.

Sleeter, C. E. & Grant, C. A. (1994). *Making choices for multicultural education: Five approaches to race, class, and gender* (2nd ed.). New York: Macmillan.

Smith, C. R. (1991). Learning disabilities: The interaction of learner, task, and setting. Boston: Allyn and Bacon.

Stewart, L. T. (1997). Readers theatre and the writing workshop: Using children's literature to prompt student writing. *The Reading Teacher, 51 (2)*, 174-175.

Terrell, T. D. (1977). A natural approach to second language acquisition and learning. *The Modern Language Journal, 61 (7)*, 325-337.

Terrell, T. D. (1981). The natural approach in bilingual education. *Schooling and language minority students: A theoretical framework*. Los Angeles: California Evaluation, Dissemination and Assessment Center, California State University, Los Angeles.

Thonis, E. (1993). Reading begins in the crib. In J. V. Tinajero & A. F. Ada (Eds.). *The power of two languages: Literacy and biliteracy for Spanish-speaking students*. New York: Macmillan/McGraw-Hill.

Tierney, R. J. (1998). Literacy assessment reform: Shifting beliefs, principled possibilities, and emerging practices. *The Reading Teacher, 51 (5)*, 374-390.

Tindall, G., Shinn, M., Walz, M. & Germann, G. (1987). Mainstream consultation in secondary settings: The Pine County model. *The Journal of Special Education, 21 (3)*, 94-106).

Tompkins, G. E. & Hoskisson, K. (1991). *Language arts: Content and teaching strategies*. New York: Macmillan.

Twomey-Fosnot, C. (1990). *Enquiring teachers, enquiring learners*. New York: Teachers College Press.

U. S. Office of Education (1977, August 23). Education of handicapped children implementation of Part B of the Education for the Handicapped Act. *Federal Register, Part II*. Washington, DC: U.S. Department of Health Education, and Welfare.

U. S. Office of Education (1977, December 29). Education of handicapped children. Assistance of the states: Procedures for evaluating specific learning disabilities. *Federal Register, Part III*. Washington, DC: U.S. Department of Health Education, and Welfare.

Wagstaff, J. (1994). *Phonics that work: New strategies for the reading/writing classroom*. Jefferson, MO: Scholastic Inc.

Wang, M. C. & Reynolds, M. C. (1986). Catch 22 and disabling help: A reply to Alan Gartner. *Exceptional Children, 53*, 77-79.

Weber, R. L. (1986). The use of imagery with learning disabled students. *Counterpoint, 3*, 9.

Weston, R. & Ingram, G. L. (1997). Whole language and technology: Opposites, or opposites in harmony? *Educational Horizons, Winter*, 83-89.

Will, M. C. (1986). Educating children with learning problems: A shared responsibility. *Exceptional Children, 52,* 411-415.

Winebrenner, S. (1966). *Teaching kids with learning difficulties in the regular classroom: Strategies and techniques every teacher can use to challenge and motivate struggling students.* Minneapolis, MN: Free Spirit Publishing.

Wishnietsky, D. H. (1992). Hypermedia: the integrated learning environment. *Fastback No. 339.* Bloomington, IN: Phi Delta Kappa Educational Foundation.

Wood, D. J., Bruner, J. & Ross, G. (1976). The role of tutoring in problem-solving. *Journal of Child Psychology and Psychiatry, 17 (2),* 89-100.

Appendixes

Appendix A
High Interest – Low Vocabulary Reading
(Many titles are available in Spanish)

Title	Publisher	Reading Level	Interest Level
		Grade	*Grade*
American Adventure Series	Harper & Row	3 - 6	4 - 8
Annie Wilkins Mysteries	High Noon Books	2	4 - 12
Basic Vocabulary Books	Garrard	2	1 - 6
Cowboy Sam Series	Benefic Press	PP - 3	1 - 6
Dan Frontier Series	Benefic Press	PP - 4	1 - 7
Deep Sea Adventures	Field Educational Publications	2 - 4	6 - 12
Ecology Series	High Noon Books	2	4 - 12
Everyreader Series	McGraw-Hill	6 - 8	5 - 12
Fastback Books	Fearon	4 - 5	6 - 12
First Reading Books	Garrard	1	1 - 4
Folklore of the World	Garrard	2	2 - 8
High Adventures	High Noon Books	3 - 4	4 - 12
High Five Series	High Noon Books	3	4 - 12
Jim Forest Readers	Field Educational Publications	1 - 3	1 - 7
Junior Science Books	Garrard	4 - 5	6 - 9
Legal Eagle Series	High Noon Books	3 - 4	4 - 12
Meg Parker Series	High Noon Books	2	4 - 12
Morgan Bay Mysteries	Field Educational Publications	2 - 4	4 - 11
Morrow's High Interest/ Easy Reading Books	William Morrow	1 - 8	4 - 10
Mystery Adventure Series	Benefic Press	2 - 6	4 - 9
On Their Own: Adventure Athletes in Solo	High Noon	3	4 - 12
Pacemaker True Adventure	Fearon	2	7 - 12
Pal Paperback Kits	Xerox Education Publications	2	7 - 12
Perspectives Sets 1-2	High Noon Books	3 - 4	4 - 12
Pleasure Reading Books	Garrard	4	3 - 7
Postcards from Series	High Noon Books	2	4 - 12
Racing Wheels Series	Benefic Press	2 - 4	4 - 9
Reading For Concepts Series	McGraw-Hill	3 - 8	5 - 12
Reading Success Paperbacks	High Noon Books	3 - 4	4 - 12
Riddle Street Mysteries	High Noon Books	1	4 - 9
Sailor Jack Series	Benefic Press	PP - 3	1 - 6
Scoreboard Series	High Noon Books	2	4 - 10
Space Science Fiction Series	Benefic Press	2 - 6	4 - 9
Sports Mystery Series	Benefic Press	2 - 4	4 - 9
Tom and Ricky Mysteries	High Noon Books	1 - 2	4 - 9
Unusual Events	High Noon Books	3 - 4	4 - 12
What Is It? - Series	Benefic Press	1 - 4	1 - 8

Appendix B
Organizations For Exceptional Children

Alexander Graham Bell Association for the Deaf, Inc. - 3417 Volta Place, NW, Washington, DC 20007

American Foundation for the Blind - 15 West 16th Street, NY, NY 10017

American Psychological Association - 1200 17th Street NW, Washington, DC 20036

American Speech-Language-Hearing Association, 10801 Rockville Pike, Rockville, MD 20852

Association for the Gifted - CEC, 1920 Association Drive, Reston, VA 22091

Association for the Severely Handicapped - 7010 Roosevelt Way NE, Seattle, WA 98115

CHADD - Children and Adults with Attention Deficit Disorder, 499 Northwest 70th Avenue, Suite 308, Plantation, FL 33317

Chicago Institute for Learning Disabilities (social adjustment, language) - University of Illinois at Chicago Circle, Box 4348, Chicago, IL 60680

Clearinghouse on the Handicapped - Rm. 3106, Switzer Bldg., Washington, DC 20202

Council for Children with Behavior Disorders - CEC, 1920 Association Drive, Reston, VA 22091

Council for Exceptional Children (CEC) - 1920 Association Drive, Reston, VA 22091

Council for Learning Disabilities (CLD) - Department of Special Education, University of Louisville, KY 40292

Division for Children with Learning Disabilities - 850 Hungerford Drive, Rockville, MD 20850

Division for Visually Handicapped - CEC, 1920 Association Drive, Reston, VA 22091

ERIC Clearinghouse on Disabilities and Gifted Education - CEC, 1920 Association Drive, Reston, VA 22091

Institute for Research on Learning Disabilities (identification, assessment, and placement), 350 Elliot Hall, 75 East River Road, University of Minnesota, Minneapolis, MN 55455

Latino Institute, Research Center, Project REACH, 1760 Reston Avenue, Suite 101, Reston, VA 22090

Learning Disabilities Association of America (LDA) - 4900 Gerard Rd., Pittsburgh, PA 15236

Learning Disabilities Research Institute (attentional deficits) University of Virginia, Department of Special Education, 152 Ruffner Hall, Charlottesville, VA 22903

National Association for Gifted Children - 217 Gregory Drive, Hot Springs, AR 71901

National Association for the Deaf - 814 Thayer Avenue, Silver Spring, MD 20910

National Federation for the Blind - 1800 Johnson Street, Baltimore, MD 21230

National Information Center for Children and Youth with Disabilities (NICHCY). P.O. Box 1492, Washington, DC 20013-1492

Orton Society, Inc. - 8415 Bellona Lane, Baltimore, MD 21204

Research Institute in Learning Disabilities (LD adolescents) - University of Kansas, Room 313, Lawrence, KS 66045

Technical Assistance for Parent Programs Project (TAPP), Federation for Children with Special Needs, 95 Berkeley St., Suite 104, Boston, MA 02116

Appendix C
Behavior Charts

The three behavior charts in this Appendix can be used to facilitate changes in behavior that will promote learning in the classroom environment.

BEHAVIOR CHART 1: The Need for Belonging, Friendship, and Love

The need to be accepted as you are; to be a sought-after member of a desired group or class.

Inappropriate Behaviors (indications that the need is not being met)	Interventions (ways to meet the need)	Actions/Responses to Avoid
• Demands much teacher attention and time; always needs help	• Recognize him for his strengths and chat with him about his outside-of-school interests to demonstrate that you care about him as a person even though he sometimes misbehaves.	• Choosing teams or cooperative groups publicly
• May be shy, fearful, tentative OR		• Threats and punishments
• May be bossy, a show-off, or class clown	• Immediately recognize positive behaviors.	• Anything that looks like a rejection
• Nosy; wants to know everyone's business	• Have her tutor younger kids.	• Ignoring the student
• May express anger; bullies others	• Use the Name Card method; occasionally paraphrase his responses.	• Giving in to power struggles
• May destroy things that belong to others	• Showcase her strengths in group learning situations.	• Giving too much help; this may enable the student into helplessness
• Complains that "no one likes me"	• Give him important jobs.	

Source: Excerpt from *Teaching Kids with Learning Difficulties in the Regular Classroom: Strategies and Techniques Every Teacher Can Use to Challenge and Motivate Struggling Students*, by Susan Winebrenner, © 1998. Used with permission from Free Spirit Publishing. Minneapolis, MN: 1-800-735-7328. ALL RIGHTS RESERVED.

BEHAVIOR CHART 2: The Need for Self-Worth

The need to feel worthy, important, and competent; to feel that your abilities are appreciated and that success is attainable.

Inappropriate Behaviors (indications that the need is not being met)	Interventions (ways to meet the need)	Actions/Responses to Avoid
• Expects and gets failure; gives up when frustrated	• Create a "risk-free" learning environment in which mistakes are invited.	• Helping too much; students can "learn helplessness."
• Speaks negatively about himself	• Teach the link between effort and outcomes.	• Doing for the student what she can do for herself
• Makes excuses—whines, cries, complains, worries	• Model positive thinking and attribution statements.	• Repetition; drill; sameness
• Procrastinates; exhibits an "I don't care" attitude	• Match learning tasks with the student's learning style strengths.	• Threats; punishment; sarcasm; public teasing
• "Puts down" other students who are successful	• Present tasks that are slightly challenging and worth doing.	• Assigning extra work when regular work has not been completed
• Rarely produces work; is disorganized; copies from others	• Connect new learning to previously mastered concepts.	• Rejection
• Directs attention away from herself; blames others; tattles	• Focus on only one deficit area at a time.	
• Withdraws; may not speak if spoken to	• Teach him how to set short-term daily goals.	
• Is frequently absent or tardy	• Uses the Name Card method; occasionally paraphrase her responses.	
	• Incorporate his interests into his schoolwork.	

BEHAVIOR CHART 3: The Need for Freedom, Autonomy, and Choices

The need to feel in control of what happens to you; The freedom to make choices and decisions about what affects you.

Inappropriate Behaviors (indications that the need is not being met)	Interventions (ways to meet the need)	Actions/Responses to Avoid
• Constantly seeks attention • Blurts or calls out; makes strange noises • Interrupts or talks loudly • Tattles; teases • Tells "tall tales" and other types of untruths • May bully or fight • Sounds angry and argumentative much of the time; challenges authority • Pushes the rules to the outer limits; seeks "exceptions" • Wears unusual clothing or hairstyles that make him "stand out" in a group • Complains "I don't want to do this. Why do we have to do this?" • Procrastinates; is forgetful • Accuses the teacher and the system of unfairness	• Offer meaningful choices whenever possible. • Learn about her personal interests and chat daily for 1-2 minutes about them. • Incorporate his interests into his schoolwork. • Demonstrate how knowledge increases personal power. • Use the Name Card method; occasionally paraphrase her responses. • Assign him important jobs in the classroom and school. • Harness her leadership ability. • Model, teach, and reinforce desirable behaviors including anger control strategies. • Help him set his own short-term goals for improvement. • Ask her to describe the consequences of inappropriate behaviors to make sure she understands them. • Use nonverbal cues to signal recognition of negative behaviors and reinforcement of positive behaviors. *Examples:* "When I tug my ear, that means you need to choose a more appropriate behavior. When I nod at you, I am noticing that you made a good choice." • Apply consequences without anger. • Let bullies know that the school's authority extends beyond the school and grounds.	• Expecting all students to do the same work in the same way • Power struggles; authoritarian statements like "Because I say so." • Threats, punishments, and extra work • Ignoring students when they are behaving appropriately • Totally negative parent conferences • Allowing students to set teachers and parents against each other by reporting information third-hand. Parents and teachers should communicate *directly* about sensitive issues.

Source: Excerpt from *Teaching Kids with Learning Difficulties in the Regular Classroom: Strategies and Techniques Every Teacher Can Use to Challenge and Motivate Struggling Students*, by Susan Winebrenner, © 1998. Used with permission from Free Spirit Publishing, Minneapolis, MN: 1-800-735-7328. ALL RIGHTS RESERVED.

BEHAVIOR CHART 4:   The Need for Fun and Enjoyment

The need to have fun; Time and opportunities for laughter, play, and entertainment.

Inappropriate Behaviors (indications that the need is not being met)	Interventions (ways to meet the need)	Actions/Responses to Avoid
• Silliness; giggling • Class clown; makes other laugh • Plays with toys and other objects • Tells lots of personal stories	• Understand that giggling is one way to release excess energy and anxiety. • Incorporate fun into regular school tasks, as well as at recess and play time. • Add variety to schoolwork. • Use game formats to teach needed information.	• Being serious all of the time • Predictable activities that rarely allow for variety • Sending messages that there is only one "correct" way to do things

Source: Excerpt from *Teaching Kids with Learning Difficulties in the Regular Classroom: Strategies and Techniques Every Teacher Can Use to Challenge and Motivate Struggling Students*, by Susan Winebrenner, © 1998. Used with permission from Free Spirit Publishing. Minneapolis, MN: 1-800-735-7328. ALL RIGHTS RESERVED.

Appendix D
Web Sites for Learning Resources

Web sites that provide information or resources relating specifically to the needs of second language learners and students with learning disabilities are listed below. New web sites are being created all the time.

American Speech-Language-Hearing Association

The American-Speech-Language-Hearing Association (ASHA) is concerned with issues in the assessment and treatment of disorders that affect speech, language, and hearing. ASHA has been actively involved in issues relating to the needs of culturally diverse populations. WEB SITE: www.asha.org

Blue Web'N

Blue Web'N is a huge index of educational sites for teachers. Links take you to activities, projects, unit and lesson plans, reference tools galore, and web-based tutorials. Each site is ranked by quality and cross-indexed by grade level and subject from art to zoology. WEB SITE: www.kn.pacbell.com/wired/bluewebn

Busy Teachers' Web Site

This award-winning site was created to help K-12 teachers find direct source materials, lesson plans, and classroom activities. Information is divided into 19 categories, such as English, math, guidance/counseling, and even recess. To make things easier, there is background information on each category. WEB SITE: www.ceismc.gatech.edu/BusyT

Classroom Connect

This searchable directory of educational sites and resources offers thousands of ideas for teachers. Includes information on learning disabilities, assertive discipline, packets for substitute teachers, to name just a few! WEB SITE: www.classroom.net

Council for Exceptional Children

The Council for Exceptional Children is one of the oldest and most respected organizations devoted to research and development in the field of special education. It is divided into several divisions, each devoted to study of specific disabilities/exceptionalities. CEC produces several journals for parents and educators, and it hosts local, state, and international conferences. WEB SITE: www.cec.sped.org/bk/tec-jour.htm

Discovery Channel School Online

Here's a monster site that includes information for K-12 teachers about resources related to science, social studies, language arts, and the humanities. Search its database of lesson plans by grade level and/or subject area and WEB SITE: www.school.discovery.com

Educational Resources Information Center (ERIC)

Sponsored by the U. S. Department of Education, ERIC is the mother of all educational web sites. It houses the largest database of educational materials in the world, including 850,000 abstracts of publications, lesson plans, a question-and-answer service, conference papers land research. WEB SITE: www.askeric.org

Education World

Offers lots of lesson-planning and curriculum resources. Information rages from outrageous women in history to Dr. Seuss. In addition to a huge education-oriented search engine, there's a message board and a searchable database of 50,000 web sites of interest to teachers. WEB SITE: www.education-world.com

Eisenhower National Clearinghouse for Mathematics and Science Education

A comprehensive database of exemplary K-12 programs for teaching science and math that even includes tips on integrating math and science with literature. A professional development exchange lists workshops, internships, journal articles, classes, and grants for educators. WEB SITE: www.enc.org

Franklin Institute

An Educational Hotlist link connects you to more than 30 major topics. Information ranges from professional development for educators to links for school librarians. Included are strategies for helping the ADD student, tips for successful science fairs, and ideas on multicultural heroes projects. WEB SITE: www.fi.edu/tfi/hotlists

International Dyslexia Association

The International Dyslexia Association maintains and distributes materials and resources on dyslexia and related reading problems. WEB SITE: www.interdys.org

Kathy Schrock's Guide for Educators

Organized by subject area, this award-winning web site contains links to over 1,400 sites for educators. There's something for every teacher from special education resources to cultural activities for the classroom. It also has connections to major search engines and instructions on how to use them. WEB SITE: www.capecod.net/schrockguide

Library of Congress

The Educator's Page and Learn More sections offer lesson plans, classroom ideas and reading lists designed to help educators teach history, creative writing, and critical thinking. Explore the American Memory Collection of texts, photos, sound recordings, movies, and maps of historic events with corresponding lesson plans. Or roam through exhibitions, databases, or up-to-date legislative information. WEB SITE: www.loc.gov

LD Online

Created and maintained by The Coordinated Campaign for Learning Disabilities ((CCLD), LD Online provides a wealth of information on learning disabilities and related topics. WEB SITE: www.ldonline.org

National Center for Learning Disabilities

NCLD provides current information on resources and services relating to learning disabilities. WEB SITE: www.ncld.org

National Geographic

You'll find lots of social studies resources, including lesson plans, units, maps, and activities searchable by grade level for K-12. A Map Machine lets you zero in on any place in the world for quick and easy access to statistics and information on individual countries. WEB SITE: www.nationalgeographic.com/resources/

Public Broadcasting Service (PBS)

PBS's Teacher Resource Service is loaded with creative ideas for using video as a tool for classroom learning. Look for the Electronic Field Trips, Mathline, and Scienceline sections. A Teacher's Digest provides success stories from teachers based upon their classroom experiences. WEB SITE: www.pbs.org/learn/

Smithsonian Education on the Web

An electronic version of our national museums, this site houses information about the Smithsonian's programs and collections, including an enormous photography database. Take note of the active-learning lesson plans and classroom activities geared especially for upper elementary school students. WEB SITE: www.si.edu/

Teachers Helping Teachers

Between 600 and 1000 teachers visit this site daily. Why? Because it's full of lesson plans and links, activities for learning, and strategies for teaching. There's also a bulletin board and a teacher's chat room for exchanging ideas with others using Internet Relay Chat (IRC). WEB SITE: www.pacificnet.net/~mandel

Appendix E
Selected Publications with Information
Relating to Special Education

American Journal of Speech-Language Pathology
ASHA Leader
Analysis and Intervention of Developmental Disabilities
Bulletin of the Orton Society
Childhood Education
Disabled U.S.A.
Early Years
Educational Horizons
Exceptional Children
Exceptional Parent
Focus on Autism and Other Developmental Disabilities
Focus on Exceptional Children
Gifted Child Quarterly
Instructor
Intervention in School and Clinic
Journal of Learning Disabilities
Journal of Special Education
Journal of Special Education Technology
Language, Speech, and Hearing Services in Schools
Learning Disabilities Focus
Learning Disabilities Quarterly
Learning Disabilities Research
Perceptual and Motor Skills
Reading Teacher
Remedial and Special Education
Teacher Education and Special Education
Teaching Behaviorally Disordered Youth
Teaching Exceptional Children
The Creative Child and Adult Quarterly
The Deaf American
Today's Education
Topics in Early Childhood Special Education
Topics in Language Disorders

Appendix F
Selected Bilingual Assessment Instruments

This listing is limited to commercially-available speech and language assessment instruments commonly used in special education evaluations. The instruments are grouped by publisher. Professionals should be cautious when using tests that are direct translations of English language measures. Moreover, norms from the English version of a test should never be used when the test is administered in a language other than English.

Publisher: Academic Communication Associates, Inc.
Address: P.O. Box 4279
            Oceanside, CA 92052-4279

    Spanish Language Assessment Procedures
    Spanish Test for Assessing Morphologic Production
    Spanish Articulation Measures
    Bilingual Classroom Communication Profile
    Bilingual Language Proficiency Questionnaire - English/Spanish
    Bilingual Language Proficiency Questionnaire - English/Vietnamese
    Bilingual Vocabulary Assessment Measure- English, Spanish, French, Italian, and Vietnamese

Publisher: Academic Therapy Publications
Address: 20 Commercial Blvd.
            Novato, CA 94949-6191

    Dos Amigos Verbal Language Scales - English/Spanish

Publisher: American Guidance Services
Address: P.O. Box 99
            Circle Pines, MN 55014-1796

    Test de Vocabulario en Imagenes Peabody (Spanish version of the Peabody Picture Vocabulary Test)
    Woodcock Language Proficiency Test - English/Spanish

Publisher: Psychological Corporation
Address: 555 Academic Court
            San Antonio, TX 78204-2498

    Boehm Test of Basic Concepts - English/Spanish
    Clinical Evaluation of Language Fundamentals - English/ Spanish
    Preschool Language Scales - English/Spanish

Appendix G
Checklist for Selecting and Evaluating Materials

Are the perspectives and contributions of people from diverse cultural and linguistic groups – both men and women, as well as people with disabilities – included in the curriculum?

Are there activities in the curriculum that will assist students in analyzing the various forms of the mass media for ethnocentrism, sexism, handicapism, and stereotyping?

Are men and women, diverse cultural/racial groups, and people with varying abilities shown in both active and passive roles?

Are men and women, diverse cultural/racial groups of people with disabilities shown in positions of power (i.e., the materials do not rely on the mainstream culture's character to achieve goals)?

Do the materials identify strengths possessed by so-called underachieving diverse populations? Do they diminish the attention given to deficits, to reinforce positive behaviors that are desired and valued?

Are members of diverse racial/cultural groups, men and women, and people with disabilities shown engaged in a broad range of social and professional activities?

Are members of a particular culture or group depicted as having a range of physical features (e.g., hair color, hair texture, variations in facial characteristics and body build)?

Do the materials represent historical events from the perspectives of the various groups involved or solely from the male, middle-class, and/or Western European perspective?

Are the materials free of ethnocentric or sexist language patterns that may make implications about persons or groups based solely on their culture, race, gender, or disability?

Will students from different ethnic and cultural backgrounds find the materials personally meaningful to their life experiences?

Are a wide variety of culturally different examples, situations, scenarios, and anecdotes used throughout the curriculum design to illustrate major intellectual concepts and principles?

Are culturally diverse content, examples, and experiences comparable in kind, significance, magnitude, and function to those selected from mainstream culture?

Source: Garcia, S.B. & Malkin, D.H. (1993). Toward Defining Programs and Services for Culturally Linguistically Diverse Learners in Special Education. *Teaching Exceptional Children, 26 (1)*, pg. 116. Reprinted with permission from the Council for Exceptional Children.

Appendix H
Recommended Readings and Resources

Assessment

Blum, R. E. & Arter, J. (1996). *A handbook for student performance assessment in an era of restructuring.* Alexandria, VA: Association for Supervision and Curriculum Development.

Butler, K. G. (Ed.) (1994). *Cross-cultural perspectives in language assessment and intervention.* Gaithersburg, MD: Aspen.

Cheng, L. L. (1991). *Assessing Asian language performance.* Oceanside, CA: Academic Communication Associates.

Danielson, C. & Abrutyn, L. (1997). *An introduction to using portfolios in the classroom.* Alexandria, VA: Association for Supervision and Curriculum Development.

Guskey, T. & Johnson, D. (1996). *Alternative ways to document and communicate student learning (audiotape).* Alexandria, VA: Association for Supervision and Curriculum Development.

Hamayan, E., & Damico, J. (1991). *Limiting bias in the assessment of bilingual students.* Austin, TX: PRO-ED.

Kranz, B. (1994). Identifying talents among multicultural children. *Fastback No 364.* Bloomington, IN: Phi Delta Kappa Educational Foundation.

Langdon, H. W. & Saenz, T. I. (Eds.). (1996). *Language assessment and intervention with multicultural students.* Oceanside, CA: Academic Communication Associates.

Mattes, L. J. & Omark, D. R. (1991). *Speech and language assessment for the bilingual handicapped.* Oceanside, CA: Academic Communication Associates.

Perrone, V. (Ed.). (1991). *Expanding student assessment.* Alexandria, VA: Association for Supervision and Curriculum Development.

Rangel, R. & Bansberg, B. (1997). S*napshot assessment system for migrant, language minority, and mobile students.* Alexandria, VA: Association for Supervision and Curriculum Development.

Seidel, S., Walters, J., Kirby, E., Olff, N., Powell, K., Scripp, L. & Veenema, S. (1997). *Portfolio practices: Thinking through the assessment of children's work.* Washington, D. C.: National Education Association.

Constructivist Approaches

Journal of Special Education (Fall 1994). Special issue. Implications of constructivism for students with disabilities and students at risk: Issues and directions.

Airasian, P. W. & Walsh, M. E. (1997). *Constructivist cautions. Phi Delta Kappan, 78* (6), *444-449.*

Brooks, J. G. & Brooks, M. G. (1993). *In search of understanding: The case for constructivist classrooms.* Alexandria, VA: Association for Supervision and Curriculum Development.

Brooks, J. G. & Brooks, M. (1997). *Constructivism* (program kit). Alexandria, VA: Association for Supervision and Curriculum Development.

Educational Leadership (December, 1999). Special topical issue on "The Constructivist Classroom."

Poplin, M. S. & Cousin, P. (Eds.). (1995). *Alternative views of learning disabilities: Issues for the 21st century*. Austin, TX: PRO-ED.

Twomey-Fosnot, C. (1989). *Enquiring teachers, enquiring learners: A constructivist approach for teaching*. New York: Teachers College Press.

Zahorik, J. A. (1995). Constructivist teaching. *Fastback No. 390*. Bloomington, IN: Phi Delta Kappan Educational Foundation.

Cooperative Learning

Johnson, D. W., Johnson, R. T. & Holubec, E. J. (1994). *Cooperative learning in the classroom*. Alexandria, VA: Association for Supervision and Curriculum Development.

Kagan, S. (1992). *Cooperative learning*. San Juan Capistrano, CA: Kagan Cooperative Learning Resources for Teachers.

Slavin, R. & Farnish, A. M. (1997). *Cooperative learning: A quarter-century of research and practice*. Alexandria, VA: Association for Supervision and Curriculum Development.

Wynne, E. A. (1995). Cooperative-competition: An instructional strategy. *Fastback No 378*. Bloomington, IN: Phi Delta Kappa Educational Foundation.

Integrating the Curriculum

Drake, S. (1993). *Planning integrated curriculum*. Alexandria, VA: Association for Supervision and Curriculum Development.

Jacobs, H. H. (1997). *Mapping the big picture – Integrating the curriculum and assessment*. Alexandria, VA: Association for Supervision and Curriculum Development.

Stepien, B. & Gallagher, S. (1997). *Problem-based learning across the curriculum* (inquiry kit). Alexandria, VA: Association for Supervision and Curriculum Development.

Learning Styles / Multiple Intelligences

Armstrong, T. (1994). *Multiple intelligences in the classroom*. Alexandria, VA: Association for Supervision and Curriculum Development.

Boyer, G. (1997). Teaching for understanding through multiple intelligences (videotape). Alexandria, VA: Association for Supervision and Curriculum Development.

Gardner, H. (1995). On multiple intelligences and education with Howard Gardner (videotape). Alexandria, VA: Association for Supervision and Curriculum Development.

Guild, P. (1995). An overview of learning styles (audiotape/kit). Alexandria, VA: Association for Supervision and Curriculum Development.

Hand, K. (1996). Using learning styles to help all children be successful (audiotape). Alexandria, VA: Association for Supervision and Curriculum Development.

Lazear, D. (1991). Seven ways of knowing: Teaching with multiple intelligences. Palatine, IL: Skylight.

Mamchur, C. (1996). A teacher's guide to cognitive type theory and learning style. Alexandria, VA: Association for Supervision and Curriculum Development.

Silver, H. & Strong, R. (1995). *Teaching to different learning styles and multiple intelligences* (audiotape). Alexandria, VA: Association for Supervision and Curriculum Development.

Multicultural Issues, Language, and Learning

Anderson, C. C., Nicklas, S. K. & Crawford, A. R. (1994). *Global understandings: A framework for teaching and learning.* Alexandria, VA: Association for Supervision and Curriculum Development.

Au, K. (1993). Literacy instruction in multicultural settings: New York: Harcourt Brace.

Baca, L., & Cervantes, H. (1984) *The bilingual special education interface.* St. Louis: Times Mirror/Mosby.

Banks, J. A. (1997). Teaching strategies for ethnic studies (6th ed.). Boston: Allyn and Bacon.

Battle, D. (Ed.). *Communication disorders in multicultural populations.* Stoneham, MA: Butterworth-Heinemann.

Bialystok, E. & Hakuta, K. (1994). In other words: The science and psychology of second language acquisition. New York: Basic Books

Cummins, J. (1984). *Bilingualism and special education: Issues in assessment and pedagogy.* Austin, TX: PRO-ED.

Delpit, L. (1995). Other people's children: Cultural conflict in the classroom. New York: The New York Press.

Fradd, S., & Weismantel, M. J. (1989). *Meeting the needs of culturally and linguistically diverse students: A guide for administrators.* San Diego, CA: Singular Publishing Group.

Jackson, F. (1996). *Creating culturally sensitive schools* (audiotape). Alexandria, VA: Association for Supervision and Curriculum Development.

Langdon, H. W., with Cheng, L. L. (Eds.) (1992). *Hispanic children and adults with communication disorders: Assessment and intervention.* Gaithersburg, MD: Aspen.

Roseberry-McKibbin, C. (1995). *Multicultural students with special language needs.* Oceanside, CA: Academic Communication Associates.

Tinajero, J. V. & Ada, A. F. (Eds.). *The power of two languages: Literacy and biliteracy for Spanish-speaking students.* Alexandria, NY: Macmillan/McGraw-Hill Publishing Company.

Parent Involvement

Bromwich, R, (1997). *Working with families and their infants at risk.* Austin, TX: PRO-ED.

Davis, B. (1996). *How to involve parents in a multicultural school.* Alexandria, VA: Association for Supervision and Curriculum Development.

Lynch, E. W. & Hanson, M. J. (1992). *Developing cross-cultural competence: A guide for working with young children and their families.* Baltimore, MD: Paul H. Brookes Publishing.

Moles, O. C. (1995). *Reaching all families: Creating family-friendly schools.* Washington, D. C.: U. S. Department of Education, Office of Educational Research and Improvement.

Simpson, R. L. (1996). *Working with parents and families of exceptional children and youth.* Austin, TX: PRO-ED.

Technology

The Association for Supervision and Curriculum Development has developed materials on video and CD-ROM that provide useful information about the use of technology in education. The following will be of interest to professionals in special education:

> *Only the Best: The Annual Guide to the Highest-Rated Educational Software and Multimedia* (book or CD-ROM).
> *Teaching and Learning with Technology* (two videotapes).
> *Teaching and Learning with the Internet* (videotape and guide).
> *Implementing a Vision for Meaningful Learning* (CD-ROM).

Two excellent references for individuals serving clients with communication disorders are the following:

Masterson, J. (Ed.). (1999). Applications of current technology in speech and language assessment. *Seminars in Speech and Language,* 20 (2).

Masterson, J. (Ed.). (1999). Applications of current technology in speech and language intervention. *Seminars in Speech and Language,* 20 (3).

Directories/Publication Guides

The following resources should prove to be especially valuable. The address of the publisher is listed.

A Guide To the Selection of Spanish Materials for the Classroom and Library. (1996). Continental Book Company, 625 E. 70th Ave. #5, Denver, CO 80229. Includes Spanish-Bilingual and ESL Publications; software, literary studies, reference books, anthologies, maps, games, professional development materials.

Annotated List of Publications in Bilingual Education. (1995). Bilingual Education Office, California Department of Education, P.O. Box 944272, Sacramento, CA 94244.

Index